Management for Professionals

The Springer series "Management for Professionals" comprises high-level business and management books for executives, MBA students, and practice-oriented business researchers. The topics cover all themes relevant to businesses and the business ecosystem. The authors are experienced business professionals and renowned professors who combine scientific backgrounds, best practices, and entrepreneurial vision to provide powerful insights into achieving business excellence.

The Series is SCOPUS-indexed.

Enrico Guarini • Markus Pasterk
Marialuisa Lavitrano
Editors

Research Infrastructure Management

Governance, Strategy Development, and Operations

Springer

Editors
Enrico Guarini
Department of Business and Law
University of Milano-Bicocca
Milano, Italy

Markus Pasterk
Department of Business and Law
University of Milano-Bicocca
Milano, Italy

Marialuisa Lavitrano
Department of Medicine and Surgery
University of Milano-Bicocca
Milano, Italy

ISSN 2192-8096 ISSN 2192-810X (electronic)
Management for Professionals
ISBN 978-3-032-20372-4 ISBN 978-3-032-20373-1 (eBook)
https://doi.org/10.1007/978-3-032-20373-1

This Springer imprint is published by the registered company Springer Nature Switzerland AG
The registered company address is: Gewerbestrasse 11, 6330 Cham, Switzerland

Preface

This book builds on the experience gained by the authors during the Horizon 2020 Project 'RItrain (Research Infrastructure training programme)'[1] (2015–2020) and through the six editions completed so far of the Executive Master in Management of Research Infrastructures (EMMRI) at the University of Milano-Bicocca, developed as a key outcome of the RItrain project. It aims to support the growing number of managers at all levels of Research Infrastructures (RIs) and Core Facilities (CFs) around the world. RIs are facilities, resources, or services of a unique nature that have been identified by pan-European research communities to conduct top-level research activities across all fields. This definition of Research Infrastructures, including the associated human resources, covers major equipment or sets of instruments, as well as knowledge-containing resources such as collections, archives, and databases[2].

Management training for leaders in research settings is seldom utilised, even though some executive MBA programmes are specifically designed for academic leadership. Only a limited number of universities require their executives to undergo formal management training. This situation reflects long-standing academic traditions in which research and scientific expertise are regarded as sufficient qualifications for leading units, departments, or universities.

As RIs are most often built by scientists or established within existing academic units, they typically follow the organisational pattern of their parent institutions. In contrast to teaching and research activities in universities or research organisations, RIs provide access to facilities and offer research services to other scientists and to industry, user management, and marketing, among others; these are new fields where staff, especially leaders of RIs, often lack formal training.

This book aims to bring together experts from both academia and RIs themselves to describe, in a scientifically sound and fit-for-purpose manner, what managers need to know to develop, steer, and lead such entities as RIs, which are public by majority, with a non-profit objective of serving other researchers in their scientific endeavours.

The book is structured along the following lines:

---

[1] http://ritrain.eu/—Grant number 654156.

[2] ESFRI - European Roadmap for Research Infrastructures Report 2006: https://www.esfri.eu/sites/default/files/esfri_roadmap_2006_en.pdf.

In Chap. 1 “The Concept of Research Infrastructure”, the co-editors explain the “Concept of Research Infrastructures’, since, for many countries—and particularly for scientists—these organisations are unique, with specific requirements and needs.

In Chap. 2 “Governance and Organisation of Research Infrastructures”, Francesca Magli, Licinio Lima, and Luca Brusati discuss different governance models, explain organisational settings, and define their relevance. In Chap. 3 “Strategic Management in Research Infrastructures”, written by Elisabetta Marafioti, Jennifer Edmond, and Ilaria Nardello. The chapter focuses on the process of building strategy within Research Infrastructures, positioning it as a core component of their development and long-term sustainability. It examines the key determinants that shape strategic design, including organisational values, mission, and vision, and analyses how these elements interact to guide decision-making and the evolution of Research Infrastructures over time. ‘Financial Management’ covers aspects ranging from bookkeeping and accounting to budgeting, reporting, and financial sustainability issues, which is why we have decided to break this field up into two chapters, namely Chap. 4 “Financial Management and Accounting in Research Infrastructures”, written by Enrico Guarini, Markus Pasterk, and Francesca Magli, and Chap. 5 “Financial Sustainability in Research Infrastructures” by Paola Bongini, Emanuele Rossi, Monica Rossolini, and Juan Arenas. This latter chapter focuses on this issue and analyses the concept of financial sustainability with specific reference to the functioning of an RI (whether single-site or distributed). Francesco Paoletti, Niklas Blomberg, and Pascale Goy have contributed to Chap. 6 “Leadership and Team Management in Research Infrastructures”. Their chapter aims to illustrate leadership in RIs by drawing on experiences from two European cases: CERN, a large single-site facility, and ELIXIR, a distributed infrastructure. By comparing these very different organisations, the authors make some general observations on RI leadership before illustrating how its development can be used to drive organisational strategies. In Chap. 7 “European Research Infrastructures’ Compliance with International and European Law”, Carla Gulotta and Ohad Graber-Soudry equip readers, particularly those with a primarily scientific background, with the skills to identify legal criticalities as they arise, anticipate necessary compliance steps and procedures, outline potential solutions, and recognise when a decision carries such delicate legal implications that consulting legal counsel is advisable.

In Chap. 8 “Service Design in Research Infrastructures”, Benedetta Trivellato and Laura Mariani propose a set of tools that can be useful to support service redesign in RIs, so as to improve quality, efficiency, and effectiveness in service provision for both external and internal users. Finally, we also want to present two real cases developed by two EMMRI’s participants, under the supervision of faculty members, as part of their Master’s field project: Chap. 9 “Sustainable Funding in EMPHASIS as a Distributed Research Infrastructure” by Sven Fahrner and Roland Pieruschka, and Chap. 10 “Developing a Data-Driven Community Engagement Plan for Integrated Carbon Observation System Research Infrastructure” by Evi-Carita Riikonen and Luca Brusati. These cases, along with others presented in this book, were conducted between 2017 and 2023; therefore, they reflect the conditions of that period and may not fully represent current practices or organisational arrangements.

We hope that reading this volume will support both newcomers and experienced staff members in deepening their understanding of how to manage and operate an RI. We also hope that it may inspire readers to pursue further training in this area.

Milano, Italy

Enrico Guarini
Markus Pasterk
Marialuisa Lavitrano

Acknowledgements

The open access publication of this book was supported by the RItrain Project. We are grateful to the European Commission, and in particular to our Project Officer, Mr. Dominik Sobczak, whose continuous support was fundamental in making this project a success.

We would like to express our gratitude to all members of the RItrain project and to the more than 300 participants who have attended the various classes of the Master's programme to date. Without the ongoing dialogue and knowledge sharing with them, this book would not have been possible.

We also wish to extend our sincere thanks to the staff at Springer for their valuable assistance and support.

Contents

About the Editors

Enrico Guarini PhD, is an associate professor of business administration and management and the coordinator of the Executive Master in Management of Research Infrastructures at the University of Milano-Bicocca (Italy). His research activities focus on public management and policy, financial management, and governance. He is co-chair of the Special Interest Group on Local Governance at the International Research Society for Public Management (IRSPM). He has been actively involved in several internationally funded projects aimed at strengthening management capacities in research infrastructures.

Markus Pasterk worked for the Austrian Science Ministry until 2006 and again since 2020, was Scientific Coordinator at the International Agency for Research on Cancer (IARC-WHO; 2006–2009), then COO/VP at the International Prevention Research Institute, Lyon (2009–2014), BBMRI-ERIC Administrative Director (2014–2018), and CEO Austrian Drug Screening Institute, Innsbruck (2018–2020). He is a Senior Management Consultant with X-Officio and Visiting Professor at the University of Milano-Bicocca, Italy.

Marialuisa Lavitrano is a full professor of Pathology and director of the Molecular Medicine Unit and of the Executive Master in Management of Research Infrastructures at the University of Milano-Bicocca (Italy), where she was vice-Rector delegate for International Affairs (2006–2013). Over the years, she has contributed to the international strategies of the Italian Ministries of Research and Health and coordinated Italy's participation in the BioMedical Sciences ESFRI roadmap. She is BBMRI.it Node-Director. She is a member of the EOSC Association Board of Directors and serves as vice-president.

The Concept of Research Infrastructure

Markus Pasterk, Enrico Guarini, and Marialuisa Lavitrano

Abstract

This chapter offers a refined overview of the concept of Research Infrastructures (RIs), clarifying their purpose, definitions, and core features across scientific domains. It synthesises the principal definitions formulated by international organisations and traces the evolution of RIs from the pioneering transnational facilities of the post-war period to the current landscape of single-sited, distributed, and virtual infrastructures. It further describes the typical life cycle of an RI, from conceptualisation and design to implementation, operation, and eventual termination, emphasising the key structural and strategic elements required at each stage. Finally, it discusses the principles guiding access and data stewardship, which underpin the provision of services and the management of research data within RIs.

M. Pasterk (✉)
Department of Business and Law, University of Milano-Bicocca, Milan, Italy

Department of Medicine and Surgery, University of Milano-Bicocca, Milan, Italy
e-mail: markus.pasterk@unimib.it

E. Guarini
Department of Business and Law, University of Milano-Bicocca, Milan, Italy
e-mail: enrico.guarini@unimib.it

M. Lavitrano
Department of Medicine and Surgery, University of Milano-Bicocca, Milan, Italy
e-mail: marialuisa.lavitrano@unimib.it

E. Guarini et al. (eds.), *Research Infrastructure Management*, Management for Professionals, https://doi.org/10.1007/978-3-032-20373-1_1

1 Definitions of Research Infrastructure

Research Infrastructures (RIs) emerged in response to the needs of numerous scientific disciplines that rely on specialised and often costly equipment, large datasets, and advanced expertise. They may operate within universities or research organisations (often referred to as core facilities), at regional or national levels, or on a transnational scale. In what follows, the term 'RI' refers exclusively to the latter category, namely transnational or international RIs.

The earliest examples are CERN[1] and ESO,[2] both created in the aftermath of the Second World War, in response to the need for transnational cooperation and investment in expensive infrastructure to be used by researchers worldwide. The creation of the European Strategy Forum on Research Infrastructures (ESFRI)[3] in 2002 triggered an even higher momentum on the discussion and implementation of transnational RIs. Within particle physics, fusion energy or space transnational cooperation with the construction of joint large facilities has long been established. Today RIs exist in almost every scientific and technological domain including in social sciences and humanities.

There exists no universally agreed-upon definition on the term 'RI', but several organisations developed similar and/or overlapping definitions or rationales. The most prominent are the following:

- *ESFRI (2006)*[4]*: 'Facilities, resources or services of a unique nature that have been identified by pan-European research communities to conduct top-level activities in all fields. This definition of Research Infrastructures, including the associated human resources, covers major equipment or sets of instruments, as well as knowledge-containing resources such as collections, archives and databases. Research Infrastructures may be "single-sited", "distributed", or "virtual" (the service being provided electronically). They often require structured information systems related to data management, enabling information and communication. These include technology-based infrastructures such as grid, computing, software and middleware.'*
- *ERIC Regulation (2009)*[5]*: 'research infrastructure means facilities, resources and related services that are used by the scientific community to conduct top-level research in their respective fields and covers major scientific equipment or sets of instruments; knowledge-based resources such as collections, archives or structures for scientific information; enabling Information and Communications Technology-based infrastructures such as Grid, computing, software and*

[1] European Organization for Nuclear Research (CERN): https://home.cern/about/who-we-are/our-history.

[2] European Southern Observatory (ESO): https://www.eso.org/public/about-eso/.

[3] ESFRI: https://www.esfri.eu/forum.

[4] European Roadmap for Research Infrastructures Report 2006: https://www.esfri.eu/sites/default/files/esfri_roadmap_2006_en.pdf.

[5] Official Journal of the European Union L 206/1 EN 8.8.2009.

communication, or any other entity of a unique nature essential to achieve excellence in research. Such infrastructures may be 'single-sited' or 'distributed' (an organised network of resources).'

- *European Commission RI website*[6]*: 'Research Infrastructures are facilities that provide resources and services for research communities to conduct research and foster innovation. They can be used beyond research e.g. for education or public services and they may be single-sited, distributed, or virtual. They include major scientific equipment or sets of instruments; collections, archives or scientific data; computing systems and communication networks; any other research and innovation infrastructure of a unique nature which is open to external users.'*
- *OECD GSF (2013)*[7]*: 'The factors that motivate scientists and science policy makers to pursue large international projects are well known. Among the potential benefits are:*
  Implementing projects that exceed the funding capacity of individual countries; Optimising the global inventory of state-of-the-art scientific facilities while avoiding unnecessary duplication; Accessing a unique geographical location, or other unique local resource; Bringing together the best scientists, engineers, technicians, and administrators; Accessing data and other resources that are distributed world-wide; Providing international experience for young scientists and engineers.'
- *OECD GSF Report (2014)*[8]*: 'An International Distributed Research Infrastructure (IDRIS) is a multi-national association of geographically-separated distinct entities that jointly perform, facilitate or sponsor basic or applied scientific research. An IDRIS should have all of the following:*
  An identity and a name. A set of international partners who are, typically, funding agencies, research institutes, academic institutions, foundations, or other research-oriented organisations from the public or private sectors. Often, only parts of these entities (as opposed to entire entities) may collectively make up the infrastructure. A formal agreement by the partners to contribute resources, expertise, equipment, services or personnel towards achieving a common scientific purpose. The agreement does not necessarily need to define a new legal entity, or be legally binding. A strategic plan, or work programme, that conveys the rationale for establishing the IDRIS and its added value over-and-above separate activities of the partners. A governance scheme (for decision-making, at a minimum) and a set of officers (not necessarily salaried staff) with well-defined responsibilities. A focus on the provision of services to its members and users.'

---

[6] https://research-and-innovation.ec.europa.eu/strategy/strategy-research-and-innovation/our-digital-future/european-research-infrastructures_en.

[7] OECD 2013; Large Research Infrastructures; part 1 Report on Roadmapping of Large Research Infrastructures (2008).

[8] OECD 2014; International distributed Research Infrastructures: Issues and Options.

2 Legal Framework of Research Infrastructures

RIs exist in various legal formats, each with its own pros and cons. The early single-sited large RIs like CERN or ESO were set up as treaty organisations. In this case, the member of the treaty organisation is a country represented by its government. Other domains utilised national legal instruments, e.g. Limited Liability Companies; examples include the ESRF, the European Synchrotron Radiation Facility in Grenoble, which operates under the French form *société civile*, or the German-based Infrafrontier GmbH. In such cases, Governments are not the shareholders, but this role is often delegated to national research funding or operating bodies, such as research councils, academies, and agencies. Other national law instruments include associations or foundations, with examples such as the Global Biodiversity Information Facility (GBIF),[9] which utilises the Association model, and the European Grid Initiative—EGI Foundation.[10] Sometimes, a very loose Collaboration Agreement is used to set up, develop, and govern an RI; an example of this is the Large Hadron Collider of CERN. During 2009, just at the point when the first new RIs of the 2006 ESFRI roadmap were in their design/preparation phase, the European Council (of Finance Ministers) together with the European Commission (EC) published the 'Council Regulation (EC) No 723/2009 of June 2009' on the Community legal framework for a European Research Infrastructure Consortium (ERIC),[11] opening the door for a dedicated legal instrument especially for distributed RIs. In 2011, the first ERIC was approved, namely SHARE-ERIC.[12] Since then (by March 2026), 32 new RIs were created using the ERIC legal instrument, and several others are in planning (for a full list of ERICs, see https://research-and-innovation.ec.europa.eu/strategy/strategy-research-and-innovation/our-digital-future/european-research-infrastructures/eric/eric-landscape_en).

Each legal form or instrument has its pros and cons. Establishing a treaty organisation will take many years, but it can provide a dedicated solution. At the same time, it will need to establish rules and processes, including those related to health insurance and pension funds, which are extremely costly. Existing Limited Liability company models or other national legal instruments, such as associations or foundations, are relatively easy to establish but have their weaknesses, e.g. being bound to national law and complicated to relocate. The ERIC model appears to bridge the divide between purely international and national models and is highly sought after for distributed RIs today. Since 2022 another European legal vehicle exists, which can be used for RIs: the European Digital Infrastructure Consortium (EDIC) introduced by Decision (EU) 2022/2481 establishing the Digital Decade Policy Programme 2030 (the 'DDPP Decision').[13] The structure is similar to that of ERICs,

[9] https://doi.org/10.15468/doc.ajz7-qt28.

[10] https://go.egi.eu/statutes-en.

[11] Official Journal of the European Union L 206/1 EN 8.8.2009.

[12] Survey of Health, Ageing and Retirement in Europe as a European Research Infrastructure Consortium (SHARE-ERIC); https://share-eric.eu/infrastructure.

[13] https://eurlex.europa.eu/eli/dec/2022/2481/oj/eng.

but there are also major differences. For details see e.g. 'The new European Digital Infrastructure Consortia (EDIC)' at https://www.xofficio.eu/post/the-new-european-digital-infrastructure-consortia-edic-uniting-europe-in-the-digital-age. By March 2026, 5 EDICs had been set up.

2.1 Single-Sited Versus Distributed Location of Research Infrastructures

RIs can be categorised according to the physical location of their facilities. In analytical sciences and astronomy, large single-sited RI predominate. They are built to provide guest researchers direct access to their equipment and/or data. Examples are CERN, ESO, ESRF, or ITER.[14] The ESFRI Strategy Report on RIs Roadmap 2018[15] describes single-sited RIs as follows: *'Single-sited RIs are central facilities geographically localised in a single site or in a few dedicated complementary sites designed for user access, whose governance is European or international. A single-sited RI needs to: i) have a legal status and a governance structure with clear responsibilities and reporting lines, including international supervisory and relevant external advisory bodies; ii) have an access policy and access point for external users facilitating the submission of proposals and a user programme absorbing a considerable fraction of the total capacity of the RI; iii) have a user support structure to optimize access to the relevant site, such as users office, ancillary laboratories, accommodation arrangements and logistics; iv) have a data management system providing metadata and data storage, retrieval tools and on-line/in situ/remote data reduction and analysis; v) identify relevant and measurable Key Performance Indicators (KPI) addressing both excellence of scientific services and sustainability; vi) enforce a human resources policy guaranteeing the necessary competences for its operation, users support, education and training by equal opportunity hiring and secondments.'*

Life and Environmental Sciences, as well as Social Sciences and Humanities, have established predominantly distributed RIs, which build on existing networks of dozens (sometimes hundreds) of smaller entities. Their governance is obviously very different from single-sited RIs. In the Roadmap 2018 report, distributed RIs are described as *'A distributed RI consists of a Central Hub and interlinked National Nodes. A distributed RI particularly needs to: i) have a unique specific name, legal status and a governance structure with clear responsibilities and reporting lines, including international supervisory and relevant external advisory bodies; ii) have legally binding attributions of coordination competences and resources to the Central Hub; iii) have a unique access policy and provide for a single point of access for all users with a support structure dedicated to optimise the access for the proposed research; iv) have a user programme absorbing a relevant fraction of the total capacity of the RI; v) identify and adopt measurable Key Performance*

[14] ITER International Fusion Energy Organization; https://www.iter.org/sites/default/files/ITERAgreement.pdf.

[15] http://roadmap2018.esfri.eu/.

Indicators addressing both excellence of scientific services and sustainability; vi) have a human resources policy adequate to guarantee the effective operation of the Central Hub supporting the research, users programme, education and training by equal opportunity hiring and secondments; vii) define a joint investment strategy aimed at strengthening the RI through the Nodes and the common/shared facilities. These features mark the difference of a RI with respect to a coordinated research network (international collaborations of fully independent research performing organizations). Nodes may be absorbed partially by the distributed RI while maintaining their national or institutional programmes, but the capacity and amount of resources engaged in the RI must be coordinated and managed by the Central Hub according to agreed statutes and common rules and procedures of the legal RI consortium.'

In addition, some combinations of both exist, with a very limited number of larger sites, e.g. the European Spallation Source ERIC[16] or CERIC-ERIC, the Central European Research Infrastructure Consortium.[17]

The fourth principal subtype is called 'virtual RI'. They exist in several scientific domains, but are the most prevalent in the humanities, e.g. DARIAH-ERIC: *'It develops, maintains and operates an infrastructure in support of ICT-based research practices and sustains researchers in using them to build, analyse and interpret digital resources'.*[18]

3 Life Cycle of Research Infrastructures

Another way to describe RIs is their timely position along the life cycle of an RI. Very often, bottom-up scientists start their thinking about the creation of a new RI on a conceptional level. During this phase, existing concepts are screened, a consortium formatted, access policy drafted, and first funding concepts developed. Such concepts are often the product of scientific associations in describing the future of a domain or can be funded by different national or international bodies.

The next phase is called the design phase and should end with a design study. This will contain a business case described with political and financial support gained. It could describe a common access policy and first high-level cost breakdowns. At this point first ideas of governance will arise. As sometimes the first two phases might be done without dedicated funding, the following phases ultimately need financial resources for completion.

Within the preparatory phase the political and financial commitments are secured, a business plan created, and (potentially) a construction plan

designed. Data policy and data management plans should be developed and a cost book outlined. For the governance to be implemented a legal instrument will be chosen and the necessary bylaws written.

[16] https://europeanspallationsource.se/about.

[17] https://www.ceric-eric.eu/.

[18] https://www.dariah.eu/about/dariah-in-nutshell/.

The next phase in the cycle is implementation. During this phase, an RI will start its construction and/or deploy the organisation and legal entity. Recruitment will start and an operations plan developed. If not yet completed, this is the time to secure funding for the operation—the next level.

During this phase, research services are developed and provided. Outreach activities will enlarge the user communities and inform other disciplines or the wider public about the operations. Instrumentations and methods will be constantly upgraded and further developed. This could be the longest phase of an existing RI.

Finally, the RI operations come to an end and termination needs to be planned and executed. The organisation needs to be dissolved, facilities dismantled, or a reuse of existing equipment for a merger or major upgrade planned.

The life cycle of an RI encompasses not only various phases of planning and operations but also requires distinct funding resources. The publication of the StR-ESFRI project, '*Guidelines on Cost Estimation of Research Infrastructures'*, describes the different cost structures of single-sited and distributed (here called virtual) RIs in a detailed and clear manner.[19] Further discussion on the different funding models will be provided in Chap. 5 "Financial Sustainability in Research Infrastructures".

4 Access to Research Infrastructures

Access to the physical site and equipment or its data is the core of an RI. Historically, many facilities in the physical sciences followed the 'ICFA Guidelines for the Interregional Utilization of Major Experimental Facilities for High-Energy Particle Physics Research'[20] that were developed decades ago for particle accelerators. According to these, international access to a national facility was to be solely based on the merits of the proposed research, and operating costs were to be covered by the facility. The European Commission has also published a Charter for Access, which sets out principles and guidelines to serve as a reference when defining access policies for RIs.[21] Many younger RIs have implemented this charter or reference it within their access policy. At the same time of publishing the charter, Wilkinson et al. (2016) published 'FAIR Guiding Principles for scientific data management and stewardship'.[22] These principles help scientists find and access data that is

[19] https://www.esfri.eu/sites/default/files/StR-ESFRI2_STUDY_RIs_COST_ESTIMATION_0.pdf.

[20] ICFA—International Committee for Future Accelerators https://inspirehep.net/files/1ecb3fd6d8df44d114f35764cd0441fb.

[21] https://research-and-innovation.ec.europa.eu/news/all-research-and-innovation-news/revised-charter-access-research-infrastructures-foster-open-science-innovation-and-research-security-2024-11-27_en.

[22] Wilkinson, M., Dumontier, M., Aalbersberg, I. et al. (2016), The FAIR Guiding Principles for scientific data management and stewardship. *Scientific Data* 3, 160018. https://doi.org/10.1038/sdata.2016.18.

interoperable and reusable. RIs as providers of massive research data fill the core of this process. Access to its data is often more important than access to its resources (for reproducing existing data).

Governance and Organisation of Research Infrastructures

Francesca Magli, Licínio C. Lima, and Luca Brusati

Abstract

This chapter examines Research Infrastructures (RIs) as complex, socially constructed meta-organisations that bring together autonomous yet interdependent partners. It explores the governance challenges arising from coordinating distributed nodes, managing common-pool resources, and balancing collective and individual interests. The chapter reviews key governance models adopted by European RIs, highlighting how formal rules, decision-making bodies, and organisational arrangements shape effectiveness and legitimacy. It argues that robust, multilayered governance is essential for sustaining collaboration.

F. Magli (✉)
Department of Business and Law, University of Milano-Bicocca, Milan, Italy
e-mail: francesca.magli@unimib.it

L. C. Lima
Institute of Education (Professor Emeritus), University of Minho, Braga, Portugal
e-mail: llima@ie.uminho.pt

L. Brusati
Department of Economics and Statistics, Udine University, Udine, Italy
e-mail: luca.brusati@uniud.it

E. Guarini et al. (eds.), *Research Infrastructure Management*, Management for Professionals, https://doi.org/10.1007/978-3-032-20373-1_2

1 Research Infrastructures as Complex Organisations[1]

On its website dedicated to Research and Innovation, the European Commission (2020a) presents a brief description of RIs, defined as 'facilities that provide resources and services for research communities to conduct research and foster innovation'. It notes that these facilities can be utilised beyond research, for example, in education, public services, and industry, and may take various organisational forms, which it categorises as single-sited, distributed, or virtual.

RIs often display a translocal character and an international configuration. The Organisation for Economic Co-operation and Development states that an International Distributed Research Infrastructure (IDRIS) is 'a multinational association of geographically-separated distinct entities that jointly perform, facilitate or sponsor basic or applied scientific research' (OECD, 2014: 7). In every case where geographically distributed organisational entities come together to cooperate and form a supra-organisational institution, a new and more complex meta-organisation emerges. The result may be the establishment of scientific umbrella organisations, clusters, consortia, or other collaborative and networked research facilities. Such new types of research facilities 'pose specific problems' (Meijer et al., 2012: 492), particularly in terms of structure, governance, coordination, and decision-making. In any case, the issue not only pertains to the emergence of a new kind of knowledge organisation but also of highly complex social units in terms of goals, technologies, structures, coordination, communication, and decision-making processes. If two decades ago R&D organisations were considered unique in terms of the coordination needs of people, ideas, funds, and culture, including the difficulties of managing autonomous researchers and creative working processes that might seem unmanageable (Jain & Triandis, 1997:19), we have to stress the magnitude of the organisational challenges now facing RIs in a knowledge-based global society. Sharing information, research data, scientific resources, and artefacts, as well as providing services and products on a large scale, are new functions that add complexity to RIs and raise unexpected demands.

1.1 Knowledge Organisations as Socially Constructed Units

RIs can host a wide variety of resources, including collections, archives, biobanks, libraries, museums, telescopes, research vessels, satellites, computing systems, and communication networks. Every scientific resource makes a difference in terms of its impact on organisational technologies, i.e. the processes used to achieve particular goals. In addition, the different scientific, technological, social, and cultural fields, as well as the diverse scientific communities and their specific epistemological and methodological paradigms, codes, and rules, strongly influence

[1] The paper is the product of the joint research study conducted by all three authors; nevertheless, in the final version, Licinio Lima wrote Sect. 1, Luca Brusati wrote Sect. 2, and Francesca Magli wrote Sect. 3.

organisational design, including such elements as structures, work processes, types of leadership and coordination, power relations, autonomy, and decision-making.

However, there is nothing natural in RIs and the above-mentioned impact cannot be understood in deterministic terms. Everything is the result of historical and social processes of construction that underscore the artificial character of RIs. As socially constructed units, RIs are neither 'things' nor anthropomorphic purposeful actors, but rather, dynamic organisations made up of people, always in process, creating and recreating structures and rules through human agency.

Biobanks, for example, may show evidence of several organisational elements that are influenced by scientific codes and professional cultures and subcultures rooted in biology. Even some organisational theorists, especially contingency theorists, have treated organisations as biological organisms. It was a metaphorical way of trying to understand organisations as living systems (Morgan, 1986: 39–76), well adapted to specific environments, surviving through the process of satisfying their needs and aspirations. But the organism metaphor has been much criticised for its reification of social and formal organisations, which are not natural beings but rather social, cultural, and political constructs. Accordingly, they show the capacity to intervene in the social environment and not just adapt to it, to choose values and policies, to change norms and rules, to cooperate and reach consensus among groups and subgroups, and to develop power relations and conflicts.

That is why the different organisational concepts we need in order to make sense of RIs are cultural and historical expressions of social theory's plurality. They are analytical tools that help us denaturalise RIs, not just as instruments to produce or to achieve something (the Greek 'organon'), but as institutions and cultural and social phenomena that are the result human agency. They are quite different from the concept of organisation related to the solar system, atoms, or cells that are not social actors with specific agendas, interests, and preferences.

1.2 Organisations in Action

Understanding RIs requires the use of two different meanings of the word organisation. On the one hand, 'organisation' as a noun is used to refer to an historically constructed social unit for achieving a minimum of cooperation between people, groups, and subgroups. This is indispensable for accomplishing work and producing goods and services in order to guarantee the 'attainment of specific goals', according to the functionalist definition of Amitai Etizioni (1961: xi). On the other hand, there is a second and more dynamic meaning of organisation that involves organisation as organised action or, simply, organisation in action and the activity of 'organising' (from the verb 'to organise'). Both meanings are crucial for the study of the organisational world: the social structure and the social action in their relationship of interdependence.

Since organisational theory offers no universal definitions due to the theoretical pluralism that marks the social sciences, the result is the plurality of organisational concepts. As Czarniawska-Joerges (1992: 17) reminded us, 'pictures of complex organizations change depending on the standpoint'. This is why the organised action performed by RIs can be interpreted in considerably different ways. At times, interpretations highlight the rational-formal elements, the standardisation of procedures, the close relationship between means and ends, and the formal structures and rules that result from more or less consensual processes of coordination. This is generally the view based on the sociological concept of bureaucracy or rational-legal authority as defined and criticised by German sociologist Max Weber (1947) in the early twentieth century. In other cases, however, lack of consensus on objectives, the existence of unclear technologies, and more ambiguous and probabilistic than formally rational decision-making processes offer us both distinct and complementary interpretative frameworks. Theoretical approaches based on the ambiguity of goals, the uncertainty of technologies, and the fluidity of participation portray organisations as 'organised anarchies' (Cohen & March, 1974) and not only as rational bureaucracies. Different patterns of order, organisation, and rationality may, however, be combined when studying RIs and seeking a deeper understanding of its dynamics.

There are often conflicts regarding organisations' goals and differing views about their official goals in particular. Important elements for understanding RIs are statutes and regulations as well as the formal structures that usually give rise to the design of methodically arranged organisational charts. But these formal views tend to be more static and official than dynamic and real. RIs in action can move considerably away from formal structures and rules through informal processes, structures, and rules that do not appear in the organisational chart. Yet these social phenomena have the capacity to change and recreate organisations, and that is why there is no theoretical advantage in treating them as simple deviations, dysfunctions, or irregular courses of organised action. Just as the pipe painted by Belgian surrealist painter René Magritte is not a pipe (*Ceci n'est pas une pipe*), but simply the pictorial representation of a pipe, so the organogram of an RI is not the RI, but only a representation of the formal structures of that particular organisation. Organised action, decisions, communication, and power relations occur in the interstices of the formal representation of the RI.

1.3 Coordination and Decision-Making Processes

RIs pose new problems of coordination, especially in the case of distributed infrastructures, which include other types of internally networked facilities, namely cyberinfrastructures. Also, depending on their size and scope as well as on policy, geographically distributed RIs tend to be more demanding than single-sited RIs in terms of coordination of their nodes. However, careful examination is required with respect to the widespread idea that single-sited facilities are by definition centralised and more bureaucratic, while distributed infrastructures tend to be decentralised and post-bureaucratic. For instance, Meijer et al. (2012: 494), when referring to some biobanks, stated that 'fully centralized facilities have a single location for samples and a unified management structure physically located at the same site'.

However, in fact, much depends on the coordination mechanisms that are adopted, similar to hierarchies, markets, or networks for example. As Barjak et al. (2013: 118) observed, 'in networks, actors are not as independent as in markets, but less interdependent than in hierarchies'. The concept of coordination, traditionally associated with control, may however comprise multiple degrees of articulation between components of the organisation as well as between objectives and actions, superiors and subordinates, and among national nodes of the same international infrastructure. RIs are not always 'rationalized, tidy, efficient coordinated structures' (Weick, 1976: 3), that is, 'tightly coupled systems'. They include elements that also allow us to understand them as 'loosely coupled systems', as organisations in which 'each event also preserves its own identity and some evidence of its physical or logical separation' (Weick, 1976: 3). Therefore, strong hierarchical coordination based on heteronomous control is not indispensable for holding together a minimally integrated and responsive RI.

In distributed infrastructures, the organisational configuration adopted may be more closely associated with the structural distribution of its nodes, showing an apparent or merely morphological decentralisation, best understood as a deconcentrated configuration. In such a case, apparent morphological decentralisation is no more than the result of a constellation of geographically dispersed partner organisations or units. That organised dispersion may be fully compatible with the centralisation of decision-making power. In tha case, power is little shared and poorly participates in decision-making terms, relatively independent from the structural configuration. In contrast, it is possible to find single-sited infrastructures whose structures of authority are participative and where the exercise of power is internally decentralised, giving considerable autonomy to social actors, departments, and units. In such circumstances, however structurally concentrated, those infrastructures may be considered internally decentralised and to some extent polycentric in terms of decision-making power. Organisational design, formal structures, authority, and power relations cannot be understood separately. That is why unified or concentrated infrastructures may be morphologically centralised into just one site, but decentralised when it comes to the autonomy of its internal units and the power of their social actors to participate in decision-making.

1.4 Just Tools in Search of Utility?

It is not possible to implement scientific policy or a large-scale research service project without resorting to an organisational apparatus. While RIs are, in this context, instruments for carrying out a specific policy programme, they are in fact far from being just technical tools in search of utility. They are also social and cultural organisations that tend towards their institutionalisation over time. Among the various institutional profiles that may emerge, three deserve mention: RIs as hierarchies, markets, and communities.

As hierarchies, RIs display elements such as instrumental rationality, order, and centrally defined universal rules. Centrality tends to be assigned to monocratic leadership, assisted by strong 'technostructures' that consist of professional advisors and other technical staff.

The market is the privileged form of institutional legitimation of RIs as market-oriented organisations. Legitimisation occurs through economic rationality, competition, flexibility, and some degree of deregulation, along with the commodification of research services and products according to an 'entrepreneurial spirit'.

Finally, as communities, RIs tend to display the sharing of goals and values, beliefs, and attitudes, through processes of socialisation, integration, and participation of their members.

The three schematically mentioned institutional profiles promote different processes of legitimation and, to some extent, the negotiation of different orders, values, norms, rituals, and organisational conceptions of RI. In practical terms, these profiles are more complementary than mutually exclusive. The community profile may require more dialogue and participation, but the values of democracy and participation are crucial to the processes of legitimation of all scientific and knowledge organisations. This is especially true for those that depend most on their reputation and social status to the public, on governmental and community budgets, and on participation of the general public, particularly the public in direct contact with the organisation. Insistence on institutional profiles based on other forms of bureaucratic domination, such as hierarchy and control, as well as on strict utility patterns in pursuit of maximum profit, can be highly questionable options for RIs. The advocacy of democratic values, ethical debates on science and its technological applications, public fundraising campaigns, and social movements in defence of human and environmental rights are increasingly relevant phenomena. Participation in terms of representative democracy and certain forms of small-scale direct democracy, including collaborative and consultative processes—especially in policymaking processes within RIs—is crucial for democratic governance and acceptance by the public.

Note also that democratic governance of RIs cannot guarantee processes of dialogue and active participation by members of the organisation, and not just in terms of information sharing, suggestion gathering, and other forms of low-intensity engagement. Participation in policymaking is irreplaceable for realising the utopia of a democratic 'scientific community' not only at the political level of the European Union Research Area (Ryan, 2015) and its member states, but also at the heart of each RI.

2 Governance in Research Infrastructures

2.1 Meta-Organisations and the Role of Governance Arrangements

RIs may share some features with all three of the institutional profiles described above, depending on their mandate, history, funding mechanisms, whether they are single-site or distributed, and other relevant factors. It is clear, though, that they fully correspond to neither hierarchies nor markets; instead, they correspond more closely to communities, networks, or clans (Ouchi, 1980). An important implication is that they cannot be managed primarily through centralised, top-down mechanisms, like superimposed procedures in hierarchies, nor through decentralised, arms-length mechanisms, like price signals in markets.

RIs share this feature with the growing number of organisations labelled as 'meta-organisations', i.e. organisations whose members are other organisations instead of individuals (Ahrne & Brunsson, 2005, 2008; Berkowitz & Dumez, 2016). Not only is the definition of RIs a close match to that of meta-organisations (OECD, 2014: 8), but their typical features also match, as described by Ahrne and Brunsson (2008: 3):

> The members have considerable autonomy. They have applied for membership by choice, and they are free to leave at any time. They cannot be forced to become members or be purchased. And as members they keep most of their autonomy and identity as independent organizations. Furthermore, in meta-organizations, as is typical for associations, members are equals.

The presence of independent organisations as part of a meta-organisation poses a specific challenge for the management of both RIs and their partners: balancing the collective interests that led to the establishment of that infrastructure with the specific objectives pursued by each partner. In a context characterised by interdependency, self-interested partners may make choices that appear rational from an individualistic perspective but ultimately lead to outcomes that leave everyone worse off. Short-term wins can trigger adverse consequences and ultimately long-term losses. This phenomenon is described in the academic literature as a collective action problem (Olson, 1965) and is especially common in the presence of 'common-pool resources', i.e. assets characterised by joint use and subtractability (withdrawal by one partner reduces the amount left for others). Opportunistic behaviours result in the 'tragedy of the commons' (Hardin, 1968), defined as a failure to avoid joint losses and the inability to secure joint gains.

This risk can be addressed by centralised governmental regulation or by privatisation, but these options are obviously incompatible with the very nature of RIs. The only option left is for partners to learn how to 'govern the commons' (Ostrom, 1990), i.e. by agreeing upon and enforcing durable cooperative arrangements that allow joint use of common-pool resources to take place in a way that keeps meeting collective objectives over time while balancing the legitimate interests of individual partners. In international relations, these arrangements among interdependent players are labelled as international policy regimes (Krasner, 1983: 2), but very similar arrangements must be developed in order to secure the governance of RIs.

Designing effective governance arrangements for joint use of common-pool resources and making sure they work have been explicitly identified by the European Commission among the most important points for the development of European RIs (European Commission, 2020b):

> State-of-the-art research infrastructures become increasingly complex and costly, often requiring integration of different equipment, services and data sources, as well as extensive transnational collaboration. (...) It is not only necessary to avoid duplication of efforts and to coordinate and rationalise the use of the facilities, but also to pool resources so that the Union can also acquire and operate research infrastructures at world level.

The importance of governance arrangements cannot be underestimated. Not surprisingly, they are often a source of disagreement, or even of conflict, among partners in an RI. For this reason, it is important to understand what challenges entailed and what solutions are available to tackle them.

2.2 What Is Governance?

The concept of 'governance' is commonly used in multiple fields of inquiry, ranging from public administration to international development. As a consequence of the multiple contexts in which it can be applied and the various perspectives through which it can be explored, defining what governance means is not straightforward. Let us begin with the problem governance is designed to address. Most societal challenges cannot be solved single-handedly by individual public authorities, through direct interventions, orders, or prohibitions. Because of their intrinsic nature, challenges such as climate change, environmental protection, or economic development require the voluntary engagement of multiple stakeholders, including other public authorities, NGOs, industry associations, and the media.

Governance is broadly defined as a 'non-hierarchical mode of governing, where non-state, private corporate actors (formal organizations) participate in the formulation and implementation of public policy' (Mayntz, 2006: 18). The presence of multiple, often heterogeneous stakeholders is intrinsic to RIs. According to the definition used by the OECD, RI partners include 'funding agencies, research institutes, academic institutions, foundations, or other research-oriented organisations from the public or private sectors' (2014: 7). Similarly, Edwards et al. define the broader concept of knowledge infrastructures as 'robust networks of people, artifacts, and institutions that generate, share, and maintain specific knowledge about the human and natural worlds' (2013: 7).

This 'non-hierarchical mode of governing' has often been touted as a miracle drug. Its proponents point out that it yields superior results, as it allows for the processing of more information, takes a broader variety of values into account, overcomes the risks associated with veto powers, builds trust and a shared vision among network participants, and, in short, makes 'better' decisions. Reality is more complex. First, not all stakeholders are created equal: they hold different amounts of information and resources, different degrees of interest, different ability to influence outcomes, and different levels of accountability. Secondly, their interests may be at odds: compromise can be the only way to keep them on board, but it may not necessarily be the best answer to societal challenges.

The way governance works, therefore, is essential for solving complex, multi-stakeholder issues. If governance is effective, then relevant stakeholders are on board, they collaborate effectively, and societal challenges are addressed efficiently. If governance is ineffective, problems remain unresolved and often worsen.

The concept of 'good governance' has been discussed at length to distill the tenets of sound multi-stakeholder decision-making. A set of eight principles has been identified by international organisations as the gold standard for good governance: respect of the rule of law, transparency, responsiveness, consensus orientation, equity and inclusiveness, effectiveness and efficiency, accountability, and participation (Young, 1999). These principles can be used as benchmarks to identify areas for improvement in the way governance is practised. They have limited usefulness in operational terms, however, especially because they are often at odds with each other.

The essence of good governance is defining suitable 'rules of the road' to facilitate interaction among different players. Effective governance is a matter of both mechanisms and management patterns, which are obviously related and deserve separate discussion.

Mechanisms are the formal rules used for decision-making. When referring to RIs, 'governance' is usually intended as 'institutional' or 'corporate' governance, i.e. the framework for decision-making established in the formal agreement that created the RI. The framework for decision-making encompasses various elements, including its mandate, the roles assigned to the General Assembly, the Director, the Secretariat, and the Scientific Advisory Board, as well as the presence of committees, voting mechanisms, and funding criteria. An overview of the corporate governance mechanisms used by European RIs is featured in paragraph 3.3.

Good governance is not determined only by formal rules, though. A systematic review of the empirical evidence in multi-stakeholder decision-making identified three sets of variables that influence effectiveness (Ianniello et al., 2019). First, contextual factors, including, in particular, information asymmetries among network participants, play a role. Secondly, formal arrangements are obviously relevant. Especially important among these are the mechanisms agreed upon to engage multiple players in the pursuit of a shared decision, stakeholder representation criteria, and the design of the process. The third set of variables is represented by process management patterns, including group dynamics and collaboration quality; although they may not be formalised, they have a significant impact on whether the involvement of multiple stakeholders actually delivers better solutions. These variables indicate that governance is not only a matter of rules, but also that managers and management patterns play a crucial role in addressing complex, multi-stakeholder challenges, such as the effective functioning of an RI.

2.3 Governance Patterns

A wide range of governance patterns can be observed when examining RIs. We focus here on two features of these patterns: the form of the network whose resources are pooled in an RI and the set of tasks the networks are expected to perform.

Antivachis and Angelis (2014: 588–589) identify three basic forms networks can take. The simplest form is polycentric governance, one that is governed by the partners themselves, without any ad hoc governance entity. The resulting networks tend to be highly decentralised and involve almost all the partners, interacting on a relatively equal basis (shared or distributed governance). This governance pattern assumes the commitment of all or a significant subset of the partners that make up the network. Partners are responsible for managing internal network relationships, as well as relationships with external stakeholders, including customers, the community, government, and funders.

Lead organisation governance (Dhanaraj & Parkher, 2006) occurs when partners share a common purpose, but one partner is more powerful than the rest in terms of size, resources, or legitimacy, allowing it to serve as the hub or central node of the network. Governance in this case is centralised instead of shared. The partner designated to undertake the lead role in network coordination may be mandated by an external funding source or may emerge among the partners, based on who they perceive to be the most effective and efficient network member to fill this role.

The third form of governance entails the presence of a dedicated Network Administrative Organisation (NAO), which is a separate central facility established, apart from network partners, with the sole purpose of governing the network and its activities (Provan & Kenis, 2007). In this case, the network is externally governed, with the NAO established either by mandate or by network partners themselves for the specific purpose of governing the network. NAOs may range in size from a single individual (the network facilitator or broker) to a formal organisation operating out of a physically distinct office with a CEO and dedicated staff.

Shared governance is typically preferred by partners, as it enables them to maintain control over the network's direction. It is most suitable when the network size and complexity are limited, and partners are similar to one another and generally agree on the goals the network should pursue. Antivachis and Angelis (2014: 590) argue that shared governance tends to become ineffective when task requirements are high because network members may not possess the required skills (e.g. communication, fundraising, lobbying). On the contrary, these conditions may favour central coordination through either the lead organisation or NAO governance forms, which are better able to develop or acquire the specific skills needed to ensure effective network governance. Obviously, more articulated solutions can be envisaged. One example is multiple operational hubs organised as national networks with a central coordinating mechanism that can be supported by one or more nodes or an NAO (OECD, 2014: 10).

A different feature of governance patterns is the nature of the institutional tasks that networks are expected to perform. This feature is relevant when analysing RIs because the activities they facilitate may be meant to support different tasks. Young

(1999) suggests a useful taxonomy in this respect, distinguishing regulatory, procedural, programmatic, and generative tasks. Regulatory tasks are the most visible. They entail the definition of the rules meant to allow participating actors to avoid joint losses or reap joint gains in situations characterised by interactive decision-making. In international relations, these rules are enshrined in treaties, conventions, and other high-profile formal arrangements. If the policy issue to be addressed is overfishing, the EU Common Fisheries Policy is a good example.

Treaties and conventions are important, but they establish broad principles that are often unsuitable for immediate implementation. Ad hoc mechanisms are necessary to make informed decisions regarding the challenges that arise when translating those principles into practice. Procedural tasks entail the administration of these mechanisms. Using the example of overfishing, it may be important to determine whether certain species should be added to the list of endangered species, thereby granting them additional protection. At times, choices are required on a regular basis, such as setting maximum catch levels for the following year.

Programmatic tasks involve establishing multi-stakeholder initiatives aimed at deepening or broadening knowledge about issues of common interest. At a minimum, concern regarding overfishing indicates that a common data collection system must be designed and implemented to assess whether the rules agreed upon are having the intended impact on fish stocks. Over time, data collection could be extended to related aspects; for example, it may be important to understand whether climate change has an impact on fish stocks, so as to determine whether maximum catch levels should be set differently.

Last but not least, generative tasks entail the establishment and merging of official and unofficial, national and transnational groups, which provide support for the development of a given regulatory framework. A component of this process is refining the conceptual frames used to discuss a given issue. For instance, early fishery regimes pursued the idea of 'maximum sustainable yields' (MSYs). More recently, the discussion of 'ecosystem management' has replaced MSYs, emphasising the interplay between harvested species with biotic and abiotic settings.

RIs are typically established to work on programmatic tasks, but they may also play a significant role in procedural and generative tasks, and ultimately may end up supporting regulatory tasks as well, especially if the latter evolve into fully developed knowledge infrastructures. As an example, LifeWatch ERIC claims that 'understanding the evolution and functions of biodiversity and ecosystem services is now of crucial importance, not only for scientific reasons, but also to meet the demand from policy makers, managers and stakeholders for scientific-based tools,' and it explicitly includes in its mission, 'supporting knowledge-based decision-making for biodiversity and ecosystem management' (LifeWatch ERIC, 2020). The actual combination of tasks performed by an RI often evolves over time based on the priority given to a set of goals, although all tasks play an important role in addressing collective action problems effectively.

3 Formal Governance in Research Infrastructure

3.1 Governance Mechanisms, Rules, and Procedures

One of the most important points in the development of European RIs for 2020 is the reinforcement of international cooperation/collaboration (European Commission, 2020b). This cooperation is vital and must be strengthened with lasting and stable agreements between the nations concerned. These agreements should take into account international differences, national objectives, but in particular, they should identify an effective system of governance (OECD, 2008, 2010).

Formal governance is the formality of governance that should be used in infrastructure (Barjak et al., 2013: 119; OECD, 2014: 11). Formal governance is characterised by material incentives, legitimacy based on rules and routines established and strengthened in contracts or binding agreements, and vertical relationships in which control is exercised by higher positions in the hierarchy (Barjak et al., 2013: 118).

Leaving aside 'material incentives', which can be of different types and refer to revenues or other resources, lower costs, opportunities for future development, etc., the other two characteristics will be examined in order to analyse which of them constitutes major governance challenges for an RI. Therefore, we will focus on the legally enforceable rules and routines established in contracts (i.e. their various legal frameworks) and the analysis of vertical hierarchical relationships (particularly the structures of governance bodies and their relationships).

According to the ESFRI Roadmap 2018, governance models for RIs should define the roles and commitments of all the different stakeholders[2] with respect to a coherent and consistent funding landscape throughout the RI lifecycle. Based on the definition of corporate governance for private companies[3] (Cadbury Committee, 1992), it is possible to extrapolate the definition of corporate governance for RIs as 'the set of structures, principles, rules, and procedures used to regulate the entities or organisms that would run RIs'.

There are different types of RIs: single-sited, e-infrastructures, and distributed RI. The latter are, of course, the most complex and will certainly have a more stratified and articulated governance structure. In distributed RIs, the various relationships between nodes and facilities are crucial. For example, there may be distributed RIs where there is a loose connection between the nodes, central coordination between the nodes (with coordinating mechanisms supported by one node or by one or more facilities or by an independent organisation), or a combination of the preceding, in which there are multiple operational hubs and the coordinating mechanisms can be supported by one or several nodes or by an independent organisation (OECD, 2014: 10).

[2] International, European, member states, associated countries, regions, research organisations, research hosting institutions, etc.

[3] The Cadbury Committee (1992) defined corporate governance as 'the system by which companies are directed and controlled".

Table 1 Legal model of RIs

International	Research infrastructures	
IGO Inter-Governmental Organisation		CERN, EMBL, ESA, ESO
European		
ERIC European Research Infrastructure Consortium		ACTRIS, AnaEE, BBMRI, CERIC, CESSDA, CLARIN, CTAO, DANUBIUS, DARIAH, EATRIS, ECCSEL, ECRIN, EHRI, ELI, EMBRC, EMSO, EPOS, E-RIHS, ESS, EU-OPENSCREEN, EU-SOLARIS, Euro-Argo, Euro-BioImaging, European Spallation Source, ICOS, INFRAFRONTIER, INSTRUCT, JIVE, LifeWatch, LOFAR, MIRRI, SHARE
National		
LIMITED LIABILITY COMPANIES		
GmbH Gesellschaft für beschränkte Haftung	DE	European X-FEL, INFRAFRONTIER (before becoming an ERIC)
Ltd Private limited Company	UK	EIBIR, SKA organisation, INSTRUCT Academic Services Limited (before becoming an ERIC)
AB Aktiebolag	SE	ESS AB (before becoming an ERIC)
Societé Civile	FR	ESRF
CONSORTIUM		
CA Consortium agreement	EU	GGP—generation and gender programme, AnaEE (national Danish consortium), DISSCo, SIOS (Svalbard), JERICO
ASSOCIATIONS		
AISBL International Belgian Association	BE	PRACE, EuroGOOS, EUFAR
FOUNDATIONS		
Stiftung des bürgerlichen Rechts	D	DESY
Stichting	NL	EGI foundation

Source: Author's elaboration

To ensure legitimacy and identify the best governance scheme for the various types of RIs, it will be necessary to begin with an analysis of the most effective legal frameworks currently in force. Regarding the latter, it is possible to identify the main rules and procedures of governance to be pursued, as well as the bodies responsible for them. During the pre-operational period of an RI, it will be crucial to identify one of the most significant sustainability issues, namely legal status and governance. 'Solid legal forms and corresponding statutes help in securing RI sustainability. Practical solutions should be adapted to the agreed needs of an RI (OECD, 2017: 22).

Table 1 shows the main legal frameworks adopted by most RIs in Europe. They are organised mainly into European Research Infrastructure Consortia (ERIC) or intergovernmental organisations (IGOs), or into alternative national legal forms, primarily Association Internationale Sans But Lucratif (AISBL), according to Belgian law (for an in-depth analysis of legal frameworks in RIs, see Chap. 7 "European Research Infrastructures' Compliance with International and European Law" in this book).

Options for governing structures are linked to the selected legal form (if applicable) (OECD, 2014: 14). Therefore, another important aspect of formal governance is represented by governance structure and vertical hierarchical relationships. A governance model used among the RIs incorporates a general assembly, which is a governing body representing the collective interests of the partners and is the ultimate decision-making body, a director or Board of Directors, in charge of implementing the decisions of the governing body, and a secretariat, which is executive management in charge of operating the infrastructure.

In order to create a more suitable governance structure to address the specific problems of an established RI, a good rule would be to clearly define the governing bodies and boundaries between supervisory and executive structures/functions directly in the articles of association (statutes) or better clarify the hierarchy and relations between the governance bodies. There could indeed be differences between the motivations and interests of associated individuals or institutions that could lead to operational or strategic difficulties. In fact, members of the general assembly are often representatives of governments, while directors or members of the Board of Directors are scientists without particular or high-level management skills. A more detailed division of tasks will therefore allow for a greater ability to separate strategy and control operations from operations management, thus ensuring more fluent and effective management.

Consequently, it is beneficial to have a clear understanding of the bodies that must be established or utilised within RI governance. In general, key tasks assigned to the main bodies can be identified by examining the main statutes of the ERIC, AISBL RIs, or the consortium as a legal framework.

The General Assembly, for example, adopts the annual work programme and budget, approves financial reports and the annual activity report, and approves Agreements and Memoranda of Understanding with Members, and any rules, regulations, guidelines, or other decisions required to ensure the performance. It also elects and dismisses members of the Board of Directors or the Executive Director or Director General, appoints members to other committees, and undertakes any other functions conferred upon it by the statutes, including any annexes or modifications thereto. These tasks represent a deliberative body, responsible for decision-making and control functions.

Having analysed all the RIs in the ESFRI landscape,[4] the tasks are those explained above. However, the denomination of this deliberative body changes from 'RI' to 'RI'. In particular, we can highlight how, both for single-sited RIs and foundations, the denomination turns out to be 'council' in most cases, while it can be 'general assembly', 'council', or 'assembly of members' for ERICs and other consortia.

The primary duties of the Director or members of the Board of Directors should be to support the General Assembly, manage day-to-day operations, follow the directions and decisions made by the General Assembly, as well as provide feedback from other boards and committees, implements the Annual Work Plans and

[4] http://roadmap2018.esfri.eu/strategy-report/the-esfri-research-infrastructures-list/.

prepare their own internal procedures for organisation and meetings. This body represents the actual management body, which has fewer tasks than the management body of private companies. Often this body is also referred to as 'executive body', but the fact of being 'executive' does not preclude strategic management and coordination activities. According to Laurent Romary (then chairman of the Board of Directors of DARIAH), the director general is not an executive of DARIAH-ERIC. The most executive part of his work is entrusted to an efficient coordinator office[5] that supports the board. The fact of being executive or not must be defined in the statutes or bylaws and, therefore, may depend on the RI (Romary, 2017).

The same analysis of the ESFRI landscape shows that most of the RIs use the denomination 'director general' for the management body (this denomination is evident in some ERICs but especially for IGOs), while in other cases 'director' or 'Board of Directors' is used. Only a few RIs analysed use names such as 'executive board', 'management board', and 'executive director'.

There are also other committees that may be relevant and assist the RIs in economic governance. One is a scientific advisory board, which is a technical body that provides consultancy. Its focus is on the mission of the RI, making sure it performs to the highest standards (Baines, 2017). It plays a significant role in providing strategic scientific advice to the RI Board. Its most important duties are to review applications for new nodes and make recommendations to the Board, ensure scientific and technical excellence and relevance, provide useful feedback, know-how, experience, ideas, and advice to develop research activities according to the latest challenges and trends, and report directly to the Board of Directors on the results of their scientific review of activities. Other committees or bodies that help manage the particularities of RIs have different names and tasks, such as the finance committee, the industry committee, the risk management director, the safety environment and health physics director, and the supervisory board (see details in Table 2).

Given the enormous disparity in terms of mission and vision, organisational structure, costs and benefits, and the type and multidimensionality of stakeholders (scientific, technological, economic, public, or policymakers), it is interesting to examine the key differences between RIs and private companies in terms of governance structure.

In private companies, the assembly has functions similar to those in RIs, namely approving financial reports, electing and removing members of the Board of Directors, and amending the statutes. In contrast, in the case of the Board of Directors/Director, the body of private companies seems to have more power, especially with regard to the task of 'governing the organization by establishing broad policies and setting out strategic objectives'. In private companies, the strategic objectives are the responsibility of the Board of Directors, while in RIs, it is more complicated to assign this task to a specific and univocal body.

[5]The National Coordinator Committee shall be one of the two operational organs of DARIAH ERIC. Its aim is to integrate and coordinate national DARIAH activities at the European level.

Table 2 Other RI committees

RI	Legal model	Names of other bodies
BBMRI	ERIC	Finance Committee, Steering Committee, Central Executive Management Office, Stakeholder Forum, Common Services (ELSI, IT, others)
CERN	IGO	Finance Committee
CESDA	ERIC	Main Office (trust support, technical, training, project working group); Service Providers Forum
DARIAH	ERIC	National Coordinators Committee, Joint Research Committee
DESY	Foundation	Desy Photon Science Committee, Physics Research Committee, Machine Advisory Committee, Scientific Committee
E. SPALLATION SOURCE	ERIC	In Kind Review Committee; Technical Advisory Committee; Administrative and Finance Committee
EATRIS	ERIC	Board of National Directors
ECCSEL	ERIC	RI coordinator Committee, Ethics and Environmental Advisory Board, other advisory committee
ECRIN	ERIC	Steering Committee
EIBIR	LLC	Industry Panel
ELI	Association	Executive Committee
ELIXIR	Consortium	Industry Advisory Committee
EMBL	IGO	Finance Committee
EMSO	ERIC	Executive Committee
ESA	IGO	Administrative and Finance Committee, Industrial Policy Committee, International Relations Committee, Security Committee, Science Programme Committee
ESO	IGO	Finance Committee, Scientific Technical Committee, Observing Programmes Committee, Users Committee
ESRF	LLC	Machine Advisory Committee
ESS ERIC	ERIC	Methods Advisory Board, Finance Committee, Core Scientific Team
ICOS	ERIC	Head Office, Carbon Portal, ICOS RI Committee
ILL	IGO	Subcommittee on Administrative Questions, Director's Services (safety environment and health physics, medical service, risk management, public relations, industrial liaison unit)
JIVE	ERIC	Head Office, Technical Operations and R&D, User Support
LIFEWATCH ERIC	ERIC	The Standing Committee, The Financial Committee, The Ethics committee
PRACE	Association	Industrial Advisory Committee, Access Committee
SHARE	ERIC	Questionnaire Committee

Certainly, one of the most challenging problems that arise in decision-making at RIs is the relationship between the decision-making body, or assembly, and the executive body, specifically the Board of Directors. The right to vote is a fundamental tool in exercising decision-making power. Therefore, it is essential to determine the most effective way to distribute voting rights in each RI. In general, it appears that RIs choose to give each member state a vote, and even if there are two representatives per country, the two usually vote as one. Another problem related to this is the extent to which a member state can contribute, particularly in terms of financial resources. Even in this case, the contribution often depends on the defined calculation basis, which is usually GDP. In such a case, wealthier countries contribute more financially but have the same voting power, which is often a cause for discussion.

References

Ahrne, G., & Brunsson, N. (2005). Organizations and meta-organizations. *Scandinavian Journal of Management, 21*(4), 429–449.

Ahrne, G., & Brunsson, N. (2008). *Meta-organizations*. Edward Elgar Publishing.

Antivachis, N. A., & Angelis, V. A. (2014). Network organizations: The question of governance. *Procedia: Social and Behavioral Sciences, 175*, 584–592.

Baines, I. (2017). *Webinar "Managing governance of RIs" in EMMRI "Executive Masters in Management of Research Infrastructures"*. University of Milano-Bicocca.

Barjak, F., Eccles, K., Meyer, E. T., Schroeder, R., & Robinson, S. (2013). The emerging governance of e-infrastructure. *Journal of Computer-Mediated Communication, 18*, 113–136.

Berkowitz, H., & Dumez, H. (2016). The concept of meta-organization: Issues for management studies. *European Management Review, 13*(2), 149–156.

Cadbury Committee. (1992). *The Cadbury report. Financial aspects of corporate governance*. Burgess Science Press.

Cohen, M. D., & March, J. G. (1974). *Leadership and ambiguity: The American college president*. McGraw Hill.

Czarniawska-Joerges, B. (1992). *Exploring complex organizations: A cultural perspective*. Sage.

Dhanaraj, C. R. C., & Parkher, A. (2006). Orchestrating innovation networks. *Academy of Management Review, 31*(3), 659–669.

Edwards, P. N., Jackson, S. J., Chalmers, M. K., Bowker, G. C., Borgman, C. L., Ribes, D., Burton, M., & Calvert, S. (2013). *Knowledge infrastructures: Intellectual frameworks and research challenges*. Deep Blue.

ESFRI. (2018). *ESFRI Roadmap 2018—strategy report on research infrastructures*, Università degli Studi di Milano.

Etzioni, A. (1961). *A comparative analysis of complex organizations*. The Free Press.

European Commission. (2020a). *European research infrastructures*. Retrieved June 7, 2020 from https://ec.europa.eu/info/research-and-innovation/strategy/european-research-infrastructures_en.

European Commission. (2020b). *European research infrastructures, including e-Infrastructures*. Retrieved June 7, 2020 from https://ec.europa.eu/programmes/horizon2020/en/h2020-section/research-infrastructures-including-e-infrastructures.

Hardin, G. (1968). The tragedy of the commons. *Science, 162*(3859), 1243–1248.

Ianniello, M., Iacuzzi, S., Fedele, P., & Brusati, L. (2019). Obstacles and solutions on the ladder of citizen participation: A systematic review. *Public Management Review, 21*(1), 21–46.

Jain, R. K., & Triandis, H. C. (1997). *Management of research and development organizations: Managing the unmanageable*. Wiley.

Krasner, S. D. (1983). *International Regimes*. Cornell University Press.

LifeWatch ERIC. (2020). *Who we are*. Retrieved June 7, 2020 from https://www.lifewatch.eu/web/guest/who-we-are.
Mayntz, R. (2006). From government to governance: Political steering in modern societies. In F. Rubik & D. Scheer (Eds.), *Governance of integrated product policy: In search of sustainable production and consumption* (pp. 18–25). Greenleaf Publishing.
Meijer, I., Molas-Gallart, J., & Mattsson, P. (2012). Networked research infrastrucures and their governance: The case of biobanking. *Science and Public Policy, 39*, 491–499.
Morgan, G. (1986). *Images of organization*. Sage Publications.
OECD. (2008). Roadmapping of large research infrastructures. Paris: OECD Global Science Forum. Retrieved June 7, 2020 from http://www.oecd.org/sti/inno/47057832.pdf.
OECD. (2010). *Establishing large international research infrastructures*. OECD Global Science Forum. Retrieved June 7, 2020 from http://www.oecd.org/sti/inno/47057832.pdf
OECD. (2014). *International distributed research infrastructures: Issues and options*. OECD. Retrieved November 18, 2019 from http://www.oecd.org/sti/inno/international-distributed-research-infrastructures.pdf
OECD. (2017). *Strengthening the effectiveness and sustainability of international research infrastructures*, OECD science technology and industry policy paper no. 48, 21 December 2017.
Olson, M. (1965). *The logic of collective action: Public goods and the theory of groups*. Harvard University Press.
Ostrom, E. (1990). *Governing the commons: The evolution of institutions for collective action*. Cambridge University Press.
Ouchi, W. G. (1980). Markets, bureaucracies, and clans. *Administrative Science Quarterly, 25*(1), 129–141.
Provan, G. K., & Kenis, P. (2007). Modes of network governance: Structure, management, and effectiveness. *Journal of Public Administration and Theory, 18*, 229–252.
Ryan, L. (2015). Governance of EU research policy: Charting forms of scientific democracy in the European research area. *Science and Public Policy, 42*, 300–314.
Romary, L. (2017). *Webinar "Governance challenges in setting up and running an ERIC" in EMMRI "Executive Masters in Management of Research Infrastructures"*. University of Milano-Bicocca.
Weber, M. (1947). *The theory of social and economic organization*. Oxford University Press.
Weick, K. (1976). Educational organizations as loosely coupled systems. *Administrative Science Quarterly, 21*(1), 1–19.
Young, O. R. (1999). *Governance in world affairs*. Cornell University Press.

Strategic Management in Research Infrastructures

Elisabetta Marafioti, Ilaria Nardello, and Jennifer Edmond

Abstract

The chapter focuses on the process of building strategy in research infrastructures as a core process in their development and future sustainability. Building common values, a mission, and a vision is just the starting point of a long and continuous process of strategic management that leads to building a business model, a strategic plan, and its consistent implementation.

1 Introduction

Strategic management is, without any doubt, a core activity for research infrastructures. In fact, it is fundamental for the process of creating and setting up a new research infrastructure. Very often, research infrastructures are the result of a joint activity managed through strict collaboration among international institutions that have previously collaborated on research projects. However, a long history of cooperation among national players is not, in itself, sufficient to lead to the creation of a research infrastructure in the form of an ERIC. The experience of RIs over the last 15 years has revealed that the turning point in the evolution of research infrastructures is always the creation of a common base, represented by shared values, mission, and vision. These are the roots on which it is possible to design a strategy and

E. Marafioti (✉)
Department of Business and Law, University of Milano-Bicocca, Milan, Italy
e-mail: elisabetta.marafioti@unimib.it

I. Nardello
School of Medicine and Surgery - University of Milano-Bicocca, Milan, Italy
e-mail: ilaria.nardello@unimib.it

J. Edmond
Trinity College Dublin, Dublin, Ireland
e-mail: edmondj@tcd.ie

E. Guarini et al. (eds.), *Research Infrastructure Management*, Management for Professionals, https://doi.org/10.1007/978-3-032-20373-1_3

then build a strategic plan aimed at guaranteeing the continuity of activities within a research infrastructure.

The chapter is built around these key concepts, with a particular focus on how a research infrastructure can be designed, built, and grown by adopting a dynamic and contingent approach.

The first paragraph provides a definition of the terms "strategic management" and "strategy", adopting a historical approach. The second is dedicated to the description of the determinants of strategy, values, mission, and vision. The third is shedding light on the importance of understanding the environment, while the fourth is on business model design, strategy formulation, and strategic planning.

2 What Are Strategic Management and Strategy

Strategic management is the evolution of what was once called "policy" or "business policies" and nowadays it is simply defined as strategy. It is about the direction of organizations and, most commonly, of businesses (Rumel et al., 1991).[1] Its main focus is the understanding of the reasons for an organization's success and failure. In the scenario described by strategic management firms/organizations are operating in an environment where they compete with other firms/organizations for factor inputs and customers/users, since the former contribute to the generation of costs and the latter to revenues that, in balance, allow them to survive over time.

Firm/organization survival is, in fact, the result of a series of complex decisions that can be defined as strategic. They can be classified as:

- The identification and choice of goals.
- The selection of products and services to offer.
- The choice and implementation of the position a firm/organization is willing to occupy in its environment and relative to other firms/organizations.
- The definition of the appropriate scope and variety of its activities and actions.
- The design of organizational structure, systems, and mechanisms adopted in order to coordinate a complex set of actors and activities.

All the previously described decisions are, in fact, interconnected and self-influential and therefore must be evaluated as a single unit. And this is, in fact, the primary role and contribution of strategy.

Strategic management originated in the 1960s with the seminal contribution of Andrews that defined strategy: "*Strategy is the pattern of decisions in a company that determines and reveals its objectives, purposes, or goals, produces the*

[1] In the field of strategic management and strategy, some terms are used interchangeably such as firm/organization/enterprise or policy/strategy/strategic management or policy/strategy/strategic management.

principal policies and plans for achieving those goals, and defines the range of business the company is to pursue, the kind of economic and human organization it is or intends to be, and the nature of the economic and noneconomic contribution it intends to make to its shareholders, employees, customers, and communities" (Andrews, 1971). According to this definition, strategy is not simply a coordination or integration of functions but rather focuses on selecting the arenas where firms/organizations are willing to confront each other ("compete" in the original version) and the key decisions on how to confront the other players in the arena.

Depending on the definition taken into consideration from the 1960s on, the emphasis has been put, alternatively, on leadership (Selznick, 1957), organizational structure (Chandler, 1962), mission, and distinctive competencies, firms' strengths and weaknesses leveraged in order to build a competitive advantage (Andrews, 1971; Ansoff, 1965).

Strategic management originated in the 1960s and flourished in the 1970s, marked by the creation of professional associations and journals that published on strategy, as well as the development of consulting companies specializing in strategy. The strong economic instability that characterized the 1970s led to a progressive abandonment of the planning approach, which was very popular during the stable and strongly growing 1960s. While originally the goal was to adopt an approach that allowed for the protection and exploitation of firm strengths, in the 1970s, firms focused on leveraging strengths to generate innovative products and services required in a dynamic environment. In the same period, new tools and concepts flourished, also thanks to the relevant contribution of consulting companies that focused their attention on multibusiness firms and how to manage their activity portfolio. It is during this period that research begins to focus attention on the link between strategy and performance, observing the heterogeneity of performance that characterizes firms/organizations belonging to the same industry or arena. It was during the 1980s that many empirical studies were published on the topic. The most influential contribution in this period is undoubtedly that of Michael E. Porter, who published the still cited and applied *Competitive Strategy* (1980). Concepts such as industry analysis, mobility barriers, competitive advantage, and generic strategies have spread quickly both in the academic and business contexts. Michael Porter also contributed to the definition of strategy (1996). According to Porter, a firm/organization generates superior performance compared to its competitors if it possesses a competitive advantage that makes it better than other actors. Rather than focusing on its definition, it is essential to emphasize that Porter aims to clarify what is not strategy: operational effectiveness is not a form of strategy. Operational effectiveness refers to performing similar activities more efficiently than rivals. This is necessary, but not sufficient, for competitive advantage. As a consequence, strategic positioning means performing different activities from rivals' or performing similar activities in different ways:

- Variety-based positioning (producing a subset of products/services)
- Needs-based positioning (serving the needs of a particular group of customers)
- Access-based positioning (using different ways to reach customers)

Most importantly, strategy involves trade-offs, choosing what not to do.

Another group of scholars has instead focused attention on uniqueness and difficult-to-imitate resources as the basis of firm/organization's superior performance. This conception was defined as a resource-based view of the firm, aimed at identifying, building, and protecting resources and competencies at the base of a firm/organization's superior performance (Wernerfelt, 1984; Teece, 1982; Rumelt et al., 1994; Barney, 1986; Teece et al., 1997; Grant, 1996).

This passage from macro to micro foundations of management further developed in the concept of dynamic capabilities that allow companies to continuously adjust to environmental changes to guarantee their durability, autonomy, and sustainability over time.

This evolution has led to a definition of strategy that is lighter than it was in its origins. As affirmed by Rivkin (2006), "*It is the integrated set of choices that positions the business in its industry so as to generate superior financial returns over the long run.*"

In broader terms, strategy is the design that defines a firm's system of activities, orienting them towards common goals and results. A strategy is what links a firm/organization to its environment. Any firm/organization possesses a strategy, whether implicit or explicit. The choice of goals is the first fundamental decision required any time a firm/organization is willing to elaborate an explicit strategy. Very often, the process of goal definition is underestimated, since many companies believe that firm goals simply relate to either generating profitability or increasing shareholder value. Goals definition is fundamental, since the success of a strategy is determined by their achievement, combined with a deep understanding of the competitive environment, objective appraisal of resources, and effective implementation (Grant, 2015) (Fig. 1).

Top management possesses a certain degree of freedom in defining firm/organization goals; however, if they are aimed at guaranteeing long-lasting life for companies, it is fundamental to define them on the basis of firm/organization stakeholders' expectations, including, among others, shareholders, employees, customers/users, partners, and a broader community. In the case of RI, the complexity of stakeholders involved is even broader, since they are multinational organizations that bring together professional interests, national interests, and public interests, all represented by hundreds of stakeholders.

While achieving shared and long-term goals, firms/organizations produce a variety of results that are aimed at rewarding and satisfying stakeholders' expectations. Results can be grouped into three main categories:

Fig. 1 What makes a successful strategy. Source: Author's elaboration

- Competitive results that measure the appreciation and consensus from customers/users
- Social results represented by consensus, approval, and loyalty from internal and external collaborators and partners and other stakeholders
- Economic and financial results that are particularly appealing to shareholders and the financial community

These three categories of results should be jointly achieved by a firm/organization with a successful strategy. The same scheme applies to RI too, even if results are weighted differently and, namely, social returns and social impact are the most relevant indicator, followed by economic-financial returns, which guarantee the sustainability of each RI and competitive results that are relevant in determining the raison d'être of an RI. In particular, in the case of RIs, relative weights are also changing depending on the stage of their life cycle. In particular, at a later stage, when economic self-sustainability becomes a priority, competitive results require special attention.

In order to define strategic goals, it is important to work on aspirations as a driver of strategy, as well as the three pillars of strategy: values, mission, and vision, which are outlined in the following paragraph.

Box 1 The Origin of DARIAH-ERIC: A Strong Common Cultural Base

The history of DARIAH (Digital Research Infrastructure for the Arts and Humanities) started in January 2006 when representatives from four European institutions (AHDS, DANS, CNRS, and the Max Planck Society) met to identify how they could join efforts in providing services to the research communities they served, with a strong focus on the arts and humanities. The idea behind this meeting was to go towards a consortium of institutions, which would ensure long-term sustainability of the underlying infrastructure and a strong political voice towards the EU. Each institution held a national role in coordinating or developing digital services in the humanities and could thus speak with a national perspective.

Establishing an infrastructure for the arts and humanities is a rather difficult task for a series of reasons:

- A research infrastructure for the arts and humanities should be able to provide concrete short-term services that may give it a scholarly recognition and at the same time have a clear vision about its general objectives that will guide the evolution of the infrastructure over the years.
- It needs to gain institutional support and demonstrate that it matches the strategic objectives of its funders.
- It needs to clearly define the manner in which it complements local initiatives to provide technical support to researchers.
- It must show its value for money in the sense that scholars do not see the infrastructure as consuming budget that would otherwise go to research.

These elements potentially apply to all scientific domains. Still, the humanities represent an even more complex environment because, on the one hand, of its highly fragmented scholarly structure, and, on the other hand, its lower levels of technical penetration. Whereas DARIAH has managed to gain institutional recognition at European and national level, it is its capacity to relate to this complex community of users that will be a real measure of its success.

DARIAH's ethos is very much driven "by researchers, for researchers". Its great strength lies therefore in its appeal to those who are at the cutting edge of new research in the humanities, based on its community-driven agenda. As stated in report presented during the General Assembly Meeting in Vienna on 4th November 2016:

"*We are therefore naturally able to support, inspire and connect a multitude of forward-looking scholarly networks across the arts and humanities. DARIAH is also very dynamic. In an era of great change, given the digital turn also in the academy, for researchers to be able to lead transformations in new technology-driven methods and forms of publication is crucial. This aspect is now as much part of the humanities researcher's activity as impact metrics, public engagement, teaching and research ethics. However, with the relevant technology becoming increasingly a commodity, humanities scholars require more than ever before new skills and competences, in order to enjoy new such digitally-enabled research opportunities to their fullest. People and skills are our most valuable infrastructure.*"

3 Aspirations, Values, Mission, and Vision

For a firm/organization that is willing to build common goals that are shared by all its stakeholders, it is important to clearly define its aspirations. **Aspirations** are the sense of purpose that motivates both individuals and organizations. In the case of organizations, aspirations are described by their mission, vision, and values that constitute their main components. Quoting Drucker (1974), one of the gurus of strategic management: "*A business is not defined by its name, statutes, or articles of incorporation. It is defined by the business mission. Only a clear definition of the mission and purpose for the organization makes possible clear and realistic business objectives.*"

In the case of RI, setting common aspirations in terms of mission, vision, and values is a fundamental and necessary step to create the basis for a successful RI as an ERIC. Building common aspirations, a mission, and a vision is, in fact, the process that allows RI to create a strong foundation for a new organization that brings together differences and coordinates them, thereby adding value to all involved institutions. This is also because aspirations are enduring and based on deep motivation.

A **mission** explains the reason an organization exists and guides and inspires it for years or even for a longer period of time (Collis & Rukstad, 2008; Casadesus-Masanell, 2014). It is strictly interconnected with the **vision** (what future we want to create) that describes how the organization, by implementing its mission, will shape the future of the industry or the context in which it operates (Casadesus-Masanell, 2014). Quoting Peter Senge (2006): *"Purpose is similar to a direction... Vision is a specific destination."*

What counts here is not what the mission and vision are formally declared on official documents published by the organization or on the website, but rather what is deeply felt by the members of the organization. And that's why mission and vision must be strongly rooted in organizational values that reflect culture (what is important to us (Casadesus-Masanell, 2014)). Values are what organizations believe in, and they are what binds all people participating in the organization. They motivate but also activate a self-selection process where stakeholders join the organization if they share the same values. Financial objectives are often clearly declared by an organization to dialogue with the financial community and stakeholders; however, even if important, they do not contribute to the creation of any motivation and commitment.

This is a very relevant issue in the case of RI, where multinationalism leads to bringing together very different national cultures that, most of the time, are mediated by professional cultures that, in the field of hard sciences, art, and humanities, are very strong and are rooted in the ethos of research. However, organizational aspirations and, therefore, culture must be constructed by individuals who possess their own aspirations and culture. In the case of RI, this potential misalignment is, generally speaking, bypassed by past experiences of collaboration involving members of the RI. It is often the case that partners willing to create an RI as an autonomous organization have collaborated for years, and in some cases for decades, on projects financed by the EU to promote transnational coordination and synergies.

Box 2 DARIAH High-Level Principles and Strategic Directions

In light of its founding as an ERIC, starting in 2014 but continuing into 2019, DARIAH began to devise some guiding high-level principles. These principles were intended to allow both researchers and those who support them to orientate themselves regarding what DARIAH is ambitious to achieve, while respecting the conditions of transformation for the arts and humanities, from analogue to digital, from national to international, from digital humanists to all those in the humanities that work in a digitally enabled way. The principles are as follows:

Science and Technology Principles
- Enable digital arts and humanities research
- Integrate existing resources, research, and services
- Use innovations from the national DARIAH partners and scale them to a European level
- Deliver methodological innovation and promote interdisciplinary research
- Stay digitally focused and analogue aware

Organizational Principles
- Operate under a sustainable business model within the larger scientific community in Europe
- Be receptive to community needs
- Deliver easy to use services and resources
- Delegate trust and share responsibilities
- Display high-quality services

Community Principles
- Governed and led by the arts and humanities research community
- Become community-driven
- Be inclusive
- Promote openness
- Enable transnational collaboration
- Promote standards and best practices

Deeply rooted in these principles are DARIAH's vision and mission.

DARIAH's vision is that the arts and humanities be firmly at the centre of a technologically evolving knowledge society.

DARIAH's mission is to empower research communities with digital methods to create, connect, and share knowledge about culture and society.

Why?

"We empower not because our communities have a deficit, but because we can help them add capacities that meet new or emerging requirements for their research and research environment.

We work for research because it is only through research that knowledge expands, but we do not see this as an exclusive activity for professionals only. Human curiosity can drive anyone to want to know more, and our remit reaches to many classes of professionals, students, and citizens.

We focus on communities, as the shared practices of a community for the baseline for the infrastructure we provide, which ensures the relevance of our work.

Digital methods are a cornerstone of what we do, ensuring we focus on how technology is transforming not objects, but activities.

To create, connect, and share knowledge reflects the stages of any research process, which we take as our own model.

Culture and society are the ultimate objects of the disciplines of the arts and humanities: we choose to name them in this way to underscore our commitment to more than academic research and jargon."

The links among strategy, mission, vision, and values are very strong because common goals are defined starting from values, and people within organizations are responsible for strategy elaboration and implementation. As we observed in the previous paragraph, strategy refers to how an organization chooses to operate in its environment in comparison with other players within the industry where they share a relationship based on a combination of cooperation and competition. While aspirations (mission, vision, and values) and strategy are addressing different issues, they must be aligned.

To support this alignment, the mission and vision should be both strategic and motivational. The reason behind this statement is that when motivations are strong and organizational aspirations are aligned with individual aspirations, the actions connected with strategy will also be activated accordingly, since strategy, as observed before, is created by people. When managers, who are responsible for providing direction to the organization, also share the same orientation, then they will be able to lead the organization while motivating its members and stakeholders.

Consequently, a mission statement should be crafted in a way that defines a set of goals that encompass the organization's purpose, its scope of operations, and the basis of its competitive advantage. Furthermore, it communicates the organization's reason for being and how it aims to serve its key stakeholders, often integrating a summary of the firm's values. Because of this broad articulation, mission statements tend to be longer than vision statements, and that's why it has the greatest impact when they reflect an organization's enduring, overarching strategic priorities and competitive positioning.

Conversely, a vision is "*massively inspiring, overarching, and long-term*" (Bart & Baetz, 1998; Collins & Ponas, 1991). It represents a destination that is driven by and evokes passion, serving as a future-oriented declaration of the organization's purpose and aspirations, addressing what a firm wants to become. Furthermore, vision statements tend to be relatively brief.

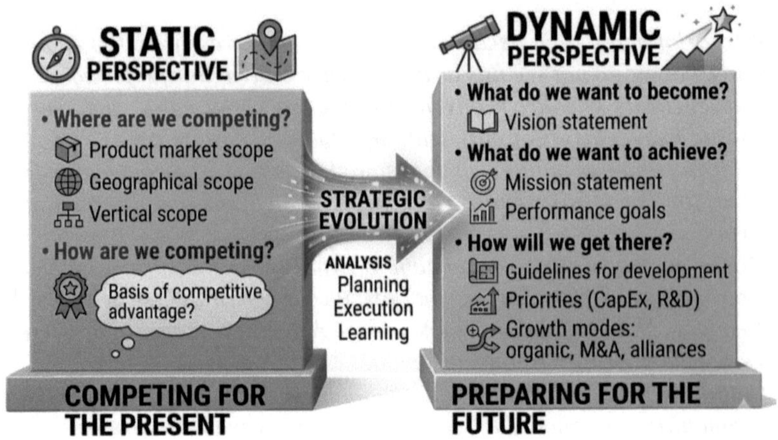

Fig. 2 Describing strategy: competing for the present; preparing for the future. Source: Author's elaboration

Combining mission, vision, and values with strategy implies a transition from a static approach, characterized by strategic choices determined by the willingness to occupy a market position, to a dynamic approach where, by focusing on aspirations, a company is constantly preparing for the future (Grant, 2015) (Fig. 2).

The deep connection between aspirations and strategy is defined as the strategy process and can be described as a feedback loop. Once an organization has defined its aspirations, it can elaborate strategic goals that can be implemented on the basis of a strategy that has been elaborated (strategy formulation) after running a strategic analysis, both internal and external to the organization.

The process is not linear, but rather iterative, and requires the simultaneous development of aspirations, strategy, and business model to achieve full consistency.

The following two paragraphs focus therefore on analysing the environment before moving to the strategic making process and the strategic plan.

3.1 Analysing the Environment

A deep understanding of the context (external analysis) in which the organization operates is very important to develop a series of actions that can favour the implementation of strategic goals. A good analysis of the environment allows us to identify the main opportunities that it is interesting to capture and, at the same time, also the risks that the organization should confront.

To collect all relevant information for organizations, it is advisable to conduct both macro and meso analyses of the environment, which requires a differentiated set of tools. This includes PESTLE analysis to understand the macro-level and industry analysis to explore the meso level.

PESTLE is an acronym for Political, Economic, Sociological, Technological, Legal, and Environmental factors; it is a useful tool for understanding the "big picture" of the environment in which RI operates, thereby taking advantage of opportunities and minimizing threats. For this reason, it is crucial to develop scenarios that are fundamental to building accurate forecasts.

This provides the context within which more detailed planning can occur to fully leverage the opportunities that present themselves. A description of the key elements and key information that are required to build a PESTLE analysis is provided in Figs. 3 and 4.

A PESTLE analysis for a research infrastructure, which typically has a transnational structure, should be developed in each market where a node is located to capture all relevant trends that support the decision-making process.

Once this analysis is completed, it is essential to proceed to the second level and focus on competitive analysis (Fig. 5), which describes the competitive and collaborative forces that drive the industry. Unlike PESTLE analysis, which is run at the national level, or, in the case of RI, can also be run at the EU level, competitive

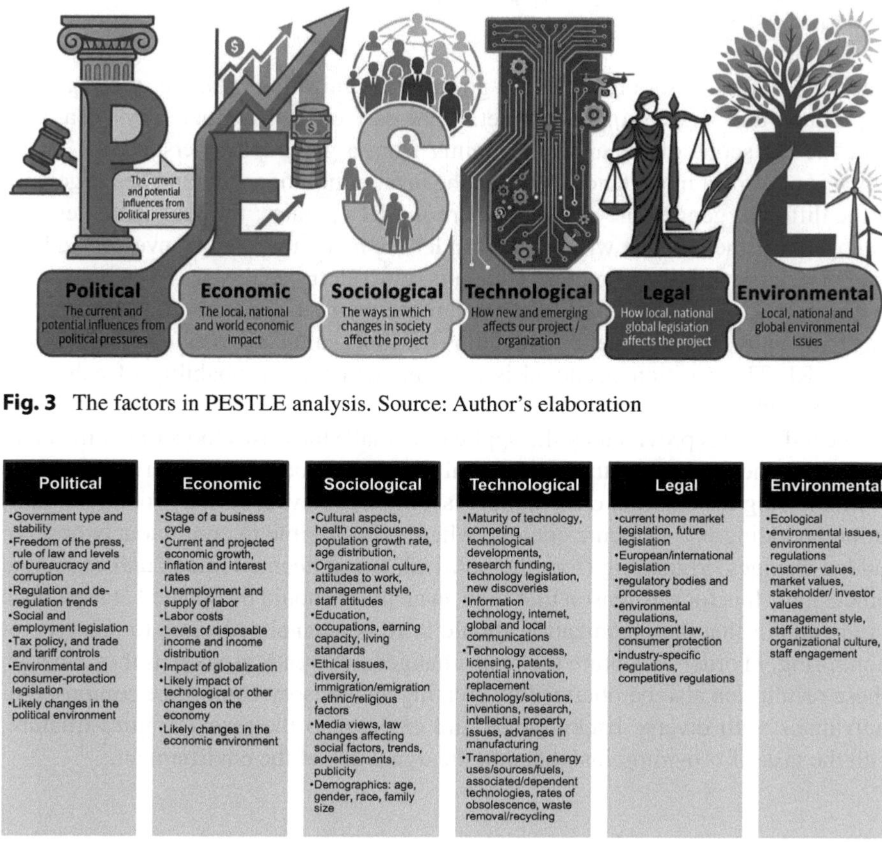

Fig. 3 The factors in PESTLE analysis. Source: Author's elaboration

Political	Economic	Sociological	Technological	Legal	Environmental
•Government type and stability •Freedom of the press, rule of law and levels of bureaucracy and corruption •Regulation and de-regulation trends •Social and employment legislation •Tax policy, and trade and tariff controls •Environmental and consumer-protection legislation •Likely changes in the political environment	•Stage of a business cycle •Current and projected economic growth, inflation and interest rates •Unemployment and supply of labor •Labor costs •Levels of disposable income and income distribution •Impact of globalization •Likely impact of technological or other changes on the economy •Likely changes in the economic environment	•Cultural aspects, health consciousness, population growth rate, age distribution, •Organizational culture, attitudes to work, management style, staff attitudes •Education, occupations, earning capacity, living standards •Ethical issues, diversity, immigration/emigration, ethnic/religious factors •Media views, law changes affecting social factors, trends, advertisements, publicity •Demographics: age, gender, race, family size	•Maturity of technology, competing technological developments, research funding, technology legislation, new discoveries •Information technology, internet, global and local communications •Technology access, licensing, patents, potential innovation, replacement technology/solutions, inventions, research, intellectual property issues, advances in manufacturing •Transportation, energy uses/sources/fuels, associated/dependent technologies, rates of obsolescence, waste removal/recycling	•current home market legislation, future legislation •European/international legislation •regulatory bodies and processes •environmental regulations, employment law, consumer protection •industry-specific regulations, competitive regulations	•Ecological •environmental issues, environmental regulations •customer values, market values, stakeholder/ investor values •management style, staff attitudes, organizational culture, staff engagement

Fig. 4 PESTLE details. Source: Author's elaboration

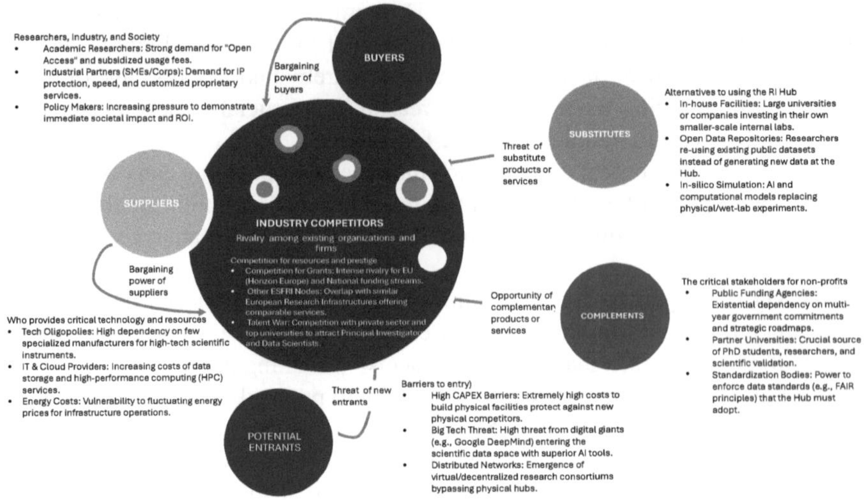

Fig. 5 Industry analysis: forces governing competition in RI ecosystems. Source: Author's elaboration based on Porter (2008)

analysis has as its unit of analysis the group or organizations that are offering similar products and services on the market. In the case of RI, it is not always clear how to define the scope of the analysis, mainly from a geographic perspective. That's why it is of utmost importance to assess the level of homogeneity and heterogeneity of the different geographic markets where the RI operates: the higher the level of homogeneity, the easier it will be to consider the market as one. Conversely, a high level of heterogeneity will require a country-by-country analysis.

The analysis of the six roles an actor can occupy in the industry aims to measure the relative power and influence and define the most suitable position in the industry for the RI. The position occupied is also impacting the probability of achieving positive results.

The indications provided by the application make these two tools fundamental to developing the first part of the SWOT analysis, which focuses on external elements.

Monitoring the external environment is a highly relevant activity for any organization operating in a dynamic context, where it is possible to continuously observe sudden changes originating from the political, social, technological, and economic dimensions. It is for this reason that such an analysis should be updated at least once a year, and/or that the organization should have personnel dedicated to this type of monitoring, in order to capture the main changes and trends as soon as they emerge. These results can also be obtained by creating an advisory committee composed of individuals with diverse backgrounds and external to the research infrastructure, with the task of providing insights into the dynamics of the environment.

4 Strategic Making Process and Strategic Plan

Once the environmental analysis is complete, the RI must select a position that facilitates its objectives. This decision then drives key operational actions, specifically the development of the business model.

These decisions and actions are outlined in a strategic plan, which serves as the "game plan" for positioning the company in its chosen market arena, competing successfully, satisfying customers, and achieving optimal business performance. A strategic plan helps firms and organizations move from where they are today to where they want to go and determines an organization's strategic position today and in the future. Insights gained through environmental and SWOT analysis help make prudent choices and select appropriate courses of action. The strategic plan serves as the "bridge" or roadmap between where the organization is now and where managers want it to be.

Box 3 DARIAH's Strategic Plan Four Pillars[2]

1. DARIAH as creator: Build a Marketplace to facilitate fluid exchange of tools, services, data, and knowledge.

   Access to tools, data, knowledge, and services that are tuned for use and reuse by arts and humanities researchers is a major challenge for them. This challenge has been at the heart of DARIAH since its earliest formulation: the statutory requirement that DARIAH members give far more in-kind than cash contribution differentiates us and speaks to our real power. Easing the flow of contributions from creator to user, for the benefit of both, and in a way that provides the rich context researchers need when evaluating how to sharpen their research, is one of the most distinct, important, and unique things we can do. The centrepoint of this commitment will be our ambitious plan to build an arts and humanities-friendly component for the European Open Science Cloud, connecting us to a major EU development and to the areas emphasized in the strategic paper developed by the NCC in 2017–2018.

2. DARIAH as transformative: Build access to education and training.

   Research in a fast-changing environment requires a sustained access to new perspectives and methods. While this happens in universities as well, research infrastructures like DARIAH are uniquely positioned to share new kinds of knowledge from broader networks in a wider variety of formats. In particular, mid-career researchers would struggle to meet their needs through traditional training, but short, focused schools and infrastructure access programmes provide alternative modes, which are a key strength and service. We do not want to reinvent ourselves as a university;

[2] Figure caption from DARIAH 2019–2026 Strategic Plan, licensed under CC-BY 3.0 US, available at: https://www.dariah.eu/wp-content/uploads/2019/08/Strategic-Plan_2019-2026.pdf.

however, so positioning DARIAH as a unique provider of or collaborator for education and training will be a significant challenge of the model we seek to realize.

3. DARIAH as connector: Build working groups, hubs, and other forms of transnational and transdisciplinary organization.

   Enabling our communities to self-organize around emerging research themes and concerns is a win-win situation: they get a structure within which to develop at an early phase, and we get an overview of the future trends and leaders in the digitally enabled humanities. Working Groups are interdisciplinary, transnational, and transverse in their approach to determining their field of enquiry. As such, they represent the fruit and the future of our research fields, although not the only one in which DARIAH might invest, given the past successes with regional hubs, the long tradition of disciplinary societies, and of course the many inspirational examples in our member countries.

   Through such mechanisms, DARIAH will build into its strategy the commitment to deepen our connection to our communities and ensure they are with us, expanding our impact on and enhancing research cultures within member countries, within key disciplines, and outside of the stereotypical researcher profiles. We will need to be creative about how we use not only the now-tested forms of organization and support (such as the Working Groups, and the funding we have dedicated to them) but also instruments we may have trialled (like the Ambassadors programme), maintained over a long time (like the theme funding or EU project consortia), or only proposed (like discipline subject centres) in order to promote a better level of awareness and service in the "long tail" of the digital humanities.

4. DARIAH as complementary: Build bridges between research policy and communities of practice.

   Brussels, or indeed one's own capital city or national research support structure, may seem a very long way from the desk of the average arts or humanist researcher. Often, however, the policies in development in these places are closer to home than that researcher may think. The arts and humanities need a voice in Europe where research policies, in particular those with a technological element, are being discussed, as well as a translator able to bring those nascent policies to the communities, to allow them to prepare and consider the impact that may be coming in 5–10 years time.

   Our position as a Europe-wide organization with a solid base and close links to a wide range of actors in Brussels is an asset we can deploy for the long-term good of our community.

   The fact that DARIAH could and should play a unique and strong role in policy and advocacy is a realization that seems obvious, and yet has only truly been operationalized recently, in particular around the policy focus on open science. We need to expand and explore this role: defining new emerging areas where the arts and humanities will be implicated; addressing key barriers to the development of digital researchers and methods, like rights and copyright in TDM, and the sustainability of "orphan" research objects; and becoming far more visible and audible in Brussels. Given that in some communities, even the digital arts and humanities are still not understood or accepted, there is much that DARIAH can achieve at the macro-level here.

There are different types of strategic plans at different levels within the organization. A strategic plan is the outcome of a structured process in five phases (Fig. 6).

It starts with examining the current situation (both internally and externally) and continues with setting objectives, developing strategies, and executing them. A tool that is often used to develop strategies is a business model. A business model is a representation of an organization's overall functioning model, resulting from the strategic choices it makes (Osterwalder & Pigneur, 2010; Zott et al., 2011). It represents a link between past strategy and future strategy and can be considered as a picture of how the strategy has been implemented. Adjustments and corrections to the business model over time, to realign it with RI's strategic goals, are possible thanks to the implementation of a KPI system. Evaluation, monitoring, and adjustments are the mechanisms activated thanks to the creation of a KPI System.

The following elements are fundamental to shaping an RI business model concept (Fig. 7):

- Value proposition. In this section, it is clarified how the research infrastructure creates and distributes value to the user segments and to society at large.
- User interface. User segments, distribution channels, and user relationship management that explain interactions and exchanges with users.
- Key activities and resources. Core activities and resources needed to produce the services.

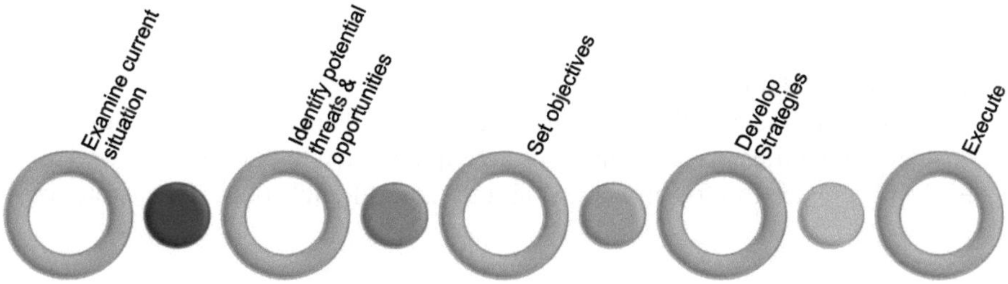

Fig. 6 The strategic planning process. Source: Author's elaboration

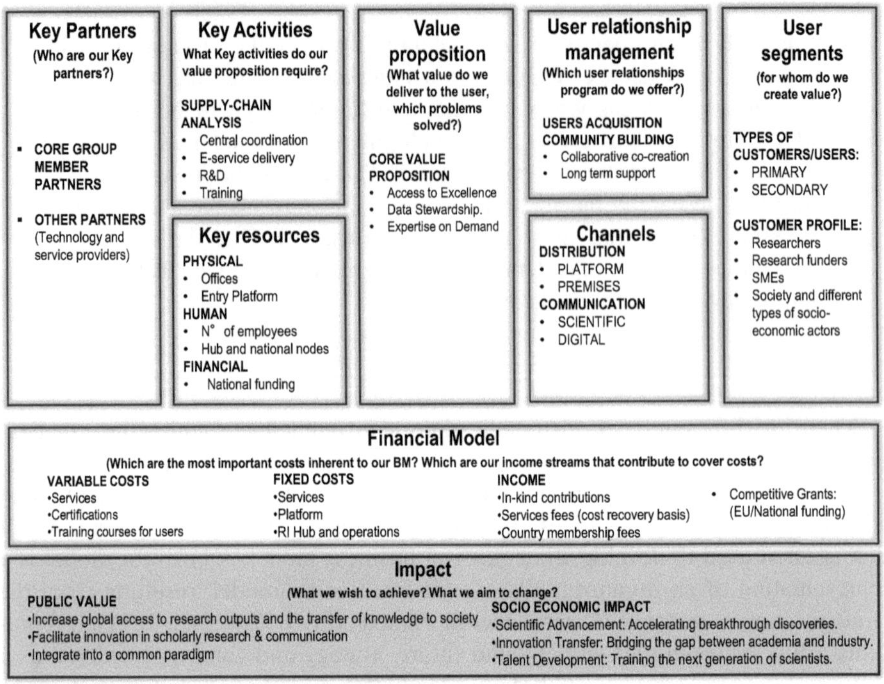

Fig. 7 The RI hub business model: adapting the canvas to mission-driven goals. Source: Authors' elaboration based on Osterwalder and Pigneur (2010)

- Partners. Which key activities the key partners perform/which key resources we are acquiring from key partners; how are upstream relationships with key partners structured and managed.
- Financial model. Costs and benefits from 1), 2), and 3) and their distribution across business model stakeholders.
- Impact. The expected societal impact/public value created by the research infrastructure.

As we observed for other tools, it is important to use the business model and business plan dynamically too. And a monitoring system built on the base of the identification of KPIs is key.

Box 4 DARIAH's Future Strategic Challenges[3]

DARIAH's ultimate goal is to ensure a better overall environment for digitally enabled humanities research that is of high quality and high impact, as well as fostering greater fluidity in accessing and using digital tools. This strategic

[3] DARIAH 2019–2026 Strategic Plan, licensed under CC-BY 3.0 US, available at: https://www.dariah.eu/wp-content/uploads/2019/08/Strategic-Plan_2019-2026.pdf.

plan aims to plot a course that uses our unique assets and position in the environment to contribute to this goal.

By making this commitment as an ERIC, we commit to increasing our value for all of our stakeholders: researchers, research policy bodies, and research contributors alike. In doing so, we believe that the second decade of the DARIAH-ERIC will continue the trajectory set by the first decade of sustained growth in both size and impact across its network of partners and beyond.

The emergence of this plan represents a significant step forward for DARIAH as an organization and as a community. Making commitments that will focus and guide our decisions for the next seven years represents a significant step forward, and is a sign of the confidence we can now claim in our value and our capacity to provide an important infrastructural layer within the European research ecosystem.

The work is not done with the agreement of this plan, however, which will be supplemented over the coming months by a number of more focused annexes, including a second Strategic Action Plan (STRAPL II), to ensure we are translating our strategic aims into clear, measurable actions, and an Impact Assessment Implementation plan (IAIP), which will clearly define how we collect and share the evidence of activity against our key performance indicators, and may also indicate areas where we might trial new indicators for potential future integration into our public reporting.

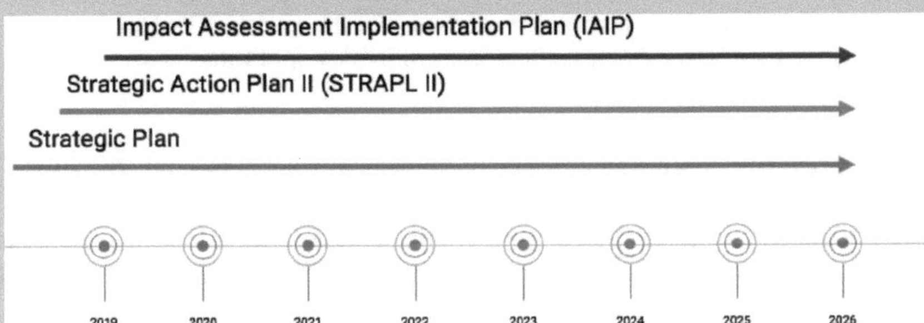

5 Conclusions

Strategy and strategic management are key activities that accompany RI throughout their life cycles, assuming different roles in each phase. During the start-up and constituency phase, strategy is creating the roots on which RI is built. It contributes to the creation of common values, mission, and vision that are continuously maintained throughout the duration of RI. At a later stage, it is fundamental to impose rhythm and impetus on action, thereby enabling the RI to reach its goals. Strategy and a strategic plan are also powerful tools for monitoring events occurring inside and outside the organization, and for adjusting them to readjust, react, or anticipate those changes.

Strategy and strategic management can therefore be conceived as a never-ending and self-renewing process that requires constant attention and commitment from managers. That's why, also, but maybe particularly in the context of research infrastructures that are richly populated by scientists and researchers, it is fundamental to build and train professional figures fully dedicated to these key activities.

Box 5 EMBRC Strategic Plan Evolution

The EMBRC concept originated from the necessity, observed with the EU FP6 Network of Excellence project ("Marine Genomics Europe"), of defragmenting the community of marine biological scientists, through sharing of relevant infrastructures, equipped with advanced technology and paired with human capacity skills and knowledge. The first step was taken with an EU FP7 "Integrating Infrastructure Initiative" (I3) project (ASSEMBLE, 2009–2014), participated by five of the nine countries who will eventually establish the initial EMBRC-ERIC consortium (Feb. 2018). Following the integration of EMBRC into the ESFRI roadmap (2008), EMBRC underwent its Preparatory Phase (2008–2014), with the support of a Preparatory Phase contract, under the 7th European Framework Programme for Research and Development (FP7), during which a blueprint of the RI was developed, including a plan for EMBRC activities and services, governance structure, and a business case. A second Preparatory Phase contract was obtained under the 8th European Framework Programme for Research and Development (H2020), which delivered a socio-economic study and other basic elements for the first step application to ERIC status, such as the EMBRC draft Statutes and Technological and Scientific Description.

In 2015, the "European Marine Biological Resource Centre" (EMBRC) was a research infrastructure project, in its Implementation Phase (2014–2018), with nine countries composing its Implementation Board (EIB). Despite almost doubling its Member-basis, and having decided on France being the host country, the legal and financial planning was stalling. In the words of the Director, who was appointed at that particular stage, EMBRC required the perspective of somebody above the parties, who could unbiasedly guide the final and decisive steps towards the EMBRC establishment, in the form of a European research Infrastructure Consortium (ERIC).

The preparatory phase business plan (2013), in fact, was mainly a business case, based on a socio-economic impact study, assessing the EMBRC Economic Net Present Value (ENPV) to be over M€300, during its lifetime, and anticipating rather general societal benefit, with contribution to several dimensions of regional, national, and European development. This was considered insufficient by the stakeholder to decide whether this initiative was worth supporting and investing in. In particular, the stakeholders would comment that the purpose of the RI appeared rather unclear and that the forecast short- and medium-term spending was not sufficiently detailed or circumstantiated. With these premises, it was proving difficult to obtain buy-in from the government level, despite the interest and the recommendations by the core scientific representatives.

The first step to bring EMBRC's purpose in light was the articulation of a vision for this RI. The vision statement was built to contain references to the main ambitions for this RI, as described by the scientific representatives, i.e. to establish EMBRC as an authoritative reference in its community of practice; to be relevant also beyond the European geographic boundaries; to be addressing both fundamental research as well as innovation opportunities, in the wide spectrum of sectors upon which marine biological sciences can be applied. The statement formulation was also sufficiently broad to avoid an explicit timeframe reference and sufficiently simple, for ease of reference: "The vision for EMBRC-ERIC is to be a global reference Research Infrastructure for fundamental and applied marine biology and ecology research."

The consensus around this vision statement was pivotal to the definition of all the other elements of relevance in the RI implementation planning and, ultimately, to obtain buy-in from its stakeholders. The fundamental planning elements included the definition of the expectations (the objectives), and of the added value (the impact) that it would produce. The effort was to imagine what the scenario would be, with respect to some specific needs of the research community, either with or without EMBRC. The core needs, against which we evaluated the potential RI, were:

- Research infrastructure/equipment/investigation capability
- Costs
- Data collection
- Data/material access
- Service provision
- Innovation and connection with industry
- Scientific Impact
- Internationalization

Following a template made available by the EU Commission, prepared with the support of authoritative economists, we went on to exemplify the EMBRC-ERIC business plan. A user strategy was defined, and services categorized. The planning of its operational deployment, including a medium-term financial plan, with a spin out and operational phase, covering six years, was the capstone of the planning phase, integrated into the "EMBRC-ERIC business plan update 2017" (Nardello et al.). This document provided the final reassurances to the EMBRC General Assembly of Ministry representatives on the bankability of EMBRC-ERIC, and gave way to the decision by all nine Members to participate in the establishment of EMBRC-ERIC.

References

Andrews, K. (1971). *The concept of corporate strategy*. Richard D. Irwin.

Ansoff, H. I. (1965). *Corporate strategy: An analytical approach to business policy for growth and expansion*. McGraw-Hill.

Barney, J. B. (1986). Strategic factor markets: Expectations, luck and business strategy'. *Management Science, 42*, 1231–1241.

Bart, C. K., & Baetz, M. C. (1998). The relationship between mission statements and h performance: An exploratory study. *The Journal of Management Studies, 36*(26), 823–853.

Casadesus-Masanell, R. (2014). Strategy reading: Setting aspirations—mission, vision, and values. Harvard Business School Publishing.

Chandler, A. (1962). *Strategy and structure: Chapters in the history of American industrial enterprise*. Harvard University Press.

Collis, D. J., & Rukstad, M. G. (2008). Can you say what your strategy is? *Harvard Business Review, 86*(4), 82–90.

Collins, J. C., & Ponas, J. I. (1991). Organizational vision and visionary organizations. *California Management Review, 34*(1), 30–52.

Drucker, P. S. (1974). *Management: Tasks, responsibilities, practices*. Harper Business.

Grant, R. M. (1996). Toward a knowledge-based theory of the firm. *Strategic Management Journal, 17*(Winter Special Issue), 109–122.

Grant, R. M. (2015). *Contemporary strategy analysis*. Wiley.

Osterwalder, A., & Pigneur, Y. (2010). *Business model generation: A handbook for visionaries, game changers, and challengers*. Wiley.

Porter, M. E. (1996). What is strategy? (HBR bestseller), Oct 31, 1996. *Harvard Business Review*.

Porter, M. E. (1980). *Competitive strategy*. The Free Press.

Porter, M. E. (2008). The five competitive forces that shape strategy. *Harvard Business Review*, 24–41.

Rivkin, J. W. (2006). *Options-led approach to making strategic choices. HBS no. 702–433*. Harvard Business School.

Rumelt, R. P., Schendel, D. E., & Teece, D. (1994). *Fundamental issues in strategy*. Harvard Business School Press.

Rumelt Richard, P., Schendel, D., & Teece, D. J. (1991). Strategic management and economics. *Strategic Management Journal, 12*(2: Special Issue, Winter 1991), 5–29.

Selznick, P. (1957). *Leadership in administration*. University of California Press.

Senge, P. M. (2006). The fifth discipline: The art & practice of the learning organization (Rev. ed.). Doubleday. p. 135.

Teece, D. J. (1982). Toward an economic theory of the multiproduct firm. *Journal of Economic Behavior and Organization, 3*, 39–63.

Teece, D. J., Pisano, G., & Shuen, A. (1997). Dynamic capabilities and strategic management. *Strategic Management Journal, 18*(7), 509–533.

Zott, C., Amit, R., & Massa, L. (2011). The business model: Recent developments and future research. *Journal of Management, 37*(4), 1019–1042.

Wernerfelt, B. (1984). A resource-based view of the firm. *Strategic Management Journal, 5*, 171–180.

Financial Management and Accounting in Research Infrastructures

Enrico Guarini, Markus Pasterk, and Francesca Magli

Abstract

This chapter examines the financial management and accounting systems required for the effective and sustainable operation of Research Infrastructures (RIs). It highlights how the hybrid nature of RIs demands both robust financial accounting for transparency and management accounting for planning and control. The chapter outlines the structure and purpose of core financial statements, the specific features of RI revenues, costs, and funding models, and the implications of diverse legal frameworks. It also explores cost-analysis tools essential for strategic decision-making. Overall, it emphasises that sound financial governance is critical to ensuring long-term viability, accountability, and efficient resource allocation in RIs.

E. Guarini (✉)
Department of Business and Law, University of Milano-Bicocca, Milan, Italy
e-mail: enrico.guarini@unimib.it

M. Pasterk
Department of Business and Law, University of Milano-Bicocca, Milan, Italy

Department of Medicine and Surgery, University of Milano-Bicocca, Milan, Italy
e-mail: markus.pasterk@unimib.it

F. Magli
Department of Business and Law, University of Milano-Bicocca, Milan, Italy
e-mail: francesca.magli@unimib.it

E. Guarini et al. (eds.), *Research Infrastructure Management*, Management for Professionals, https://doi.org/10.1007/978-3-032-20373-1_4

1 Introduction[1]

Research Infrastructures (RIs) constitute a distinctive class of organisations characterised by significant heterogeneity, as outlined in Chap. 2 "Governance and Organisation of Research Infrastructures" in this book. This diversity is reflected in the particular challenges they encounter, among which financial management is especially prominent. In this context, financial management encompasses the systematic processes of planning, organising, directing, controlling, and monitoring financial resources to ensure the effective and efficient achievement of organisational objectives. According to the British Columbia Cancer Agency scholars "*the financial management on research activities is complex. Monies may come from multiple sources, such as collaborative research groups, industry, grant competitions, or donated funds. In addition, monies may have to be disbursed to multiple groups....*" (French et al., 2009:167).

Even in the world of research, and particularly in making research infrastructures function efficiently, a robust system of financial management and accounting is essential. Indeed, it could ensure that:

- "the amount of financial resources available is sufficient to finance all the costs;
- the funds are properly spent;
- measures are in place to ensure accountability...." (French et al., 2009).

A research infrastructure typically exhibits characteristics that situate it halfway between a traditional research project and a real private enterprise.

To build a fitting financial management and accounting system, it is essential to consider this positioning and understand, among the various tools, procedures, and items, which are the most suitable and useful to utilise and replicate.

2 Financial and Managerial Accounting

The starting point for constructing a suitable financial management system is to identify the primary tools to be used in solving financial and economic problems and satisfying the information needs of all stakeholders.

One of the most important tools is surely accounting, which involves identifying, measuring, and communicating financial information. It can be divided into two subsystems, each with its own report: one called financial accounting and the other managerial or management accounting, both with distinct characteristics. Financial accounting refers to communication with users external to the entity, whereas management accounting serves the particular needs of management (Weetman, 2006; Stittle & Wearing, 2008).

Other important distinctive features of the two subsystems are:

[1] Paragraphs 1–3 were developed by Francesca Magli, Paragraph 4 by Markus Pasterk, and Paragraph 5 by Enrico Guarini.

- *Financial accounting* deals with the creation of financial statements; therefore, it requires that the records are kept with remarkable accuracy, reports on the profitability of the organisation, and is concerned with showing the financial results that it has already achieved; therefore, it has a historical orientation.
- *Management accounting*, on the other hand, is more interested in highlighting operational reports, including financial (e.g. product/service costs and revenues) and non-financial information (e.g. performance metrics for projects or services), which are useful for management within an organisation, often deals with estimates, reports on what is causing problems and how to solve them, and can drive budgets and forecasts, and therefore it can have a future orientation. Moreover, management accounting focuses on small parts of the organisation, such as products, services, activities, and departments.

Which of these subsystems is most important for building an RI's financial management?

Surely the definition of a budget and the definition or estimate of the costs and funds to be used are fundamental, but also the final analysis of what occurred in the previous period can be important, both to verify if the objectives of the RI have been achieved and to structure the subsequent budget, that is the subsequent estimates of costs and needs in terms of funds.

Often, more importance is given to management accounting; however, we must remember that, even in the context of RIs, the estimation of costs and the definition of funding needs can only be defined by knowing what actually happened in the past and whether our strategies have been implemented.

Hence, both management accounting (to estimate costs and identify future funding needs) and financial management (to identify actual economic and financial events in the RI) are important.

To achieve financial sustainability and ensure effective financial management, it is necessary to employ both forms of accounting, with the aim of identifying the key characteristics that are specific to RIs. As noted previously, financial accounting provides the essential foundation for the development and application of management accounting. Accordingly, our analysis will begin with an examination of this instrument.

3 Financial Accounting

Accounting is the language of business used by managers to report financial information:

- It helps decision-makers make good economic decisions.
- It communicates the financial consequences of business decisions.

Financial accounting allows owners to make better decisions about capital allocation because vital information about costs, revenue, assets, and debt is disclosed to them (Power, 2018:33). The financial accounting is, in detail, the process of taking financial data from the firm's accounting records, making a summary in the form of an annual report/financial statements, and publishing it for the benefit of people outside the firm. It is accounting for external decision-makers (Libby et al., 2011, p. 4).

The purpose of financial accounting is to summarise the financial activity of the organisation in accounting records. It records accounting transactions and converts the resulting information into financial statements. But financial accounting is not just processes or methodology, "*accountants create a picture of an organization..... and on the basis of that picture.... people think and act*" (Hines, 1988: 257).

Accounting records and bookkeeping constitute the foundation of an organisation's financial accounting. Typically, these records are structured into three principal components: the income statement (also referred to as the profit and loss statement), the balance sheet, and the cash flow statement. The principal function of this process is to produce financial statements and accompanying disclosures that offer transparency regarding an organisation's financial performance and position, thereby supporting efficient and effective operational decision-making. As noted above, the primary beneficiaries of these outputs are external stakeholders, including investors, creditors, and lenders. "*Financial accounting can be viewed as a window between the "inner" operational world of the organization and its outside*" (Power, 2018:32).

Financial accounting comprises the core financial statements together with the accompanying notes that provide essential contextual and explanatory information. Within the annual report—where these financial accounting elements are formally presented—additional disclosures may also be included. These can encompass, for example, social impact metrics or other forms of non-financial reporting, which extend beyond traditional financial statements to reflect a broader conception of the organisation as a social entity. (Power, 2018:50; Elliot & Elliott, 2011:838). In fact, "*financial accounting has been receptive and creative in the face of social pressures for more representation of the social exterior, provided that these internalized accounting elements have a degree of measurability and auditability*" (Power, 2018:43).

3.1 The Financial Statements (US) or Accounts (UK)

Usually, the financial statements include a balance sheet, an income statement, and a cash flow statement (Griffin, 2015).

The *balance sheet* has a very simple structure and is divided into two parts, namely assets, liabilities, and capital (see Fig. 1). The balance sheet reflects the financial position of an organisation at a specific point in time. In the balance sheet, assets are in the left part and represent the investments, liabilities, and owners' equity are in the right part and represent the capital.

The assets are direct investment activities or resources that are expected to provide future economic benefit and are represented by a lot of items, some of which are depicted in Fig. 1. Assets are classified into two categories: current assets and

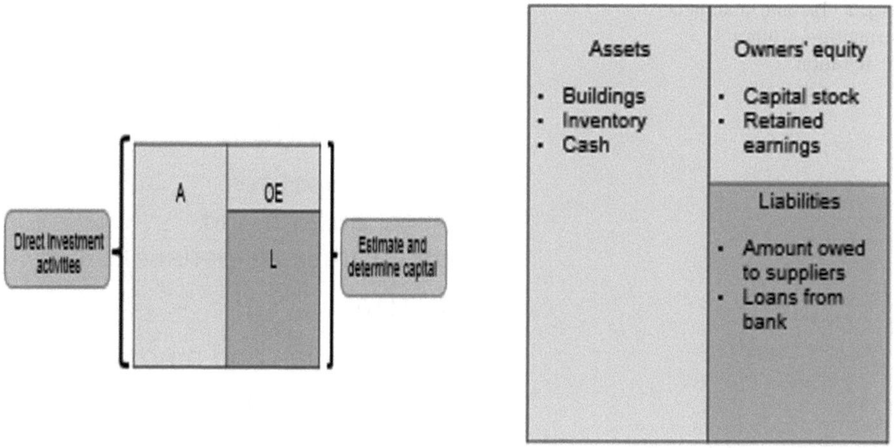

Fig. 1 Balance sheet structure—Author's elaboration

non-current assets. Current assets are the resources of the firm that are either cash or that the firm expects to convert into cash, to sell, or to consume during the next 12 months or during the firm's operating cycle, whichever is longer. Non-current assets refer to resources that an organisation expects to utilise over an extended period in the course of its operations. These typically include items such as land, buildings, equipment, and other long-lived operational facilities. Owners' equity and liabilities represent the sources of capital available to the organisation and indicate how the entity finances its assets. Together, they reflect the claims on the organisation's resources, distinguishing between the residual interest of owners and the obligations owed to external parties. Examples of components included within owners' equity include contributed capital (i.e. capital stock invested by owners) and retained earnings, representing accumulated profits that have been reinvested in the organisation. Typical categories of liabilities include long-term obligations, such as mortgages and bank loans, as well as current liabilities, including accounts payable and deferred revenue.

The organisation acquires capital from both owners (owners' equity, OE) and external lenders (liabilities, L). These financial resources are then allocated to investments in productive assets (A). Any portion of the capital that has not yet been deployed in such investments appears as cash on the balance sheet, an asset of central importance to the organisation's liquidity and operational flexibility.

The *income statement (US),* also known as the "profits and losses statement/account" (UK) or the "statement of revenues and expenses", is a statement that measures the performance of the firm over a period of time. It includes revenues, an increase in owners' equity resulting from selling products or services to customers, expenses, and a decrease in owners' equity due to costs incurred to generate revenues. The difference between revenues and expenses is the net profit/loss, or the increase/decrease in owners' equity, resulting from the company's operating activities. Net profit indicates whether the organisation is generating a financial surplus or

Fig. 2 Income statement structure—Author's elaboration

Sales

- COGS (cost of goods sold)

GROSS MARGIN

- SG&A expenses (sales, general and administrative expenses)

EBITDA

- Depreciation and amortization

OPERATING PROFIT

+ Financial income
- Interest expenses

PROFIT BEFORE TAXES

- Tax expenses

NET PROFIT

deficit over a given reporting period, serving as a key summary measure of overall organisational performance. The structure shown in Fig. 2 identifies the most used items:

To facilitate a more detailed analysis of cash, organisations prepare a cash flow statement. This statement provides insight into the organisation's ability to generate cash, demonstrating how effectively it can meet debt obligations, finance operating expenses, and support investment activities.

Given that the United Kingdom employs slightly different terminology for certain components of financial statements, Table 1 presents key terms alongside their commonly used equivalents.

3.2 Main Features of Financial Statements in Research Infrastructures

> *"Financial accounting continues to be challenged by conceptual and measurement difficulties in dealing with the rise of the intangible economy and in representing more fluid and hybrid organizational forms that are increasingly prevalent in the twenty-first century"* (Power, 2018:33).

It is therefore essential that even large organisations, such as Research Infrastructures, have their own financial accounting that accurately represents them.

Table 1 Terminology differences in UK and US financial statements

UK term	US equivalent
Accounts	Financial statements
Capital allowances	Tax depreciation
Creditors	Accounts payable
Debtors	Accounts receivable
Financial year	Fiscal year
Fixed tangible assets	Property, plant and equipment
Gearing	Leverage
Loan capital	Long-term debt
Net asset value	Book value
Profit	Income (or earnings)
Profit and loss account	Income statement
Profit attributable to ordinary stakeholders	Net income
Reserves	Stockholder's equity (other than capital stock)
Share capital	Ordinary shares, capital stock
Share premium account	Additional paid-up capital relating to proceeds of sale of stock in excess of par value
Shares in issue	Shares outstanding
Stocks	Inventory
Turnover	Revenues (or sales)

Source: Author's elaboration

The financial management of research infrastructures is largely determined by specific characteristics related to their location and ability to attract funding.

Depending on whether RIs are single-sited or distributed, and the location of hubs/headquarters, the RIs must comply with different legal systems and accounting frameworks. For example, ICOS-ERIC has its headquarters in Finland and central facilities located in several European countries. Thus, ICOS-ERIC will be run in accordance with Finnish accounting legislation, standards, and principles, whereas its central facilities shall comply with the the applicable legal and accounting frameworks of their hosting countries. These different legal systems identify specific financial and economic rules and regulations that reflect the typical features of the hosting country or the type of treaty signed. For example, an ERIC (European Research Infrastructure Consortium) takes advantage of the VAT exemption, and there are specific principles and rules concerning budgets, financial statements, and liabilities of the RIs (see Fig. 3).

To economically support the presence of various facilities, each national node with a large number of personnel, equipment, and other resources should have a robust funding model. A large part of the funding model is certainly made up of mandatory contributions of Member States, but it is important that each RI can identify other typologies and contributors to its funding model. To obtain more funds and ensure contributors, RI should efficiently estimate costs/expenses through the structuring of reporting and auditing processes.

Article 13

Budgetary principles, accounts and audit

1. All items of revenue and expenditure of an ERIC shall be included in estimates to be drawn up for each financial year and shall be shown in the budget. The revenue and expenditure shown in the budget shall be in balance.
2. The members of an ERIC shall ensure that the appropriations are used in accordance with the principles of sound financial management.
3. The budget shall be established and implemented and the accounts presented in compliance with the principle of transparency.
4. The accounts of an ERIC shall be accompanied by a report on budgetary and financial management of the financial year.
5. An ERIC shall be subject to the requirements of the applicable law as regards preparation, filing, auditing and publication of accounts.

Article 14

Liability and insurance

1. An ERIC shall be liable for its debts.
2. The financial liability of the members for the debts of the ERIC shall be limited to their respective contributions provided to the ERIC. The members may specify in the Statutes that they will assume a fixed liability above their respective contributions or unlimited liability.
3. If the financial liability of the members is not unlimited, the ERIC shall take appropriate insurance to cover the risks specific to the construction and operation of the infrastructure.
4. The Community shall not be liable for any debt of the ERIC.

Fig. 3 Figure caption from European Union (2013), licensed under CC-BY 3.0 US

3.2.1 Balance Sheet

As discussed in the preceding subsection, the balance sheet is composed of two main sections: assets and liabilities and the owners' equity.

Assets are categorised into non-current and current assets, following the general organisational structure commonly adopted in financial reporting. Non-current assets typically include:

- Land and buildings (tangible assets)
- Property, plant, and equipment available for use (tangible assets)
- Property, plant, and equipment under construction
- Intangible assets, such as software

Current assets, by contrast, typically comprise:

- Inventories
- Receivables (including amounts due from Member States, taxes, project teams, and collaborative partners)
- Prepaid expenses
- Cash and cash equivalents

In RIs, owners' equity differs from that of private companies. It typically consists solely of the net surplus or deficit for the current period, together with accumulated surpluses and deficits from previous years. In certain cases, these accumulated surpluses may be designated as reserves, similar to the practice in private sector organisations.

In the owners' equity of RIs, there is typically no item corresponding to shareholders' or owners' capital. This is because RIs are primarily financed through contributions from member countries rather than capital investments from owners or shareholders. The exception occurs in RIs established under private law entities, such as limited companies (Ltd) and GmbHs. Contributions from member countries are generally allocated on an annual basis, recorded in the income statement, and recognised as revenue.

Liabilities in RIs are generally classified into non-current and current liabilities and are primarily composed of various forms of loans and debts. The most commonly encountered items include long-term and short-term debts, convertible debenture loans, other debenture loans, bank borrowings, bank overdrafts, other financial borrowings and debts (e.g. amounts owed by partners), accounts payable, and deferred or prepaid income.

3.2.2 Income Statement

The primary macro-categories of the income statement in RIs, as in other organisations in general, are:

- Revenues
- Expenses/costs

The main specific items in RI revenues are:

- Membership contribution/fee from Member States
- Contributions from host states
- Other contributions (e.g. from associate Member States, EU contributions, third-party contributions)
- In-kind contributions

Grants

- Other income (interest, sales, and donations).

Contributions, in general, refer to cash donations. They are used to cover the activity costs of the whole community (users, members, observers, etc.). In-kind contributions are non-cash contributions in the form of goods, work, or the use of services. A grant is, instead, an amount of money given by a government or other funding institutions to a person or organisation for a special purpose (e.g. grants for projects).

The costs/expenses for RIs are more general and similar to those of traditional organisations or specific scientific projects. The principal cost items for RIs typically include:

Material Costs

- Costs for consumables, raw materials, suppliers, and goods (cash and in kind)
- Costs for services (cash and in-kind). For example, insurance, travel expenses, electricity, heating, gas, and water
- Maintenance
- Staff costs (cash and in-kind)
- Costs of rents, concessions, and royalties (cash and in kind)
- Legal and consulting costs
- Other operating costs (e.g. costs for institutional activities, office and administration costs)

Personnel Costs

- Remuneration (salaries and wages)
- Other costs for personnel

3.3 Financial Expenses

3.3.1 Depreciation and Amortisation

The difference between revenues (or income) and expenditures (or expenses/costs) represents the net result of the organisation's operations. A positive balance indicates a net surplus or profit, whereas a negative balance reflects a deficit or loss.

4 Reporting

Financial reporting is the process of publishing an organisation's financial results to its stakeholders and the public. It typically encompasses the following documents:

- Financial statements, which include the income statement, balance sheet, and statement of cash flows
- Accompanying footnote disclosures, which can include detailed information on specific topics
- Annual Reports
- Financial project reports for grant funders
- Internal monitoring reports
- (For commercial companies) any documents, flyers, or prospectuses issued to potential investors

Financial reporting in Research Infrastructures (RIs) is always governed by the legal and regulatory requirements associated with their organisational form and the jurisdiction of their statutory seat or founding convention.

In the case of RIs using the ERIC model (i) their accounts shall be accompanied by a report on budgetary and financial management of the financial year and (ii) they have to produce an Annual Activity Report which shall include in particular, scientific, operational, and financial aspects to be approved by the Assembly of Members and submitted within 6 months to the EC[2]:

In the case of using a commercial legal instrument, such as a Limited Company and GmbH, the RI will need to follow the country's requested reporting requirements.

As in many existing cases, the members of the Governing Board are scientists or scientific officers of Ministries or funding agencies, and the Annual Report's financial chapter will need to be carefully translated into layperson's language.

Depending on the different stakeholders, many RIs are producing specific reports that aim to fulfil the information needs of that group.

For funded grants, detailed specific reporting guidelines exist.

[2] Council Regulation (EU) No. 1261/2013 of 2 December 2013 amending Regulation (EC) No 723/2009 concerning the Community legal framework for a European Research Infrastructures Consortium (ERIC).

5 Management Accounting Concepts for Research Infrastructures

As outlined previously, management accounting is concerned with providing information to individuals within the organisation to help them make informed decisions and enhance the efficiency and effectiveness of operations.

In the context of RIs, the planning and control cycle, as articulated by Anthony and Young (2003), constitutes a core management accounting framework for ensuring coherence between strategic intent and operational execution (Fig. 4). The cycle begins with strategic planning, in which long-term missions and priorities are defined, followed by programming, where these strategic objectives are translated into medium-term plans, service portfolios, and resource trajectories. At this stage, one of the major functions of management accounting is the provision of information that facilitates the selection of appropriate alternative course of actions. Once the programmes have been selected, they should then be operationalised through budgeting, which allocates financial and non-financial resources to specific activities and services. The budget is a financial plan for implementing the various decisions that the governance bodies of the RI have made. Budgets are expressed in terms of revenue and expenses, as well as cash inflows and outflows. These budgets are merged into a single, unified statement for the entire organisation, which communicates to

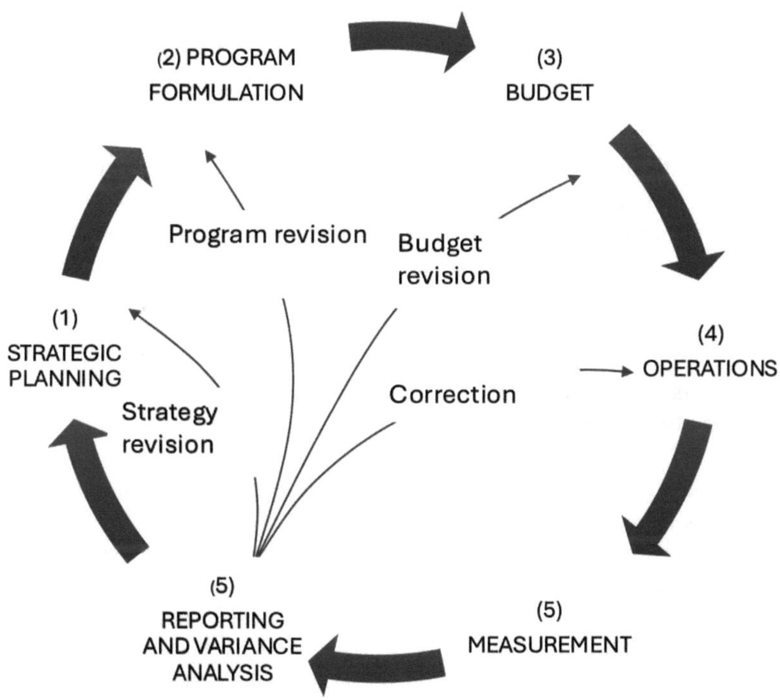

Fig. 4 Planning and control cycle of an organisation. Source: Author's elaboration

organisational units the part they are expected to play in implementing the budgeted decisions. The final stages in the process depicted in Fig. 4, namely, comparing actual outcomes with planned targets, constitute the managerial function of control. This function encompasses the systematic measurement, reporting, and correction of performance with the aim of ensuring that organisational objectives are attained and that plans are effectively executed. The process of taking corrective action to ensure that actual outcomes conform to planned outcomes, or of modifying the plans when comparisons indicate that actual results diverge from expectations, is depicted by the arrowed lines in the Figure, which underscore the dynamic nature of the process and highlight the interdependencies among its various stages.

The establishment of a Research Infrastructure to meet the scientific demands of various domains requires either the construction of new facilities or the sharing of existing ones, often exceeding the operational and financial capacity of individual institutions or countries. Decisions regarding such investments are driven not only by scientific and technical requirements but also by political and financial considerations. This means that cost and revenue information are relevant for decision-making throughout the entire life cycle of Research Infrastructures, from the initial design and construction phases through operational activities to the eventual decommissioning or termination phase (European Commission, 2020). For example, during the realisation phase, cost data supports budgeting for construction, equipment acquisition, and initial staffing; in the operational phase, revenue and cost tracking guide day-to-day resource allocation and service and project funding decisions; and in the termination phase, financial information is essential for managing decommissioning costs, asset disposal, and final reporting to stakeholders, ensuring transparency and accountability. The major theme is that different management accounting information is required for different purposes. Thus, the RI management must ensure that political decision-makers are made fully aware of the cost of running the RI and the funding conditions required to maintain its financial viability over time. The following section outlines the fundamental accounting terms and concepts employed in the management accounting literature and considers their relevance for RIs, particularly in support of informed decision-making.

5.1 Measuring Relevant Costs and Revenues for Decision-Making

The provision of relevant information for decision-making is one of the most important functions of management accounting. For example, managers face decisions regarding whether to allow transnational access to an existing service, introduce a new service, calculate the related costs to assess the conditions under which it can be provided for free, or apply a recovery charge to users, and/or replace existing equipment. A distinguishing feature of these decisions is that they are not routinely made at frequent intervals. For example, a relevant issue in the planning of RIs is the budget required to build the facility, or to pool existing facilities, and to operate it once it is in service.

A key distinction between long-term and short-term decisions is that the former cannot be easily reversed, whereas the latter can often be modified with relative ease. The actions that arise from short-term decisions are frequently repeated, allowing alternative courses of action to be adopted in the future; for example, the configuration of a particular service mix can typically be adjusted within a short time frame. By contrast, long-term decisions, such as those concerning capital investments, including the acquisition of new scientific equipment and facilities, are far less flexible. Resources for major capital expenditures are usually available only at extended intervals, and decisions related to plant or equipment replacement are unlikely to be repeated or revised in the short term.

Making decisions requires considering the relevant costs and revenues. We focus on the basic concept of cost structures, which can have a significant impact on the RI's financial sustainability. The costs of an RI should be assessed over its entire life cycle, typically 15–25 years, although a longer horizon may be justified for certain RIs. A long-term perspective enables a comprehensive assessment of all expected or generated costs, including those that arise in the long run. Such an approach helps ensure that significant but less immediately visible costs (e.g. replacement costs) are not overlooked, supporting advance planning to secure long-term financial sustainability. Moreover, RIs may generate effects and associated financial consequences that extend beyond their operational life cycle—for example, in cases involving nuclear waste requiring costly decommissioning and long-term liability, or environmental impacts such as air, soil, or water pollution that entail remediation costs.[3]

Moreover, it is essential to clarify at the outset that the analysis of the cost structure may pertain to either the RI as a whole or a specific service or organisational unit. Moreover, differences in analytical focus naturally arise between single-sited and distributed RIs, given their distinct organisational configurations and modes of service provision. For example, in single-sited RIs, all the costs apply to the single plant where the facilities are located, as well as to each of the services delivered. In distributed RIs, where the shared facilities are located in different countries and institutions, the cost structure should be referred to the headquarter/hub itself or to each of the autonomous institutions hosting the facilities. In such cases, most of the service costs incurred at the local level are influenced by the cost structure of the local hosting institution and are measured primarily as in-kind contributions for transnational access, including onsite or remote services (e.g. laser beam time at a national facility, staff hours made available) (see Fig. 5).

5.1.1 Cost Behaviour and Cost–Volume–Profit Analysis

A thorough understanding of the cost structure is fundamental to the financial sustainability of RIs, as it enables managers to analyse how costs evolve in relation to changes in activity levels across the organisation and within specific services provided to the research community. Activity of volume may be measured in terms of units of services delivered, hours of equipment use, number of users, tests

[3] Guidelines on cost estimation of Research Infrastructures, August 2019, available at: https://www.esfri.eu/sites/default/files/StR-ESFRI2_STUDY_RIs_COST_ESTIMATION.pdf.

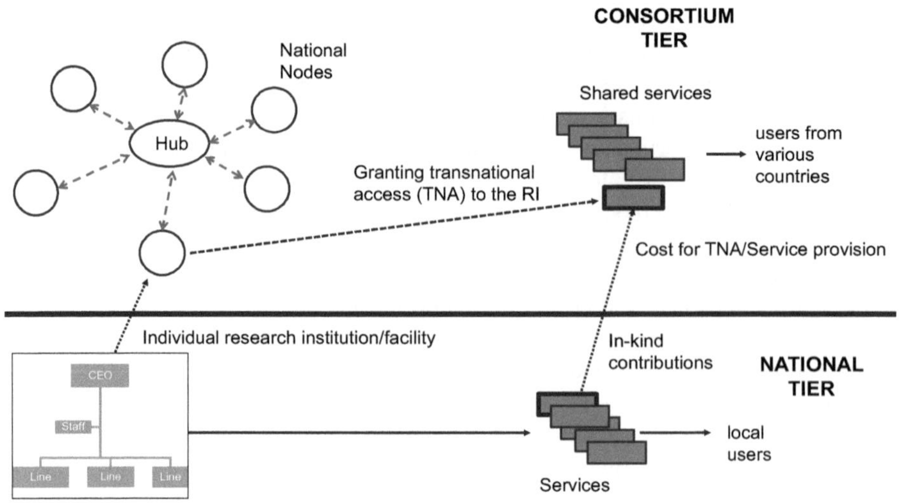

Fig. 5 Cost objects and analysis in distributed RIs. Source: Author's elaboration

processed, or any other appropriate measure of the activity of an RI. Examples of decisions that require information on how costs and revenues vary with different levels of activity include the following: how will costs and revenues change if activity is increased or decreased by a certain level? What will be the impact on financial viability if government funding is reduced by a certain level or if the level of services provided increases? What is the level of fee that can be charged to users to cover service costs if no other funding is provided?

Such analysis is crucial for determining whether planned activities can be supported by the funding typically received from government sources, for appropriately sizing services and capacity, and for identifying key financial thresholds that inform prudent operational and strategic decision-making. Figure 6, 8 illustrates how cost behaviours react with changes in activity.

The terms "variable", "fixed", and "semi-fixed" have traditionally been used in the management accounting literature to describe how a cost reacts to a change in activity. Variable costs vary in direct proportion to the volume of activity; that is, doubling the level of activity will double the total variable cost. Thus, total variable costs may exhibit linear behaviour, and the unit variable cost remains constant. Examples of variable costs in a research institution include direct consumables used to run an experiment, as well as energy to operate the equipment, which is assumed to fluctuate in proportion to the level of related activity.

Fixed costs remain constant over a broad range of activity within a specified time period. They therefore differ from variable costs in that total fixed costs are not influenced by fluctuations in activity levels. Typical examples include depreciation of scientific equipment, insurance premiums, maintenance expenditures, heating, and administrative salaries. The distinction between fixed and variable costs must be made relative to the time period under consideration as well as the level of activity itself. Over an extended time horizon of several years, particularly when establishing a new service, nearly all costs can be considered variable. For instance, staff can be released, equipment replaced, and even buildings or land divested. Likewise, increases in activity will ultimately lead to a rise in all categories of costs. In shorter time frames, once technical capacity and service offerings have been established, costs can be classified as either fixed or variable with respect to changes in activity. Some fixed costs, such as research staff salaries, can be adjusted in the short term to reflect variations in demand. For example, if service demand surpasses a critical threshold, additional personnel may be hired. Costs exhibiting this pattern are typically referred to as semi-fixed or step-fixed costs, as illustrated in Fig. 6.

Building on the analysis of cost behaviour, cost–volume–profit (CVP) analysis provides a framework for examining the relationship between costs, activity levels, and revenues, enabling managers to assess what will happen to financial results if a specified level of revenue, costs, or activity fluctuates. This information is vital to RI management, as one of the most important variables influencing financial sustainability is the level of revenue, which is largely fixed and depends on government subsidies. For this reason, understanding this relationship receives particular emphasis, as it enables management to determine the level of activity at which neither net surplus nor loss is incurred, namely, the break-even point (BEP). This analysis can be applied either to the RI as a whole or to specific services, supporting informed decision-making at both organisational and service levels.

CVP analysis is based on the relationship between units of output or activity and the corresponding revenues, costs, and financial outcome in the short run. The short run is typically considered a period of 1 year or less, during which an organisation's output is generally constrained by existing operating capacity. Moreover, the majority of costs and revenues are predetermined over this period, so the principal source of uncertainty affecting the RI's net result is the volume of services delivered and the associated costs. CVP analysis thus highlights the effects of changes in service volume on the level of net result in the short run.

A diagram showing CVP behaviour is presented in Fig. 7. In the left chart (a), the line of revenue assumes, within a certain relevant range, that these are composed of

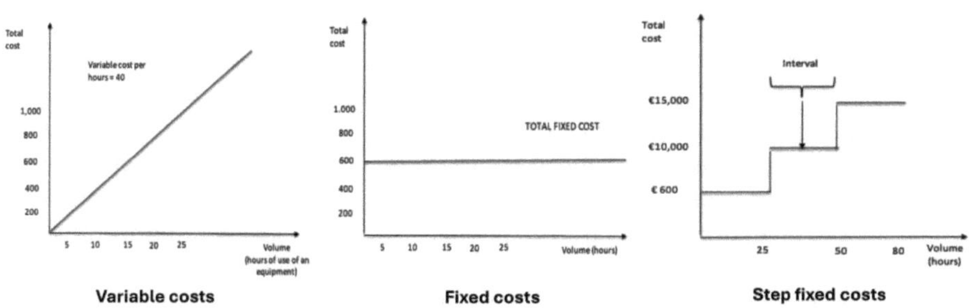

Fig. 6 Cost behaviours in relation to activity level. Source: Author's elaboration

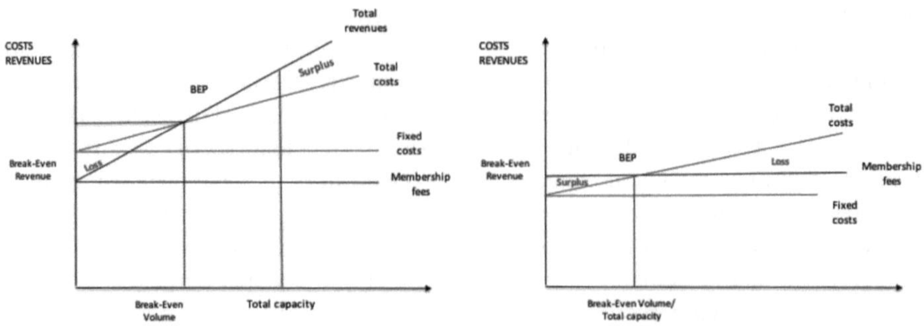

(a) RIs funded through Member State fees and service fees

(b) RI funded through Member State fees only

Fig. 7 Net result-volume graph. Source: Author's elaboration

fixed revenue, such as Member State fees, and variable revenue, such as service fees, which assume a linear relationship (i.e. a straight line) for total revenue as output/volume changes. The total revenue line is the result of the fixed revenue line, which is drawn parallel to the horizontal axis, and the variable revenue line. The cost line, in turn, results from the sum of the fixed costs line and the variable cost line. In cases where no service fees are applied, the maximum operating capacity—and the corresponding break-even point—is determined by the level of fixed revenue available to cover both fixed and variable service costs. In the right chart (b), this point is depicted at the intersection between fixed revenue and total costs (Fig. 7).

The following reporting examples illustrate how the financial implications differ between the two cases, highlighting the distinct patterns of cost coverage and break-even conditions that arise under each scenario, assuming a simple mix of three research services delivered by the RI (Fig. 8).

5.1.2 The Role of Cost Information in Pricing Decisions

Break-even analysis can also be undertaken at the level of individual services, enabling managers to assess their financial viability by examining how service-specific revenues and costs interact at varying levels of activity. RIs are typically funded through public funding, which justifies the fact that scientific users will not be charged any fee. However, determining the cost of services is particularly important for determining the value of in-kind contributions of individual research institutions within shared facility agreements between countries, and for setting appropriate cost-recovery prices in contexts where services are reimbursed through transnational access grants or provided to industrial users. RIs are required to establish prices for their services in contexts where no conventional market exists for those services. In this context, cost information constitutes a crucial input to pricing decisions, and RIs retain a degree of discretion in setting prices, particularly with respect to the time horizon over which such decisions are made. It is possible to express the CVP relationships in numerical terms, allowing them to serve as input for

Performance	Service			Total Services	TOTAL
	A	B	C		
a. Membership fee					20,000
b. Service fee	20,000	10,000	20,000	50,000	
Full cost of delivery:					
Personnel	10,000	4,000	20,000	34,000	
Services	3,000	4,000	3,000	10,000	
Other costs	3,000	2,000	1,000	6,000	
c. Full cost of Delivery	16,000	10,000	24,000	50,000	
d. Services Gross Margin (b-c)	4,000	-	-4,000	-	-
e. Overheads					20,000
Net result (a-d-e)					-

(a) RIs funded through Member State fees and service fees

Performance	Service			Total Services	TOTAL
	A	B	C		
a. Membership fee					70,000
b. Service fee	-	-	-	-	-
Full cost of delivery:					
Personnel	10,000	4,000	20,000	34,000	
Services	3,000	4,000	3,000	10,000	
Other costs	3,000	2,000	1,000	6,000	
c. Full cost of Delivery	16,000	10,000	24,000	50,000	
d. Services Gross Margin (b-c)	-16,000	-10,000	-24,000	-50,000	-50,000
e. Overheads					-20,000
Net result (a-d-e)					-

(b) RI funded through Member State fees only

Fig. 8 Comparison of management accounting reports for an RI under different funding models. Source: Author's elaboration

computer-based financial models. One important variable to consider is the contribution margin, which equals total revenues minus variable expenses. It represents the capacity of available service fees to cover variable service costs and contribute to the coverage of fixed costs. This implies that, to avoid incurring a loss, service fees must, at a minimum, cover the associated variable costs; in other words, the contribution margin must be positive. The greater the contribution margin, the higher the capacity of the service fees to cover fixed costs.

For example, assume a research laboratory conducts experiments that utilise equipment, staff time, energy, and consumables. The RI is examining the viability of providing access to external users for running experiments in accordance with its cost structure. The estimated fixed cost of the laboratory is €100,000, which includes the director's salary, equipment depreciation, and maintenance costs. The variable costs per hour are calculated as 80€ and consist of the technician's salary for supervision, energy, and supplies. The laboratory has a maximum capacity of 5,000 hours. To calculate the price per hour of use, we should first determine the break-even contribution margin/hour to cover all laboratory costs at some target volume. As a first approximation, the target volume could be set at the maximum capacity, so that the contribution margin/hour is 100,000/5,000 = 20€. Thus, the price to break even should be set as follows: Price per hour = Variable costs + Contribution Margin per hour, that is, 80 + 20 = 100€. By operating at full capacity, this price level enables reaching € 500,000 in revenues and the RI to break even (see Fig. 9). However, it should be emphasised that pricing each service at full cost does not guarantee that revenues will equal costs. Even if prices are based on estimated fixed costs at maximum capacity, as illustrated earlier, a lower-than-expected service volume will result in a loss. A more prudent approach is to set the target volume slightly below the maximum available capacity, thereby providing a margin of safety and increasing the likelihood of achieving the break-even point.

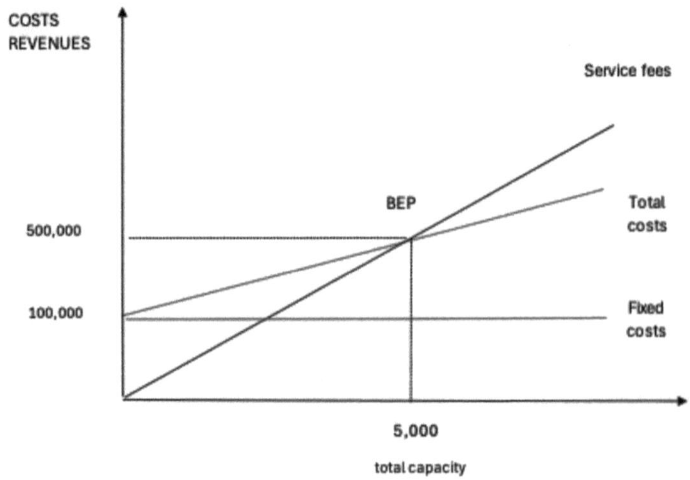

Fig. 9 Break even at the full operating capacity. Source: Author's elaboration

5.1.3 Cost Configurations

The long-term viability of an RI depends not only on its ability to recover the costs associated with its services through fees, but also on its capacity to cover broader organisational costs and to generate a surplus for future investments that cannot be attributed to any single service. This does not mean that the markup on variable costs must be the same for every service. Different services are provided to different users, and the RI management must adapt its pricing policy to fit each user segment and market conditions. Moreover, general funding from the government ensures that the majority of the RI's fixed costs are covered, including those directly associated with specific services delivered. This analysis requires that costs and revenues be attributed to individual services. Unlike private companies, where profitability analysis seeks to distinguish profitable from unprofitable products, the purpose in RIs is to understand the factors that drive the net result. In this context, it becomes essential to determine which costs can be clearly associated with specific services and to assess how those costs, together with the corresponding revenues, contribute to the overall net result.

The cost accounting system that assigns costs to services typically accounts for costs in two broad stages. First, it accumulates costs by classifying them into specific categories, such as by type of expense (e.g. salaries, consumables) or by cost behaviour (e.g. fixed and variable costs). Second, it then assigns these costs to services. Costs that are assigned to services can be divided into two broad categories: direct and indirect costs. Direct costs are those expenses that can be specifically and exclusively attributed to a particular service. For example, the cost of reagents or other laboratory supplies, as well as the hours of technician time required to run experiments, can be directly assigned to individual services because their consumption can be measured through physical observation. Conversely, indirect costs are those that cannot be specifically and exclusively attributed to a given service.

Examples include the costs for maintaining and repairing scientific equipment, the expenses for lighting and heating, or the rental of an office. Variable costs are frequently direct, although they may also be indirect when they cannot be traced to a specific cost object (e.g. energy costs that vary with activity but cannot be traced to a specific service are variable indirect costs). Fixed costs may be either direct (e.g. a dedicated piece of equipment for one service) or indirect (e.g. administrative overheads), depending on whether they can be uniquely attributed to the service or activity under consideration. The term overheads is widely used as an alternative to indirect costs and can be referred to specifically as the provision of services (production overheads) or as general administration (administrative overheads). For example, for a research facility, the full cost can be identified as follows:

Production Direct Costs
- Cost of materials to run an experiment (variable cost)
- Cost of processing time (variable cost)

Production Overhead Costs
- Salary of the facility manager (fixed cost)
- Depreciation of equipment (fixed cost)

Administrative Overhead Costs
- Salary of the research institute director (fixed cost)
- Administrative costs (fixed cost)

References

Anthony, R. N., & Young, D. W. (2003). *Management control in nonprofit organizations* (7th ed.). McGraw-Hill.

Elliott, B., & Elliott, J. (2011). *Financial accounting and reporting*. Pearson - Prentice Hall—Financial Times.

European Commission. (2020). *Cost control and management issues of global research infrastructures*—report of the European expert group on cost control and management issues of global research infrastructures, Publications Office. https://data.europa.eu/doi/10.2777/15246.

European Union. (2013). COUNCIL REGULATION (EC) No 723/2009 of 25 June 2009 on the Community legal framework for a European Research Infrastructure Consortium (ERIC). https://eurlex.europa.eu/eli/reg/2009/723/oj/eng.

French, J., Fcamrt, C., & Poznanski, D. (2009). Managing research—a guide to research infrastructure. *Journal of Medical Imaging and Radiation Sciences, 40*, 165–169.

Griffin, M. P. (2015). *How to read and interpret financial statements—second edition. A guide to understanding what the numbers really mean*. AMA—American Management Association.

Hines, R. (1988). Financial accounting: In communicating reality, we construct reality. *Accounting, Organizations and Society, 13*(3), 251–261.

Libby, R., Libby, P. A., & Short, D. G. (2011). *Financial accounting*. McGraw-Hill.

Power, M. (2018). Accounting, boundary-making, and organizational permeability. In L. Ringel, P. Hiller, & C. Zietsma (Eds.), *Toward permeable boundaries of organizations?* (Vol. 57). Research in the Sociology of Organizations.

Stittle, J., & Wearing, R. (2008). *Financial accounting*. SAGE Publication.

Weetman, P. (2006). *Financial and management accounting. An introduction* (4th ed.). Prentice Hall—Financial Times, Pearson Education.

Financial Sustainability in Research Infrastructures

Paola Bongini, Emanuele Rossi, Monica Rossolini, and Juan Arenas Màrquez

Abstract

This chapter examines the concept of financial sustainability within Research Infrastructures (RIs), a critical yet often underexplored dimension of their long-term viability. Positioned as long-term, publicly funded, non-profit entities, RIs must balance scientific excellence with effective managerial and business-oriented practices. The chapter defines financial sustainability in the RI context, outlines the primary conditions necessary to achieve financial stability, and describes the role of robust financial planning in supporting informed strategic decision-making. A concrete example illustrates how financial planning tools can enhance RI management.

1 Introduction

"Sustainability" has become a mantra that encompasses our personal and professional lives, and this also applies to Research Infrastructures (RIs) due to their specific nature as not-for-profit organizations, heavily dependent on public funding, and committed to demonstrating their economic and broader social value. As a matter of fact, "*Research infrastructures are long-term enterprises, often being operational for several decades. They represent long term strategic investments which are indispensable for enabling and developing research in all scientific domains and also often have broader socio-economic impacts. They require careful planning and*

P. Bongini (✉) · E. Rossi · M. Rossolini
Department of Business and Law, University of Milano-Bicocca, Milan, Italy
e-mail: paola.bongini@unimib.it; emanuele.rossi@unimib.it; monica.rossolini@unimib.it

J. A. Màrquez
ELIXIR, Hinxton, UK
e-mail: juan.arenas@elixir-europe.org

E. Guarini et al. (eds.), *Research Infrastructure Management*, Management for Professionals, https://doi.org/10.1007/978-3-032-20373-1_5

continuous and stable support, which is not limited to financial considerations" (OECD policy paper. 48/2017).

In this context, the sustainability of RIs has a broader meaning, extending beyond financial aspects, as it refers to the "capacity to remain operative, effective and competitive over the lifetime" (OECD, ibidem).

Although each RI has its own specificities, they share the same challenges to ensure the above-mentioned capacity, as identified by the European Commission and the European Strategy Forum on Research Infrastructures:

1. Ensuring scientific excellence
2. Attracting and training the managers, operators, and users of tomorrow
3. Unlocking the innovation potential of RI
4. Measuring socio-economic impact of RI
5. Exploiting better the data generated by the RI
6. Establishing adequate framework conditions for effective governance and sustainable long-term funding for RI at every stage in their life cycle
7. Structuring the international outreach of RI

that have also prompted related main recommendations (ESFRI, 2017).

As the National Research Center (2014) has pointed out, Research Infrastructures are in the "business" of scientific research, innovation, education, and public outreach; as such, the management of these organizations requires not only scientific excellence but also skills and experience in the running of a successful business, which include strategies that contribute to the RI's financial sustainability.

This chapter focuses on this issue and analyses the concept of financial sustainability with specific reference to the functioning of an RI (whether single-site or distributed).

The remainder of the chapter is organized as follows. Section 2 defines the concept of financial sustainability and reviews the main conditions to ensure financial stability in RIs. Section 3 outlines the characteristics of a financial plan, while Sect. 4 provides a concrete example of how financial planning can be applied in the management of an RI. Finally, Sect. 5 concludes.

2 The Five Conditions to Ensure Financial Sustainability

2.1 Definition of Financial Sustainability

A broader definition of financial sustainability that could be applied to any context, be it at the macro level (e.g. a country's financial sustainability) or at the micro level (to a local community, a private enterprise, an NGO), refers to the capacity of an organization to continue a defined behaviour indefinitely. In other words, it means the smooth operation of the entity (i.e. its operational efficiency) with adequate resources to overcome unfavourable financial conditions, such as a lack of liquidity, without incurring the risk of bankruptcy. It refers to a reasonable expectation of covering operating costs through stable financial resources (either internally generated or externally obtained).

Financial stability is considered the basis of survival for any enterprise: each enterprise must maintain the ability to continuously fulfil its financial obligations to its stakeholders (suppliers, state, owners, employees, etc.) while guaranteeing, in the foreseeable future, its solvency, economic independence, and investment attractiveness within the permitted level of risk.

In the case of for-profit enterprises, financial sustainability means earning enough revenues to cover expenses, to pay obligations on a timely basis, to continue operations in the future, and to allow for appropriate growth while delivering the enterprise's mission and a return on investments (Keating et al., 2005; Ng & Rezaee, 2018).

Achieving financial sustainability is a goal that any organization should strive for. In fact, this is the condition where an organization is able to cover operating costs and prioritize activities so as to accomplish its mission, without the need to depend on external funds. In the case of not-for-profit (RIs) organizations it means avoiding negotiations with donors (or Member States in the case of RIs) who may or may not agree with the vision and/or the cost structure of the institution (León, 2001). The main difference with the corporate sector is that in this case the surplus generated is used to create individual wealth, while in the RI/not-for-profit sector is reinvested to accomplish "the mission" of the organization.

With specific referral to not-for-profit organizations, as RIs can be ascribed to, financial sustainability has been similarly defined as the organization's capacity to obtain revenues in order to sustain its projects at a steady or growing rate with the final goal to obtain its stated results, i.e. accomplish its mission (León, 2001; Sontag-Padilla et al., 2012). Other scholars have mostly emphasized the aspect of unexpected threats stemming from the strong dependence on external funding sources that characterize not-for-profit entities. For instance, according to Gajdovà and Majduchovà (2018) it is "the position in which non-profit organizations ensure stable financial resources well and continuously pursue their own functions, and financial stability is sufficiently resistant to unfavorable financial conditions"; analogously, Bowman (2011) relates financial sustainability to the ability to maintain a financial capacity over time (both in the short and long period), where financial capacity consists of resources that give an organization the ability to seize opportunities and react to unexpected threats.

In addition, Research Infrastructures present their own specificities. As a matter of fact, RIs differ at least in three main aspects from large-scale projects in other fields.

First, they are long-term initiatives: for the purpose of the costing exercise and the definition of financial sustainability, it is important to look at the entire life cycle of the RI, while "dividing" it into phases, the ones that traditionally characterize the development of an RI (conceptual design, design, preparation, implementation, operation, decommissioning) as described in Chap. 1 "The Concept of Research Infrastructure" of this book.

In this respect, RIs are similar to enterprises, whose life cycle (and corresponding modes of funding) is depicted in Fig. 1. The business life cycle is the

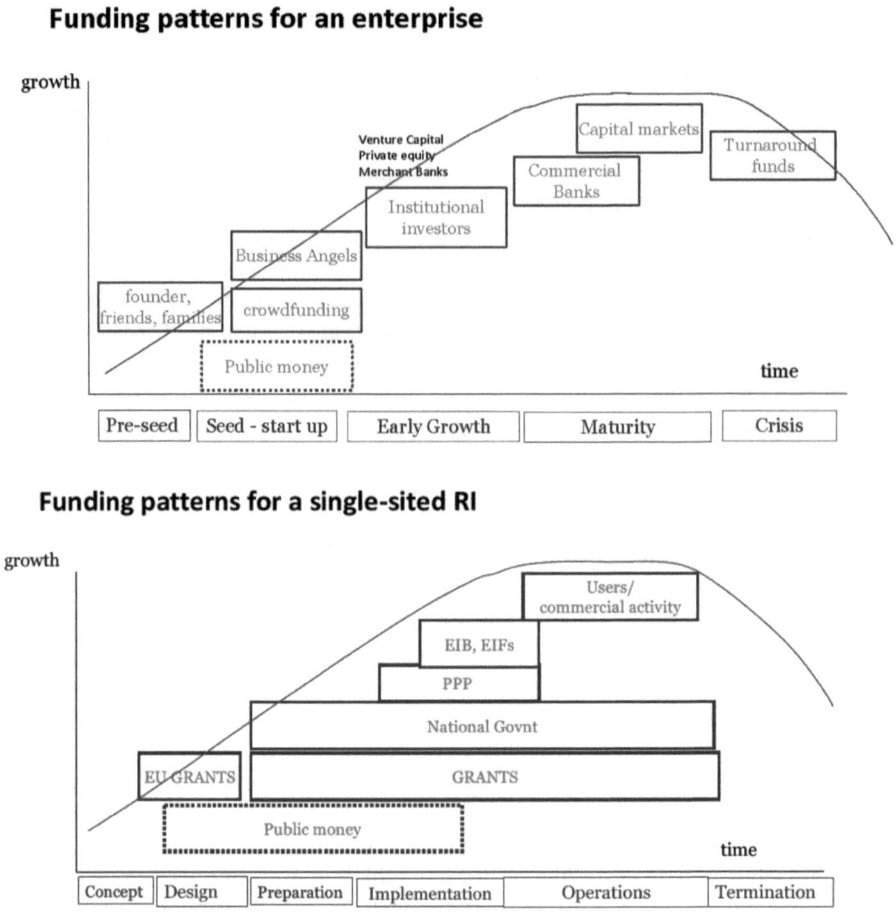

Fig. 1 Life cycle and funding patterns—Author's elaboration

progression of a business over time and is most commonly divided into different phases: launch (pre-seed and seed-start-up phase), growth, maturity, and decline. In the case of businesses, at launch when sales are the lowest and business risk is the highest, it is almost impossible to finance operations and investments with debt, due to its unproven business model. Financial resources mainly consist of self-funding (founders' capital) and loans from friends and family members; over time, still in the start-up phase, these funds can be complemented by other options that include government grants (typically devoted to promote young or female entrepreneurship), angel investors (high net worth individual who provides financial backing for small start-ups, typically in exchange for ownership equity in the company), and the crowd (crowdfunding, see Box 3). When the start-up is ready to launch its products or services to the market, it might begin looking for institutional investors (as opposed to individual investors) such as venture capital funds and private equity funds. These types of formal investors are able to provide both capital and mentorship from their experience in the field. Once the business has proven successful, and gained its maturity, more established and traditional funders come to play: commercial banks will be inclined to offer bank debt, not accessible in earlier stages, and financial markets (stock exchange) will help to raise money from the public. In case of decline, turnaround funds will come into play, with the specific task of revamping the business (and starting a new one) or liquidating it.

Similarly, as depicted in the ESFRI roadmap (2018), the life cycle of an RI consists of different phases which are each characterized by specific funding and decision-making processes, which start with generic preparation activities (which may go from concept screening to consortium creation) and end with decommissioning. Specifically, there are six RI life-cycle stages:

1. Conceptual development stage
2. Design stage
3. Preparation stage
4. Implementation stage
5. Operation stage
6. Termination stage

The long preparation and duration of an infrastructure implies that the funding model is likely to evolve from one phase to the next as depicted in Fig. 1: firstly, because the needs will be different in nature (non-investment costs vs. investment costs, for instance) and in amount (investment peak during implementation/operation and upgrades for some infrastructures, versus fairly stable running costs), and secondly, because the landscape of funding opportunities and the funding policies, as well as the scientific requirements and the available technologies, are likely to evolve dramatically over the course of, say, 20 years (RAMIRI Handbook, 2013, (https://www.ceric-eric.eu/project/ramiri-handbook/).

As highlighted by the OECD working paper n.48/2017, government funding represents the predominant source for the first three initial phases. In the preparatory phase up to the design and decision to proceed, the funding in single-site RIs is often provided by an existing RI which aims to implement major extensions or upgrades. More diverse is the initial funding for distributed-site RIs, depending on their subnational or international nature. Similarly, depending on the nature of the RI and the scientific discipline it covers, income from partner countries and private sources such as charities or foundations could represent an additional income stream. For RIs of pan-European relevance, design and preparatory phases can be funded through the EU Framework Programmes (for the EU priority projects listed in the ESFRI roadmap and beyond), while construction remains a national prerogative although it can sometimes be supported by structural funds (which play a very important role in some European countries), including the involvement of the European Investment Bank as a financing body (e.g. European Spallation Source ERIC). In a small number of cases, private foundations may be involved in funding new facilities, and large RIs often rely on funding from multiple partners. Users' fees at cost-cover levels and sometimes commercial activity come into play when the RI has entered an established path, in its operational phase.

Besides, the context, type of infrastructure (single-site or distributed), and the related cost structure can influence this phasing. In fact, Fig. 1 depicts the typical life cycle of a virtual RI with limited fixed assets investments; however, the cost structure and related funding needs can take two different patterns (as described in Guidelines on cost estimation of Research Infrastructure, StR-ESFRI study, 2019), namely when RIs are involved in tasks which are performed cyclically (wave like cost structure) or when RIs face a rump-up phase after launch which implies a relatively large investment peak (and related funding needs) that decreases during the operation (Fig. 1).

It would be quite natural to consider each phase as the relevant financial horizon over which to make the relevant financial decision (on top of the annual budgetary exercise); however, as for any enterprise meant to live indefinitely, it is necessary, from the design phase, to address the overall and long-term financial issues of the RI. This translates into the need to define a "business model" that creates the optimal conditions for the future sustainability of the infrastructure.

Second, RIs are mainly funded by public money; an essential aspect of this funding model is that it could imply a strong political "interference", in particular through the issue of the "just retour", i.e. the request to "demonstrate" that it is worth investing in the RI. This is why a business case (i.e. a document that outlines the why, what, how, and who and is necessary to decide if it is worthwhile starting a project/creating an infrastructure) and a business plan (i.e. a statement of quantifiable objectives, together with the resources required to achieve them) are so crucial in the life of an RI. It is the management team's responsibility to demonstrate the scientific excellence of the RI and that it is worth investing in the organization. This also implies the definition of a credible organization and governance model, the establishment of KPIs, and the outlining of staff planning. The business plan/case becomes the best passport to demonstrate the value and the ability to deliver scientific and societal value.

Third, many RIs are based on complex technological systems and/or innovative solutions, which in turn require excellent financial management to avoid cost overruns and the waste of public money. Risk management techniques become crucial.

2.2 Five Conditions to Ensure Sustainability

Literature on the financial sustainability of not-for-profit organizations has highlighted the main conditions to ensure their financial stability (León, 2001; Sontag-Padilla et al., 2012) that can be summarized in five conditions or pillars (see Fig. 2):

1. Long-term commitment of founders
2. Diversification of financial resources
3. Own income generation
4. Strategic and financial planning
5. Measurement of impact

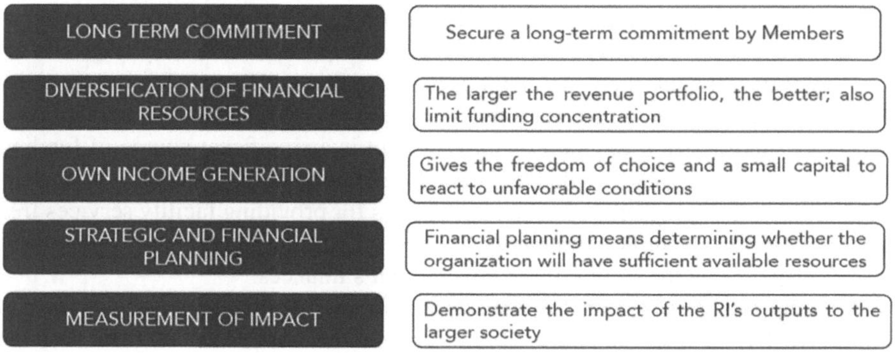

Fig. 2 Five pillars to ensure sustainability—Author's adaptation from León (2001), and Sontag-Padilla et al. (2012)

Condition n.1 has to do with the fact that any organization needs "capital" to absorb financial and operational risks. In the corporate sector, shareholders provide capital, which is, by definition, a long-term and stable resource (as long as the organization remains profitable, in the case of listed companies). In the case of RIs, there is no true "shareholder capital" as in the corporate sector; however, the members of the RI consortium can be considered as "shareholders" and their contributions (cash or in-kind) should secure long-term viability and longevity of the RI itself.

Questions to Ponder

1. How stable are the founders' resources?
2. How long is the initial commitment of Member States?
3. For how long are the founders legally bound to contribute to the RI?
4. What are the rules that govern the withdrawal options of the founders?
5. What is the required notice period for founders to withdraw funding?
6. What is the RI policy to maintain long-term and stable relations with members?
7. Should the RI consider the possibility of starting negotiations with the Member to secure a longer timeframe for legally binding contributions from Member States?

Condition n.2: The second condition of financial sustainability is the development of a diversified portfolio of funding sources, which involves increasing the number of sources that provide funding and decreasing the reliance on each individual source. The larger the revenue portfolio, the better a Research Infrastructure will comply with its mission and be less vulnerable to fluctuations in any source of funding. However, financial vulnerability cannot be avoided if, although tapping multiple sources of funding, a large portion of the RI's budget is financed by a single source of income. Organizations are financially stable if the core of their activity remains unchanged when major financing sources decrease.

RIs typically have funding models that involve government funds and international contributions (mainly at the EC level): their support is essential for RIs' financial viability, although there are challenges associated with heavy, if not complete, reliance on direct government funding, Member States' contributions, and grants.

Direct funding from the national government is a significant source of funding for large, single-site research facilities and large international consortia. It is desirable because it is long term in nature and allows for providing facility services free of charge to the scientific community. However, it could be a volatile source as it strictly depends on the health of the government's finances.

Funding also comes from member organizations' own budgets, usually for less expensive RIs or distributed RIs. Typically, members take care of their national nodes and infrastructures, providing support for the coordination, governance, and organization of joint operations and the headquarters (OECD, 2017). As seen in condition n.1, the long-term engagement of members could be a critical point, as in several cases, the withdrawal notice may be as short as 3 months.

Grants are also a mainstream funding option for RIs, which apply to this form of project-based funding at the international, European, and national levels. These funds are awarded based on a selection process that can be lengthy, while calls may not align with the funding needs of the RI.

Revenues from the market at large (user fees or commercialization of RI's results or equipment) can also be an option, which is being implemented in a number of cases to cover a part or all the operating costs (see Condition n.3).

As members' funding is somewhat volatile, there is a need to diversify the income and tap into alternative sources that can go under the hat of "funding from the private sector", which entails finding donations outside the framework of grant agreements (from private foundations), involving industrial partners, access to private–public partnerships (PPP), and access to traditional form of bank financing (for instance EIB loans) or modern form of funding (crowdfunding). These diverse options are described in Boxes 1, 2, and 3.

Box 1 Bank Loans and the Role of the European Investment Bank

In the business world, a typical source of funding is bank loans, which can have either a short-term or long-term time horizon. Short-term loans are typically related closely to the borrowers' need for short-term cash to finance the purchase of inventories, cover production costs, and pay taxes, interest on debt, and dividend to stockholders. Long-term loans are designed to fund longer-term business investments, such as the purchase of equipment or the construction of fixed assets intended to generate a stream of revenue in future periods; for these reasons, they span a period longer than one year.

From the point of view of the financing bank, what is relevant is the issue of "bankability". A bankable project or business can be defined as a project or proposal that has future cash flows, sufficient collateral, and high probability of success to be acceptable to institutional lenders (like a bank) for financing. Lenders are in search of the "ideal loan applicant", who typically meets these requirements: i) a cash flow sufficient to make the loan payment (for existing businesses); ii) an owner who has a track record of profitably owning and operating the same sort of business (for new ventures); iii) the presence of a sound, well-thought-out business plan; and iv) financial reserves and personal collateral sufficient to solve the unexpected problems and fluctuations that affect all businesses.

In other words, the lender requires and searches sufficient comfort from the borrower for proper servicing of the loan (that is paying the capital, the due interests, and any other potential charges—like fees and commissions). To this end, the lender considers financial, economic, legal, and political considerations to estimate and evaluate whether the borrower has the means and the willingness (or duty) to repay the loan. In bank terms, the lender evaluates the Capacity (i.e. ability to repay the loan generating enough cash flow in the future) and the Character (i.e. the lender's opinion of a borrower's general trustworthiness, credibility, and personality) of the borrower. The lender also takes into consideration: Capital (i.e. the amount of money invested by the business owner or management team), Collateral (i.e. assets that are used to guarantee or secure a loan), and Conditions (i.e. the state of the economy, the industry, and sector trends, and how these factors might affect the borrower's ability to repay the loan).

In the case of RIs, what is particularly challenging is the definition of whether the organization has the authority to request a loan and the legal standing to sign a binding loan agreement. From the RI and the lending bank point of view, it means to verify whether its management is allowed to contract a loan and, if positive, whether there are any limitations on the value of the loan—also, and above all, whether members will be liable for the loan (and this provides enough comfort for the lending bank). This piece of information could be found in the RI's Statute, in those articles defining the organization's liability regime (i.e. the conditions under which it is considered responsible of answerable in law, or legally obligated to deliver what has been promised in a contract), along with the articles defining the conditions under which the winding up of the organization should be completed, in particular with regard to the liabilities remaining after including the organization's assets and how these should be apportioned among members.

A prominent role in offering loans to RIs is played by the European Investment Bank, which represents the lending arm of the European Union. It is a multilateral financial institution whose aim is to "help the economy, create jobs, promote equality and improve lives for EU citizens and for people in developing countries". Given its specific nature and mission, the Bank offers a wide range of financial products at favorable terms. For certain projects that support innovation and skills in Europe, EIB accepts more risk than a commercial bank. Differently from a traditional commercial bank, EIB also offers technical assistance to help prepare and implement projects

An instrument specifically tailored to support the financial needs of an RI goes under the name of *InnovFin Science,* which supports research and innovation (R&I) investments by research institutes, universities, and research organizations (public or private).

Box 2 Public–Private Partnerships (PPPs)

Public–private partnerships (PPPs) can be broadly defined as arrangements between public and private actors for the delivery of goods, services, and/or facilities (Caselli et al., 2015). More specifically, the PPP is "a long-term contract between a private party and a government entity for the provision of public services and/or development of public infrastructure in which responsibilities and rewards are shared" (United Nations ESCAAP).

PPPs have been implemented in many policy areas of intervention, such as infrastructure, water supply, transportation (Wettenhall, 2003), and also Research Infrastructures (VanOmmen et al., 2015). PPP advocates argue that these partnerships deal with the managerial bias that frequently characterizes government entities. Indeed, PPPs bring the public sector's organizational culture closer to private sector's in order to address perceived inefficiencies in direct state service provision. For well-functioning of PPPs, it is essential that clear governance and functioning rules are defined so as to stimulate the effectiveness of the instrument (Oakey, 2003; Hallberg, 1999).

There are four main characteristics that distinguish PPP from the traditional procurement approach (summarized in Table 1):

1. Funding sources

   With a traditional procurement approach, specific projects such as infrastructure projects are financed by the national budget of a country. The government entity selects a contractor and pays a budget in the construction phase (upfront payment). In the PPP, the private investors finance the project, and it receives remuneration from the government. In this case, the public disbursement is not concentrated in the construction phase, but rather is distributed throughout the project's life. The remuneration of the private actor can depend on a) user fees paid by the users of the asset or b) the public part pays a fee to the private investors for the availability of assets (called availability payment) after controlling that the asset can be used and meet the quality criteria defined in the contract. This is an incentive for the private investors to maintain a high standard for assets.
2. Duration

   In traditional procurement, the relationship between the government agency and the private contractor typically ends once the construction phase is complete. In the PPP model, the relationship extends beyond the construction phase, as the private contractor is responsible not only for building the infrastructure but also for operating it for many years (typically more than 20 years). The public authority has a role in monitoring during the life of the contract, and at the end, ownership of the asset returns to the public.

3. Requirements

In conventional procurement, the requirements are defined by input (for instance, which characteristics are required in the construction phase, how many resources will be employed, etc.), whereas in PPP, the requirements are defined in terms of outputs (how many users will be satisfied, what is the goal of the project). Focuses on outputs provide the opportunity for the private sector to adopt innovative solutions to achieve the project's objectives.

4. Risk allocation

In PPPs, the risks are shared between public and private partners. Frequently, the operational risk (i.e. the risk that the construction and operational costs exceed the estimated budget) is supported by the private sector.

The PPPs exhibit both benefits and limitations compared to traditional procurement. The main benefits are to overcome public budget constraints, improve efficiency, profitability, and quality of public services and assets, and transfer project risks.

The most significant advantage of the PPP is its ability to attract private capital, which means the possibility of realizing a project that would not be feasible due to public budget constraints. Another important benefit is that the private view can help discover and develop efficiently the possibility of additional profitability from the asset. Private investors are accustomed to seeking additional sources of revenue beyond those generated from the traditional use of an asset. For instance, considering a PPP that finances a new airport, traditionally, public entities focus on transportation services, whereas private investors can generate additional revenues from shops, hotels, parking, and other sources. PPPs benefit from the efficiency of the private sector in terms of quality of public services, managerial experience, and use of technology. Another important benefit relates to the project's duration. PPP is a long-term contract that, if well-defined, can avoid the problems of poor construction and poor maintenance, as the private investor is responsible for operating an asset over a long period, and in the same way, its return depends on the asset's quality. The last important benefit relates to risk transfer. With PPP, the government entity transfers the operating risk to the private sector, thereby protecting the public budget from the possibility that costs will be higher than the expected project budget.

The PPPs also face several limitations, including complexity, the managerial skills of the private actors involved, limited flexibility, and political interference.

PPP is a complex operation that requires high transaction costs for procurements; for this reason, it is applicable only to large projects (more than $ 20 million). PPPs perform well in sectors that do not undergo rapid change. This type of contract is more effective when there are long-term, predictable needs for these services. The success of PPP also depends on the managerial skills of the private sector operating in the country, particularly on the capacity of private actors involved in managing the project's risk. PPP is a funding solution with limited flexibility, and it could be affected by political and social sensitivity. On one side, public players might be politically influenced by the search for consensus rather than by an economic assessment of the transactions (Florida & Smith, 1993), and this could impact the functioning of the contracts (for instance, they shall not introduce user fees to avoid political dissents) (Table 1).

Table 1 The PPPs main characteristics

	Traditional procurement	PPP
Funding	National budget	Private investment with remuneration in terms of user fees or availability payment
Duration	Construction phase	Construction and operating phase
Requirements	Defined by inputs	Defined by outputs
Risk allocation	Operational risks are supported by public actor	Operational risks are supported by private actor

Box 3 Crowdfunding

Crowdfunding can be defined as "an open call – mostly through the Internet – for the provision of financial resources by a group of individuals instead of professional parties either in the form of donations, in exchange for a future product or in exchange for some sort of reward" (Belleflamme et al., 2014).

The most innovative feature of crowdfunding is the establishment of an online platform that creates funding opportunities by effectively matching innovative projects with a large number of small investors seeking some kind of "return" (not necessarily economic) on their investment. This simple yet striking idea, which brings together a potentially large number of small capital providers, typically benefits start-ups and small businesses. However, its scope is not limited to businesses; it also involves individuals, research organizations, or NGOs.

In fact, any innovative project typically requires capital in the short term to initiate a new business, product, or research endeavour, but it generates value (both economically and socially) in the medium to long term. This temporal asymmetry generates the need for financing, and crowdfunding represents a new approach to fill this funding gap, which is increasingly used even to fund research.

Several crowdfunding sites have emerged to help fund impactful scientific research that might otherwise lack funding. Some examples are the sites of Experiment.com (experimental research), Consano (medical projects), Useed (experiential learning), Medstartr (medical and healthcare innovation), or CrowdScience (any scientific project) which are helping match scientist doing cutting-edge research with individuals interested in backing their important work. For instance, Consano was founded in 2012 by a breast cancer survivor who wanted to provide researchers with alternatives to very large nonprofits that tend to fund general research. Consano, like other specialized sites, provides a platform that enables individuals to donate directly to specific research projects and programmes, thus enabling scientific progress and empowering individual action.

Along with these examples of specialized platforms, which target a more focused audience, generalist platforms (like Indiegogo or Kickstarter, to name the most famous) can also be addressed, and this could make more sense when the research project is of broader interest and could potentially affect a larger share of the society. Crowdfunding for scientific research may significantly change the way science evolves moving forward.

Through crowdfunding, fundraisers can:

- Collect feedback that can be useful to develop the project (Dushnitsky & Marron, 2013)
- Build a community of users (customers) interested in the project
- Signal the quality of the project to other prospective funders
- Evaluate the size of the market of an innovative product/service (Agrawal et al., 2014)

Among the different crowdfunding models, the two mostly applicable to the science case are: i) *reward-based platforms*, where financing is provided in the expectation of a reward or prize (material or not), and ii) *donation-based platforms*: project funding motivated by philanthropy or sponsorship, without any other remuneration for crowdfunders.

Incentives that could be envisaged to reward funders span from a "thank-you" card, to online seminar, to live seminars, and even to dinner with scientists (see https://crowd.science/crowdfunding-guidelines/).

The main idea is to engage funders with the researchers' vision and help them understand that their money and support could make a difference, a difference they can trace and constantly monitor.

Academic research is also increasingly studying this new phenomenon; a recent paper by Sauermann et al. (2019) specifically analysed data from over 700 campaigns on the largest dedicated platform (Experiment.com), highlighting important differences between crowdfunding and traditional funding mechanisms for research such as grants from government agencies. Success rates of crowdfunding campaigns are comparatively high, students and junior investigators are more likely to succeed than senior scientists, and women have higher success rates than men. Conventional signals of quality–including scientists' prior publications–have little relationship with funding success, suggesting that the crowd may apply different decision criteria than traditional funding agencies. Fundraising is also faster than the traditional grant-based system. At the same time, the amounts raised with crowdfunding tend to be much smaller and funds are used primarily for materials and travel rather than salaries or tuition. This study's results support the view that crowdfunding of scientific research broadens access to resources for groups that have been excluded or disadvantaged in traditional funding systems, similar to what has been shown in crowdfunding of business initiatives. However, the amount of resources raised—at the level of individual projects but also the platform as a whole—is presently too small for crowdfunding to serve as a substitute for traditional funding mechanisms. As such, crowdfunding for research may best be seen as a complement to such traditional sources. Platforms for crowdfunding will not fix the rigidities and difficulties in accessing traditional research funds, but may represent an interesting way to promote work (and demonstrate impact) as well as gain funds.

However, in order to seize the opportunities to diversify and supplement sources of funding, the first step is the development of a solid business plan to convince potential funders to contribute, especially if they come from the private sector. The business plan can also help secure and stabilize the support of core founders.

Questions to Ponder

1. What is the list of the RIs' income sources each year, with approximate amounts?
2. How many funders' contacts does the RI have? Is the list regularly updated?
3. Does the RI have procedures for following up with founders, donors, and industrial partners?
4. Does the RI have procedures to scout for grants?
5. Has the RI considered establishing a public relations team?
6. What is the RI's proposal in terms of voting rights, governance, access for scientists, and socio-economic impact? Is this business model compelling enough to attract funding partners?
7. Does the RI have a detailed legal framework in place? What are the plans for it when negotiations begin?
8. Does the RI have a detailed, regularly updated business plan and financial plan?

Condition n.3: Alongside the need to diversify their funding sources, there is an increasing need to generate their own income flows, which can provide additional means for diversification and represent a monetization of the outcomes or impact of the activities performed by the RI (see condition number 5). Income generation can come from the sale of goods and/or services (developing commercial activities, also in partnership with private corporations) and the implementation of a service-fee structure (for instance, users' fee access to laboratory equipment, biological collections, or more in general, access to data that have been collected and stored by the RI).

Services could include the delivery of educational programmes (for instance, via MOOC), the provision of expert advice and consulting services to the public and private sectors, and sharing personnel and research equipment with interested industries. Private entities may negotiate physical access to the RI's (and nodes') platform/physical site to support their own R&D, retrieve data, exploit models, consult with experts, and refine in-house protocols. It could also be the case for the establishment of a new company in partnership with private corporations to exploit specific competences and knowledge of the RI's personnel and data.

Condition n.3 requires the acquaintance of the RI's types of users and their needs (related to products and services provided), remembering that users can be as diversified as the research community, the policy makers, the national funding agencies, the industry(ies), the educators, and civil society at large. There is also a need to highlight the market trends and outlook in the field of operation of the RI, as well as the innovation potential that can be delivered. Also, data policy and access should be clarified and defined whether users' fees should be the standard or the exception.

Questions to Ponder

1. Which market segments do you serve?
2. How can you offer services to these markets?
3. How much of the RI's income comes from the selling of products/services?
4. Is the organization trying to create alliances with corporations?
5. Does the RI have a communication and branding policy?

Condition n.4: The fourth condition refers to the need to implement a strategic and financial plan. The strategic plan outlines the "how" and "when" of an organization's mission and vision. It is useful for communicating the organization's direction to its stakeholders. It sets long-term objectives and helps prioritize the actions needed to accomplish them (León, 2001). The financial plan, i.e. the financial section of an organization's business plan, helps to determine whether the strategy is viable and adequately takes into account the available resources and the RI's capacity to obtain new sources of funding. Section 3 of this chapter will detail the characteristics of a financial plan with an example of an FP for an RI. The financial plan consists of projected revenues and expenditures and should highlight the capacity of the organization to have sufficient resources available in the medium term to meet the mission described in the strategic plan. The financial plan outlines various scenarios, ranging from the ideal to the minimum feasible, which quantifies the fixed and operational costs required to deliver the minimum level of services and research that justifies the operation of the RI.

Questions to Ponder

1. Does the RI have a strategic plan?
2. Have the RI defined scenarios of operation?

3. Does the RI have an idea of the revenues and costs associated with the actions defined in the strategic plan?
4. How often does the RI update its financial plan?
5. What kind of instrument (spreadsheet or other?) does the RI uses to implement the financial plan?

Condition n.5: The fifth pillar refers to the capacity of the RI to define and communicate its impact to the wider community of stakeholders.

The main goal of the planning effort just described in Condition n.3 is not only to identify and communicate the strategic vision and mission of the RI but also to pinpoint the future research challenges that the RI is uniquely positioned to address and its unique education and outreach goals (impact), define the metrics that should be used for measuring progress towards such goals, and, more generally, state the RI's value proposition (National Research Center, 2014). The value proposition, in a nutshell, represents the reasons why a company or a product is attractive to customers and stakeholders at large; in particular it is directed to clarify and underline the benefits of the products or services delivered from the outset.

In the case of RIs, the value proposition can include a variety of elements, spanning from creation of longitudinal datasets, outreach on learning opportunities and knowledge transfer for local communities, being an enabling facility that supports innovation, providing scientific support to public policies, etc.; the value proposition should answer the logical demand for understanding and evaluating the return on investments on (costly) research facilities. Where the return is not in terms of performance (operational or financial) but in terms of impact, i.e. opportunities for innovation and market development and broad contribution to socio-economic development.

As a matter of fact, funding agencies and RI management are increasingly expected to justify key decisions about implementing new projects or investing in existing ones; as a consequence, there is a strong demand for credible methodologies for assessing the overall impact of RIs as outlined in the recent OECD policy paper (n.65/2019) that provides useful tools and templates on how to evaluate the achievement, whether they be scientific, technological, training, and educational or socio-economic, of the RI's objectives.

Fostering scientific knowledge *per sé* (i.e. for the benefit of the scientific world) is no longer considered a sufficient justification to support and fund RIs. There is a need for an observable and measurable impact at societal and economic level. The very *reason d'etre* of an RI is to impact the environment, socially and economically. What is needed (and the four pillars of sustainability are meant to highlight this) is to clarify this impact and communicate it in the simple language of the policy makers and taxpayers.

A number of challenges have been detected that make it difficult to assess the outcomes of a Research Infrastructure. RIs in fact exist to deliver high-quality scientific output to the scientific community and many of their outcomes are indirect and not directly produced by RIs themselves but rather by their users; besides, RIs have different stakeholders—Member States, scientific community, national and

Table 2 Interested stakeholders and their interest in RI

Interested stakeholders	Main interest
National authorities	Justify large investment to finance ministry and to other political authorities (parliament…). Demonstrate, maintain or develop leadership and attractiveness at national/international level. National authorities are usually interested in a limited number of generic indicators which provide an overall picture of the impact, in particular the "scientific and economic return on public investment"
Regioanl/local authorities	Justify investment, increased attractiveness of the area; benefit to local businesses and the development of local/regional innovation ecosystems; raise attractiveness and quality of local higher education institutions
RI funders	Value for money; maximum return or investment. Top priority is usually the scientific and technological impact but funders often require RIs to demonstrate additional benefits
RI initiators (individuals and institutions at the origin of the RI)	*Ex ante* assessment to demonstrate potential impact for funders, national authorities and local authorities and help raise funding
RI management	Monitor impact on as regular basis to improve performance and gather information to make the case to funders when upgrades are required.
RI hosts	Demonstrate the value of the RI in terms of scientific attractiveness, training or education
Scientific community	Advocate for new (*ex ante* assessment) or updated RIs to foster new scientific knowledge and developments
Civil society/ general public	Value for money, new scientific knowledge, general benefit to society (e.g. health, energy, environmental topics). On case by case basis, impact on the environment and/or on local populations

Source: OECD (2019)

local communities, etc.—with different strategic visions and objectives; this means that there are different expectations from different audiences (see Table 2).

Being long-term initiatives, RIs' outcomes often result from cumulative effects over time. Indicators usually provide snapshot information; hence, there is a need to use consistent indicators over time; besides, merely relying on quantitative indicators can offer a limited view of the true impact of an RI; narratives can help illustrate the transformative effects of an RI; time plus adequate competences should be devoted to this task (even considering using social media).

Questions to Ponder

1. Does the RI have defined the main objectives (and expectations) relevant stakeholders/funders have in the infrastructure?
2. Are indicators of impact linked to the strategic objectives?
3. Who is in charge of selecting impact indicators? Are these discussed and agreed upon with relevant founders?
4. Does the RI regularly review the system of impact indicators according to its life cycle?

2.3 A Look at the European Research Infrastructures' Landscape

How are the EU RIs positioned with respect to the above-mentioned five conditions of financial sustainability?

In this section, we attempt to answer such a question based on the data, information, and discussions gathered during past editions of the Executive Master in Management of Research Infrastructures (EMMRI). Although the data gathered cannot be considered representative in a strict statistical sense, however, given the number of European RIs participating in the EMMRI editions, the discussions during class and information gathered through Module assignments and field projects are valuable and relevant in delivering a significant picture of the challenges faced by EU RIs in terms of financial sustainability.

Specifically, considering the statutes of the 32 existing ERICs (https://research-and-innovation.ec.europa.eu/strategy/strategy-research-and-innovation/our-digital-future/european-research-infrastructures/eric/eric-landscape_en) as of March 2026, the field project by Arnaud Roi (DARIAH-ERIC) highlighted both the presence of a limited framework for a long-term commitment and a scarce diversification of financial resources (Criteria n.1 and n.2 of our list).

In fact, the withdrawal conditions of the analysed statutes spanned from a minimum of 6 months—for instance in the case of DARIAH, CESSDA, or EPOS—to a maximum of 36 months (as in ESS or ECRIN), with the majority of ERICs falling into the 12 months withdrawal window, which cannot be considered a signal of long-term commitment by members. As a consequence, meeting the targets set by condition n.1 appears to pose a challenge for EU RIs.

Similar considerations can be drawn when analysing condition n. 2 (diversification of financial sources). Based on the DARIAH field project and the EMMRI participants' answers to a questionnaire distributed at the beginning of the Module on the Financial Sustainability of Research Infrastructures, we can highlight a generalized concentration of financial resources in terms of a limited number of sources and their uneven relevance across the total. Members' funds represent the majority of available sources of finance, accounting for over 80% of total funds in many cases.

User fees and commercial activity are more an exception than a rule, although there is a growing attention towards the need and possibilities to generate one's own income (condition n.3).

Apart from the case of RIs at their initial stage of life, business and financial plans are sometimes available and publicly accessible, and yet few cases exist where a formal commitment to regular updates is made every assigned number of years. Similarly, scenario analysis and risk management techniques are not as widespread, probably due to the fact that many RIs have just entered the implementation phase (in which these tools appear to deliver the most of their usefulness), and management teams tend to be mostly science-based and not trained in the principles of business administration.

Finally, as far as the measurement of impact concerns, the condition seems to be generally met, given the increased expectations for value and impact by Member States: RIs tend to break down their strategic plan into concrete action points that become part of the KPI set used to measure impact. Studies published in 2019, e.g. the StR-ESFRI study "Guidelines on Cost Estimation of Research Infrastructures" and the OECD Policy Paper No 65/2019, deal with the issue of measurement and impact. The guideline on cost estimation is especially important, as many distributed RIs, which base their services on local nodes in various countries and organizations, face challenges in defining the financial situation of the overall infrastructure and continue to report mainly the income and expenses of the secretariat or headquarters. An updated and verifiable evaluation of the costs of an RI could and should form the basis for a continuous assessment of the socio-economic impact of RIs (particularly, with the use of cost-benefit analysis).

The Reference framework, on the other hand, focuses on impact assessment and not performance evaluation. It defines Core Impact Indicators, which provide a general picture of the socio-economic impact of RIs, and a more detailed list of standard indicators, which represent the traditional approach used by several RIs, but are adapted.

Figure 3 summarizes the challenges that EU Research Infrastructures face with respect to meeting the five pillars of financial sustainability. Strategies to address such challenges are also depicted, which will be further commented on in the final section of this chapter.

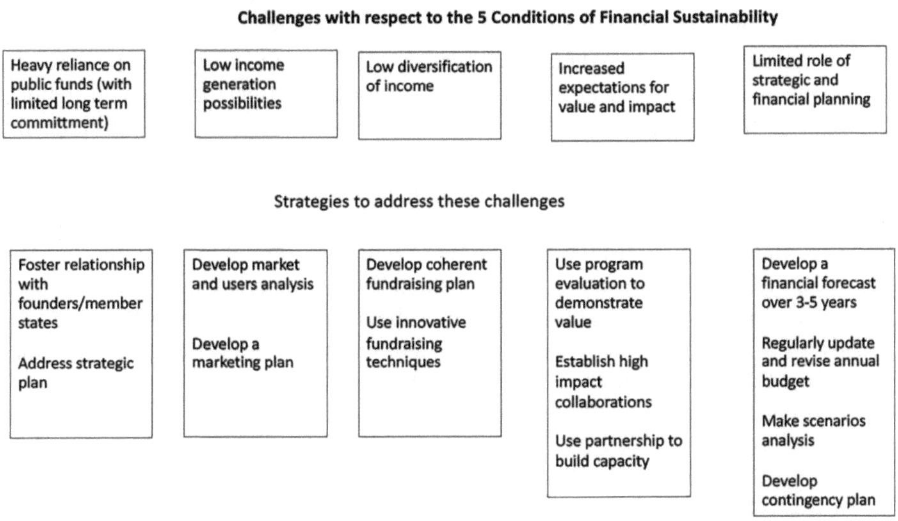

Fig. 3 Challenges and strategies to address financial sustainability—Author's adaptation from OECD (2019)

3 The Financial Plan: A Tool for Sustainability

3.1 Financial Planning for RIs

The purpose of the financial plan (FP) should be to ascertain that the formation of the financial needs resulting from the strategic plan stated in the Business Plan is consistent with the entity's financing capacity. The financial plan is a statement of quantifiable objectives, together with the resources required to achieve them. The objectives are different between profit and not-for-profit entities. For profit entity the main goal is to obtain income, market share, and return on investment, whereas for not-for-profit institutions, like RIs, the objectives could be to obtain new funding sources, or convincing the country members to keep paying their fees. The resources that each entity employs to achieve these objectives are of a different nature; we can mention (but the list is not exhaustive) human resources, property plant and equipment (PPE), and services, but also capital, cash, etc.

As presented in Chap. 4 "Financial Management and Accounting in Research Infrastructures", the RI financial analysis process begins with the preparation of the financial and income statement; this is the starting point for the analysis of the past results. Even if the historical financial analysis of the entity is fundamental to verify the results achieved, another important step of financial analysis is the planning, forecasting, and assessing of future results. "Planning is required when the future state that we desire, involves a set of interdependent decisions; that is, a system of decisions. …The principal complexity in planning derives from the interrelatedness of the decisions rather than from the decisions themselves …" (Ackoff, 1970).

If financial statements and ratios are the main tools for the analysis of past results, the financial plan is the typical tool used in management best practices to help in forecasting future business results (Helfert, 2000). The financial plan highlights the inflows and outflows, allows improving the evaluation of the economic and financial balances, and permits making sensitivity analysis considering different possible future scenarios. It involves the prediction of what could happen in the future so that business planning includes the calculation of what is required to fulfil the forecast, i.e. make the future happen as it is forecasted. Thus, a financial plan uses a forecast as an initial point of departure and then adds the details to reflect how the particular process or project is intended to proceed. It involves making a series of assumptions about how the variables in the plan will behave in future periods.

The financial plan has a strategic role in the business plan feasibility for different reasons.

Firstly, *to achieve the goal defined in the strategic plan, adequate funds have to be ensured*. The financial plan highlights the presence of a financing gap, namely the difference between firms' investments and the amount of available funds. When the financing gap is positive, this means that the use of existing funds is not sufficient to support the company investments; thus, some other forms of external finance have to been activated.

Secondly, *financial plan helps in ensuring a reasonable balance between outflow and inflow of funds so that stability is maintained*. In this sense, FP provides the opportunity to monitoring the equilibrium between outflows (for instance, cost for employees, administrative expenses, services, PPE, etc.) and inflows (for instance, in RI context, Member State fees, user fees, or grants).

A third important role of the FP is *to ensure that the suppliers of funds are persuaded in investing in the RI entity. The FP is also an instrument for anticipating their judgements/valuations*. Indeed, the FP is a tool that can be used internally as self-evaluation instrument to check the sustainability of the investment projects and, from an external point of view, it allows to refine some aspects and decisions in order to solve worries or critical views arising from the potential or existing funders.

The fourth aspect concerns the RI survivorship. *FP helps in making growth and expansion plans that improve the likelihood long-run survival of the Research Infrastructure*. With the business plan, managers define the development strategy of the RI; with the FP, the management can show to the funders that the RI has not only a sound strategy but also that is financially sustainable. In other words, this means that the resources to finance the RI's growth are attainable.

The last aspect regards the capacity of the FP *to mitigate uncertainties concerning changing market conditions, uncertainties that can be a hindrance to growth.* FP is a helpful tool to realize scenario analysis, which allows us to monitor what happens to the RI's financing gap or overall sustainability if some conditions change. For instance, managers can verify in advance what happens to the RI's income and financial statements if the interest rates on the market increase (and they have a bank debt), or if one of the Member State decides to not renew its fee.

The FP plays a strategic role in the RIs' management activity. Considering external relations, it is a fundamental instrument to demonstrate the sustainability of your business strategy to potential external funders (i.e. EIB). As described in the previous section, the diversification of sources of funding is important for RIs as well as for other types of firms. The availability of different sources of funding avoids being excessively dependent on governments and members' funding or grants. To diversify their income RIs can ask for "funding from the private sector": industrial partners, access to private–public partnerships (PPP), and access to traditional form of bank financing (EIB loans) or modern form of funding (crowdfunding). In order to convince potential funders to invest in the RI, the preparation of a complete and informative business plan is fundamental. Certainly, funders are interested in the RI strategic plan but a precondition is to demonstrate, through an FP, that this strategy is financially sustainable.

The FP is also an important tool for the day-by-day management of a RI since it can be useful for the budgeting activity aiming to achieve interim, short-term targets on a yearly basis. Therefore, FP serves as a valid support for providing the budgets of all areas/divisions within an institution (e.g. a single-site RI). In the distributed RIs model, the different areas can correspond to the network nodes. In general terms, the budget is a detailed estimate of future transactions on a short-term basis (typically annual). The essence of a budget is that it sets targets for management to keep within, achieve, or surpass (for control purposes). Thus, a budget is always associated with a specific departmental/node accountability centre within the institution. This might be a division that has a sales budget, a facility with a capital budget, or an individual cost centre (office) with an expense budget.

Budgetary control provides some benefits: i) a budget obliges management to set in detailed quantitative objectives its future intentions (planning function); ii) it provides a yardstick by which individuals or groups can be measured and rewarded (incentive function); iii) it allows some responsibility and authority to be decentralized without loss of information (delegation function); iv) it provides a mechanism to oversee in detail the revenues, costs, cash flows, and capital expenditures of the organization; hence, it promotes an environment of cost awareness (monitoring function); and v) it creates the conditions to react timely to deviations from targets (control function).

3.2 Developing a Financial Plan

3.2.1 Introduction

Financial management best practices may consider different approaches to the building up of a financial plan. The two most popular are the *traditional approach* and the *zero-based budgeting approach*. Moreover, both methods can be implemented using a procedure that can be deterministic or stochastic. In the latter case, the financial plan is developed through a scenario analysis (baseline scenario plus, at least, two scenarios that play a role as the best and the worst case) or, more rarely, a Monte Carlo simulation.

Within the *traditional approach* some institutions formulate their financial plan forecasts starting from last year or the previous administrative period data, adjusted for expected growth and/or for inflation. This approach relies on the notion that all the business variables will remain more or less the same in relation to one another and from one period to the next. This is the typical situation, for example, for an RI during the operational or maturity phase of its life cycle. For this type of financial planning, just a minimal amount of maintenance is required, after collecting the initial set of last available accounting data and basic assumptions (Helfert, 2000).

On the other hand, the *zero-based budgeting* approach (ZBB) assumes that it is necessary to start the budgeting process from scratch each time. The main advantage of this approach is that it ensures a deep rethinking of the basic business assumptions on which the organization relies (e.g. in preparatory or construction RI phases). With a ZBB system, each functional section/area in the business will plan in detail all revenues/incomes, expenditure, and capital items, and these items will be ordered according to the relative significance for the long-term sustainability of the business. Through this selection process, the financial plan will be set up with the aim of achieving a sound financial equilibrium between cash inflows and outflows.

ZBB is clearly more pertinent for start-up and new ventures; meanwhile, the *traditional approach* is less demanding and more useful for established, more mature organizations where the business and RI environment uncertainty is lower (see Fig. 4).

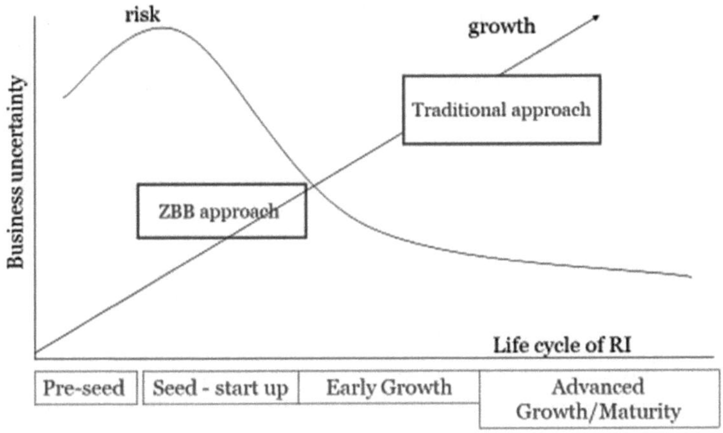

Fig. 4 Different approaches to financial plan and RI life cycle—Author's elaboration

3.2.2 Financial Planning in Practice

In this section, we examine the development of a financial plan from a technical perspective in more detail. The aim is to provide a general overview of the topic with a particular adaptation to the environment and characteristics of a typical RI. In Sect. 4, a real case example of financial planning for a specific RI is provided.

From a technical point of view, the financial plan is essentially a **spreadsheet application**, which often involves acquiring a revenue forecast and then specifying all the necessary resources and their related costs to ensure that the forecasted targets are met, as well as assessing the potential funding gap. A financial plan can be performed for an entire organization, or for a department, network node, or a single investment project. When separate divisional or network node financial plans are developed, they must subsequently be incorporated into an overall corporate plan. The critical aspect is not the actual tool chosen (mainly spreadsheets) but the methodology employed that must be sound, consistent, and possibly easy to share with all internal and external stakeholders (i.e. transparent).

Another key aspect is that the methodology selected should allow an easy implementation of several functions.

I. Facilitate the execution of alternative simulations, allowing changes in the basic key assumptions (scenario analysis, stress testing, what-if analysis, risk analysis carried out through sensitivity analysis).
II. Permit rolling financial planning activity (allowing periodic—yearly, semi-annual, or quarterly—updating and revisions of the projections), also for budgeting control purposes in order to check at fixed future dates potential gaps between expected and actual results.
III. Enable tests on different funding alternatives of prospective financial needs (funding gap), i.e. defining the *financial policy.* The financial policy addresses the overall funding sources and their mix that the RI aims to obtain, looking at

the amount and the expected inflows' time of each financial source. Achieving a good diversification of funding sources is one of the main targets of the overall financial policy, ensuring in this way the appropriate level of *financial flexibility*.

Among alternative existing approaches commonly used in practice, we propose here a simplified methodology that has the following features:

- Traditional approach (last year available data plus growth assumptions)
- Deterministic (most probable scenario—so-called *baseline scenario*)
- Best suited for an established RI in its maturity phase
- Synthetic (it does not rely on infra-annual cash budgets)
- Parsimonious and cost-effective (it does not use a huge amount of data)
- More easy to grasp for non-specialists in financial planning techniques

The methodology builds pro forma financial statements over each year of the planned horizon (minimum 3–5 years). For starting the process, a set of yearly key indicators and business variables assumptions regarding the major items of the entity standard operations are needed. For example, we must surely consider in the case of a RI: expected revenues (or incomes) growth rates that include Member State fees, external grants, and/or fees for commissioned services; main operating cost categories growth rates relating to staff, external services, office rents, and administrative and general costs; and inflation rates assumptions and interest rates if lending or financial debt is introduced. We also need as initial inputs the last period/year financial report (balance sheet and income statement at time T, i.e. the historical accounting data). The last available historical accounting data are taken as the current base for the first year of the projection exercise.

The pro forma procedure is structured into 7 main steps or phases (for each year of the forecasted financial statements—years T + 1, T + 2, T + 3, or more). Thus, we have to repeat the process 3–5 times as the number of years considered in the planning horizon.

Here below we present the pro forma financial statements through the 7 steps sequential approach. They are the following:

1. Estimate of EBITDA (starting from expected revenues and operating monetary costs—i.e. the first half of the income statement)
2. Projection of end of period net operating working capital (NOWC)
3. Estimate of the cash flow from operations
4. Estimate the end of period cash equivalents (or short-term financial debt), i.e. net financial position (NFP)
5. Estimate of interest charges (or financial income) on net financial position
6. Closing of projected income statement (from EBITDA until net income, i.e. the second half of P&L account)
7. Closing of projected balance sheet (all assets and liabilities)

Each phase warrants a deeper discussion. We begin with Step 1.

1. *Estimate of expected EBITDA (i.e. gross operating income)*

+ Expected Revenues (i.e. Revenues at time T * (1 + expected growth rate))
– Variable monetary costs (using expected costs growth rate and inflation assumptions)
– Fixed monetary costs (mainly, salaries for employees)
= Expected EBITDA (Earnings before interest, taxes, depreciation, and amortization)

We do not close the income account, here in the first step, because we have to estimate financial expenses or income. For doing that we need cash flows projections.

2. *Projection of end of period net operating working capital*

In general terms, the net operating working capital (NOWC) is normally defined in financial accounting as the difference between operating current assets (the sum of Receivables, Inventory, other minor current assets) and operating current liabilities (the sum of Payables, Debt vs employees, and other minor current liabilities). These accounting items are taken directly from the balance sheet of the entity financial report. In the specific case of RIs and other services provider businesses, Inventory (raw materials and/or finished products) is not existing; thus, we can assume that NOWC for a typical RI is formed by only three major items (excluding, in a simple framework, other minor items): Receivables, Payables, and Debt vs employees.

As we need to project the end of period forecasted NOWC, we have to estimate the end of period Receivables, Payables, and Debt vs employees. The first two items can be estimated using the average payment delays given (on Receivables account) to customers (mainly, Member State contributors for RIs) or obtained (Payables account) by services suppliers (the so-called CDO and SDO, which are, respectively, the customers days outstanding and suppliers days outstanding metrics). These average days indicators are well known in the financial accounting profession as valuable working capital financial ratios (Walsh, 2003), as they provide the managers with a quick indication about how long (on average) is the mismatch between revenues and cash inflows (Receivables) and services costs and cash outflows (Payables).

Under these circumstances, CDO are computed using last available accounting data (at time T) as the ratio between the receivables and the daily revenues (using 360 days of the commercial annual calendar), whereas SDO are calculated as the ratio between the payables and the daily services expenses (still using 360 days).

Thus, using the historical last available accounting data at time T, we can define:

$$\text{CDO} = \text{Receivable T} / (\text{Revenues T} / 360); \text{and}$$

$$\text{SDO} = \text{Payables T} / (\text{Services expenses T} / 360)$$

Then, we can use historical CDO and SDO values in order to project end of period Receivables and Payables on the assumptions that the average days indicators will remain constant in the forecasted period/year.

Thus, expected Receivable is equal to CDO times the daily revenues T + 1 and expected Payables is equal to SDO times the daily services expenses T+ 1.

$$\text{Receivables}_{\text{T+1}} = \text{CDO}^{*}\text{Revenues}_{\text{T+1}} / 360; \text{and}$$

$$\text{Payables}_{\text{T+1}} = \text{SDO}^{*}\text{Services Expenses}_{\text{T+1}} / 360$$

In the case of the other items included in the operating working capital (in our case Debt vs employees) that do not have time delays metrics, a rule of thumb often used in practice is to use a constant fixed percentage (versus revenues) based on historical and more recent accounting data.

At the end, in order to compute the net operating working capital, we sum each item being careful that current liabilities maintain a negative sign in the algebraic sum.

RIs normally display a negative NOWC with an inverted sign of cash conversion cycle (i.e. inflows precede outflows).

3. *Estimate of the cash flow from operations*

Cash flow from operations (CFO) is the most relevant cash flow generated by the operating cycle (inputs acquisition–production and services selling) of a business. It is also an important indicator of the entity self-financing capacity since a positive CFO means that cash inflows are higher than outflows, indicating that the typical business operations do not cause financial needs or a funding gap that requires finding a source of external funding.

As the CFO definition is:

$$\text{CFO}_{\text{T+1}} = \text{EBITDA}_{\text{T+1}} + / - \text{Net operating working capital change}_{(\text{T+1}-\text{T})}$$

we can have the two following cases.

If NOWC **increases** in the period under investigation, we have to subtract the NOWC change from the EBITDA as the net working capital produces net outflows; meanwhile if NOWC **decreases** we have to sum EBITDA and the NOWC change as the reduction of NOWC underlines a net disinvestment or partial liquidation of assets that causes a net cash inflow.

As RIs are typically cash-generating entities, when there is growth, we have cash accumulation, but in a revenue decline phase, we can quickly develop financial needs (RIs turn out to be a **cash absorber** entity).

4. *Estimation of end of period net financial position (NFP)*

In this phase of the procedure, we need to estimate the end of period net financial position (NFP) which is defined as accumulated cash net of short-term bank overdraft (if present). For accumulated cash, we refer to total cash and cash equivalents we can find in the current assets side of the balance sheet. Besides normal cash, cash equivalents include whatever temporary investment in short-term safe financial assets such as liquid and default risk-free government bonds.

The aim of the estimation of NFP is to assess whether typical cash outflows arising from new planned investments in fixed assets (CAPEX), such as in property, plant, and equipment (PPE), cause financial needs that must be funded by new external sources. Let us suppose that a given entity, starting at time T with an initial cash of 100, needs to carry out an investment in fixed asset (equipment) equal to 50 plus an obligation to pay annual tax for 10. Which is the expected end of period NFP if the cash flow from operation is positive and equal to 30?

Here below, we present the effects that the cash from operations and the other cash flows from investment and financial activities (including tax cash outflows) produce on the final (end of period) net financial position.

$$+\text{Initial cash equivalents}\left(\text{short-term bank overdraft}\right) = +100\left(\text{at time T}\right)$$

$$+/-\text{Cash flow from operation}\left(\text{see step 3}\right) = +30$$

$$-\text{CAPEX}\left(\text{New investments in PPE}\right) = -50$$

$$-\text{Repayment installments of previous bank loans} = 0$$

$$+\text{New long term bank loan}\left(\text{if planned}\right) = 0$$

$$-\text{Tax payments} = -10$$

$$= \text{End of period NFP}\left(\text{cash equivalents}\right) = +70$$

In the above numerical example, the initial cash is reduced by 30 to reach an end of period value of 70. In other terms, the new investment in fixed asset and the tax payments are financed by internal financial sources (i.e. CFO) and, residually, by a reduction of cash equivalents. No external financial needs or funding gap arises from this situation.

5. *Estimate of interest charges (if existing)*

In this step, we proceed to estimate the annual interest expenses we might be charged by a financial institution (i.e. a bank or EIB), in case of financial debt (e.g. with a negative NFP).

Given an assumption on the interest rate charged on short-term bank overdraft (= i %), we can compute the financial expenses if our net financial position turns out to be a net short-term bank exposure.

Interest charges (IC) can be estimated on the simple average NFP across the period/year as:

$$\mathrm{IC} = \mathrm{i}\%^{*}\left(\left(\text{Beginning of period NFP} + \text{End of period NFP}\right)/2\right)$$

This step is omitted if we observe a positive end of period cash equivalents, as it is common in the majority of RIs that do not use bank lending (see step 4).

6. *Closing of projected income statement*

In this step, we close the income statement account fulfilling the second (bottom) half of the income statement.

We start with the expected EBITDA projected in step 1 and we complete the income statement after considering non-monetary costs, such as depreciation and amortization on fixed assets, and other non-operating costs, such as financial expenses and corporate taxes (if relevant).

Bottom half of the income statement

+ Expected EBITDA (see step 1)
– Depreciation (average depreciation rate * gross PPE)
= Expected EBIT (Earnings before interest and taxes)
– Financial expenses (IC on short-term debt - see step 5- + IC on long-term loans, if existing)
= Before tax income
– Taxes (= current corporate tax rate * before tax income)
= Net income

7. *Closing of projected balance sheet*

The last step consists in putting together all assets and liabilities of the balance sheet at time T + 1.

Some assets and liabilities have already been estimated in previous steps (see NOWC, Cash equivalents, or NFP). The residual items to be added are PPE (or net fixed assets) including new capital expenditures net of depreciation of the period; NFP including interest charges (IC) on short-term bank overdraft, if NFP turns out to be negative; long-term loans if any; tax debt if estimated annual tax in the income statement is higher than tax liquidation outflows charged in step 4; and, finally, equity calculated as sum of initial equity plus net income of the period. Here, below, we summarize all assets and liabilities of the balance sheet.

Balance sheet

Assets	Liabilities
+ PPE (PPE $_{T}$ + CAPEX $_{T+1}$—Dep $_{T+1}$)	+ NOWC (if negative) (see step 2)
+ Cash equivalents (see step 4)	+ (NFP if negative) (NFP post IC)
+ (Tax credit, if tax payments >taxes)	+ Long-term bank loans (if existing)
+ (NOWC (if positive))	+Tax debt (= Taxes$_{T+1}$—Tax payments >0, see steps 6,4)
–	+ Equity (initial equity + net income $_{T+1}$, see step 6)
= Total assets	= Total liabilities

At the end, we have to check the accounting consistency of the first-year financial plan forecasts verifying that the total assets are equal to the total liabilities.

After completing first-year projections, we have to repeat the process for the subsequent years of the horizon considered (using the previous forecasted year as platform for the next one).

At the end of the process, we obtain a *baseline projection or scenario* (most probable). We can interpret the results looking at some relevant financial ratios (e.g. current ratio) trying to *predict the financial stakeholders' assessment* on our solvency/creditworthiness (Walsh, 2003). We can also implement the necessary adjustments (e.g. reducing some cost items not deemed essential).

We may employ a *what-if analysis* simulating alternative scenarios (e.g. considering a *worst-case or a stress test scenario*) changing the inputs/values of the key indicators/variables assumptions (e.g. revenues growth, inflation, operating cost development, investment in PPE, and interest rates). Thus, we can ascertain the role of the most sensitive variables and *assess the corporate risks*. Hence, we can better prepare for contingencies.

Thanks to the financial plan obtained through the described methodology, we can achieve the following additional objectives:

- We can gain valuable information on how to design our RI's *financial policy* (i.e. how to fund the financial needs, for example: do we need a bank loan, this year or the next and for which maturity?) We can also test the effects of alternative financial policies (inserting different funding solutions in step 4 of the above procedure).
- We can use the pro forma financial statements tools for updating at regular intervals our projections (applying *rolling forecasts*).
- A similar approach can be used to the financial planning of a *single investment project* (but, here, the cash outflows precede the inflows).
- Finally, last but not least, we can use the information set arising from our financial planning exercise to finalize the financial and funding framework part of a business plan and/or the documents requested by potential lenders (such as EIB, or other potential financial resources providers from the private sector).

In conclusion, the financial plan plays a key role in conveying and sharing the RIs' financial sustainability with all its stakeholders and, in the same time, allows the management to carry out a very broad set of planning tasks.

4 The ELIXIR Case Study

The ELIXIR Financial Plan 2019-23 accompanies the development of the ELIXIR Scientific Programme 2019-23. It was the result of a process that spanned 18 months, from the initial discussions until approval by the ELIXIR Board. The process involved all ELIXIR stakeholders and, in particular, the ELIXIR nodes following bottom-up and top-down approaches (see Fig. 5).

All ELIXIR Nodes and Stakeholders were involved in providing input for the definition of the priorities and goals for the Scientific Programme. In addition, a consultation on the actual allocation of financial resources was carried out with ELIXIR Platforms, Head of Nodes, the ELIXIR Director, and the ELIXIR Board that finally approved both the Scientific Programme and the Financial Plan on 13 November 2018.

It is important to note that the Financial Plan provides a reality check on the ambition of the Scientific Programme contributing to the prioritization and the phasing of the scientific and technical activities along the duration of the Scientific Programme. Neither the Financial Plan nor the Scientific Programme can be developed in isolation as one complements the other.

4.1 The Development of ELIXIR Financial Plan

The following sections describe the process followed in ELIXIR to develop the ELIXIR Financial Plan 2019-23 including the following steps:

1. Understanding the RI context and constraints it imposes on the development of the Financial Plan
2. Identifying the financial scenarios

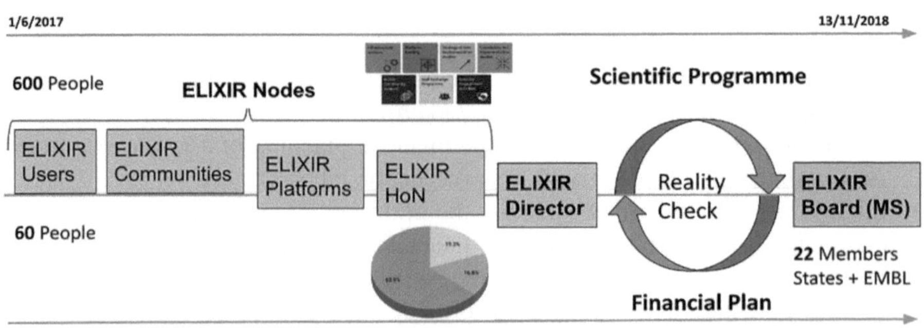

Fig. 5 Developing the ELIXIR Scientific Programme 2019–23 and the ELIXIR Financial Plan 2019–23—Author's elaboration

3. Building a financial model to test the different financial scenarios
   (a) Income streams
   (b) Constraints to be incorporated into the Financial Plan
   (c) Contingencies to be incorporated into the Financial Plan
   (d) Allocation of financial resources to support the ELIXIR Scientific Programme
4. Analysis of the different scenario ("what if?")
5. Financial Plan execution and monitoring

4.1.1 Understanding the Context

ELIXIR coordinates and develops life science resources across Europe so that researchers can more easily find, analyse, and share data; exchange expertise; and implement best practices. This makes it possible for them to gain greater insights into how living organisms work.

ELIXIR is a treaty-based consortium of countries (Belgium, the Czech Republic, Denmark, Estonia, Finland, France, Germany, Greece, Hungary, Ireland, Israel, Italy, Luxembourg, the Netherlands, Norway, Portugal, Slovenia, Spain, Sweden, Switzerland, the UK, and an intergovernmental organization, the European Molecular Biology Laboratory (EMBL). Cyprus is currently an Observer country. The ELIXIR Consortium Agreement (ECA) is the legal treaty that established ELIXIR.

The ECA covers e.g. ELIXIR's mission, membership, obligations of the members and the ELIXIR Hub, the governance structure between the ELIXIR Hub and the ELIXIR Nodes, and the internal governance structure of the ELIXIR Hub itself.

The ECA establishes the relationship between ELIXIR and EMBL. EMBL's role within ELIXIR is threefold: EMBL is a member of the ELIXIR Consortium; it serves as the host of the ELIXIR Hub providing administrative services; and EMBL provides technical services to ELIXIR. In the activities carried out within ELIXIR, EMBL is bound by the provisions of the ECA and the decisions of the ELIXIR Board.

- *As an ELIXIR Member*, EMBL sends its delegates to the ELIXIR Board, ELIXIR's decision-making body, having one vote like all other members of the ELIXIR Consortium.
- *As the host of the ELIXIR Hub*, EMBL recognizes that ELIXIR is part of EMBL. EMBL provides to ELIXIR all those services essential for the operation and management of the ELIXIR Hub and the accomplishment of ELIXIR's goals taking into account that ELIXIR exists as a Consortium, which does not have its own legal personality. In the ECA, these activities are referred to as "Core Responsibilities", and they are funded by the ELIXIR Budget. These include employing ELIXIR Staff and making available facilities, infrastructure, and services to the ELIXIR Hub, such as services provided by EMBL's Administration (e.g. procurement and financial management). In addition, EMBL, as part of and as mandated by the ELIXIR Consortium, enters into agreements with third parties or acts as party to legal disputes.

- *EMBL also takes on the role of an ELIXIR Node.* In this function, it provides technical services to ELIXIR as approved by the ELIXIR Board just like any other ELIXIR Node.

The Core Responsibilities and technical services of EMBL to ELIXIR as a Node are defined in "Work Programmes".

The ELIXIR Governance structure is defined in the ECA:

- *ELIXIR Board:* the highest decision-making body in ELIXIR.
- *Scientific Advisory Board (SAB):* constitutional advisory body that advises the Board and the ELIXIR Director on ELIXIR's scientific strategy and reviews ELIXIR Nodes.
- *Industry Advisory Committee:* gives advice and guidance on industry needs.
- *Director:* responsible to the ELIXIR Board for implementing its decisions and in particular ELIXIR's Scientific Programme.
- *Heads of Nodes Committee:* consists of the Director and the heads of the ELIXIR national infrastructures (Nodes). The Committee helps the ELIXIR Director to develop ELIXIR's scientific and technical strategy, including its programme.

This structure has a number of implications for developing a financial plan:

- ELIXIR does not have a balance sheet as it consolidates with EMBL accounts.
- ELIXIR has to maintain a positive cash balance at all times. ELIXIR can't enter into loans.
- ELIXIR Financial Plan has to be approved by all members of the ELIXIR Board; it requires unanimity.

4.1.2 Identifying Financial Scenarios

Possibly the most important limiting factor when preparing a financial plan is the identification of a realistic budget you can expect your Member States will agree to. This is an iterative process that requires working in close collaboration with your Member States to build and test different financial scenarios until there is enough consensus to agree on the final scenario.

During the preparation of the ELIXIR Financial Plan 2019–23 a total of seven different scenarios were considered; for illustration purposes, we present two of them below. The first scenario represents a flat budget (0% increase on budget), while the second one represents a budget + inflation scenario (2% increase) (Fig. 6).

Each of the scenarios implies a different commitment, in the form of a yearly financial contribution, from the Member States (MS). The exact commitment from each Member State will depend on how the scale of the contributions is calculated for each RI. In the case of ELIXIR, the scale of contribution of ECA signatories is calculated based on the average Net National Income (NNI) at factor cost based on OECD data. In the case of observer countries, no contribution is required during the first 2 years, but if the observership is extended for another 2 years, they will contribute with 30% of their full contribution assuming their membership. While a

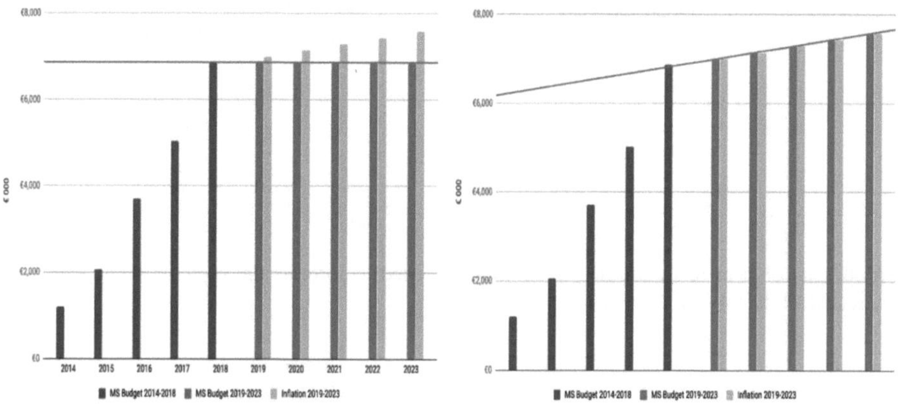

Fig. 6 ELIXIR 2019–23 Financial Scenarios. Examples—Author's elaboration

MS	Scale	2019	2020	2021	2021	2023
Total:	100.00%	€ 6,864,441	€ 6,864,441	€ 6,864,441	€ 6,864,441	€ 6,864,441
Country 1	2.79%	€ 191,518	€ 191,518	€ 191,518	€ 191,518	€ 191,518
Country 2	0.98%	€ 67,272	€ 67,272	€ 67,272	€ 67,272	€ 67,272
Country 3	1.91%	€ 131,111	€ 131,111	€ 131,111	€ 131,111	€ 131,111
Country 4	0.13%	€ 8,924	€ 8,924	€ 8,924	€ 8,924	€ 8,924
Country 5	1.37%	€ 94,043	€ 94,043	€ 94,043	€ 94,043	€ 94,043
Country 6	15.46%	€ 1,061,243	€ 1,061,243	€ 1,061,243	€ 1,061,243	€ 1,061,243
Country 7	21.41%	€ 1,469,677	€ 1,469,677	€ 1,469,677	€ 1,469,677	€ 1,469,677
Country 8	0.65%	€ 44,619	€ 44,619	€ 44,619	€ 44,619	€ 44,619
Country 9	1.14%	€ 78,255	€ 78,255	€ 78,255	€ 78,255	€ 78,255
Country 10	1.77%	€ 121,501	€ 121,501	€ 121,501	€ 121,501	€ 121,501
Country 11	11.43%	€ 784,606	€ 784,606	€ 784,606	€ 784,606	€ 784,606
Country 12	0.21%	€ 14,415	€ 14,415	€ 14,415	€ 14,415	€ 14,415
Country 13	4.83%	€ 331,553	€ 331,553	€ 331,553	€ 331,553	€ 331,553
Country 14	2.79%	€ 191,518	€ 191,518	€ 191,518	€ 191,518	€ 191,518
Country 15	1.17%	€ 80,314	€ 80,314	€ 80,314	€ 80,314	€ 80,314
Country 16	0.24%	€ 16,475	€ 16,475	€ 16,475	€ 16,475	€ 16,475
Country 17	7.51%	€ 515,520	€ 515,520	€ 515,520	€ 515,520	€ 515,520
Country 18	3.19%	€ 218,976	€ 218,976	€ 218,976	€ 218,976	€ 218,976
Country 19	4.21%	€ 288,993	€ 288,993	€ 288,993	€ 288,993	€ 288,993
Country 20	16.81%	€ 1,153,913	€ 1,153,913	€ 1,153,913	€ 1,153,913	€ 1,153,913

MS	Scale	2019	2020	2021	2021	2023
Total:	100.00%	€ 7,001,730	€ 7,141,765	€ 7,284,600	€ 7,430,292	€ 7,578,898
Country 1	2.79%	€ 195,348	€ 199,255	€ 203,240	€ 207,305	€ 211,451
Country 2	0.98%	€ 68,617	€ 69,989	€ 71,389	€ 72,817	€ 74,273
Country 3	1.91%	€ 133,733	€ 136,408	€ 139,136	€ 141,919	€ 144,757
Country 4	0.13%	€ 9,102	€ 9,284	€ 9,470	€ 9,659	€ 9,853
Country 5	1.37%	€ 95,924	€ 97,842	€ 99,799	€ 101,795	€ 103,831
Country 6	15.46%	€ 1,082,467	€ 1,104,117	€ 1,126,199	€ 1,148,723	€ 1,171,698
Country 7	21.41%	€ 1,499,070	€ 1,529,052	€ 1,559,633	€ 1,590,826	€ 1,622,642
Country 8	0.65%	€ 45,511	€ 46,421	€ 47,350	€ 48,297	€ 49,263
Country 9	1.14%	€ 79,820	€ 81,416	€ 83,044	€ 84,705	€ 86,399
Country 10	1.77%	€ 123,931	€ 126,409	€ 128,937	€ 131,516	€ 134,146
Country 11	11.43%	€ 800,298	€ 816,304	€ 832,630	€ 849,282	€ 866,268
Country 12	0.21%	€ 14,704	€ 14,998	€ 15,298	€ 15,604	€ 15,916
Country 13	4.83%	€ 338,184	€ 344,947	€ 351,846	€ 358,883	€ 366,061
Country 14	2.79%	€ 195,348	€ 199,255	€ 203,240	€ 207,305	€ 211,451
Country 15	1.17%	€ 81,920	€ 83,559	€ 85,230	€ 86,934	€ 88,673
Country 16	0.24%	€ 16,804	€ 17,140	€ 17,483	€ 17,833	€ 18,189
Country 17	7.51%	€ 525,830	€ 536,347	€ 547,073	€ 558,015	€ 569,175
Country 18	3.19%	€ 223,355	€ 227,822	€ 232,379	€ 237,026	€ 241,767
Country 19	4.21%	€ 294,773	€ 300,668	€ 306,682	€ 312,815	€ 319,072
Country 20	16.81%	€ 1,176,991	€ 1,200,531	€ 1,224,541	€ 1,249,032	€ 1,274,013

Fig. 7 ELIXIR 2019–23 MS contributions corresponding to the financial scenarios—Author's elaboration

financial scenario can be acceptable for a Member State, it can be completely unfeasible to others, and therefore, building a financial model that allows you to easily benchmark the different scenarios and hypothesis is highly recommended.

For illustrative purposes, the contribution corresponding to the two scenarios above is presented in Fig. 7.

4.1.3 Building the ELIXIR Financial Model

Income Stream

Each RI has different income streams. In the case of ELIXIR, they are limited to Member States' contributions and external grants (EC, IMI grants).

The Member State contributions are forecasted based on the financial scenarios discussed in Sect. 4.1.2.

Grants income is forecasted based on the current grant portfolio that includes:

Ilustrative example (Mock Data)		2019	2020	2021	2022	2023	
GRANTS (EXT funded)		€ 635,043	€ 614,327	€ 591,391	€ 607,668	€ 619,218	Type
Current Portfolio	EXT. RUNING 1	€ 249,784	€ 0	€ 0	€ 0	€ 0	H2020
	EXT. RUNING 2	€ 84,672	€ 60,997	€ 0	€ 0	€ 0	H2020
	EXT. RUNING 3	€ 12,701	€ 13,071	€ 26,881	€ 41,432	€ 0	IMI
	EXT. RUNING 4	€ 4,234	€ 0	€ 0	€ 0	€ 0	H2020
	EXT. RUNING 5	€ 16,934	€ 60,997	€ 0	€ 0	€ 0	H2020
Proposal to identified calls	EXT. proposal 1	€ 55,037	€ 108,923	€ 147,848	€ 170,331	€ 0	H2020
	EXT. proposal 2	€ 25,402	€ 34,855	€ 49,283	€ 27,621	€ 0	H2020
	EXT. proposal 3	€ 4,234	€ 4,357	€ 4,480	€ 4,604	€ 42,542	H2020
	EXT. proposal 4	€ 93,140	€ 104,566	€ 116,486	€ 78,260	€ 0	H2020
	EXT. proposal 5	€ 88,906	€ 209,133	€ 228,492	€ 220,970	€ 0	IMI
Funding soruce to be identifed	To be defined	€ 0	€ 17,428	€ 17,921	€ 64,450	€ 576,677	H2020

Fig. 8 Snapshot of the simplified modelling tool used to forecast personnel cost income from grants (Mock Data)—Author's elaboration

Scenarios =>	0% increase					2% Increase				
Financial Plan 2019-23	2019 €000	2020 €000	2021 €000	2022 €000	2023 €000	2019 €000	2020 €000	2021 €000	2022 €000	2023 €000
Income										
Member State Contributions										
Ordinary Contributions	€ 6,864	€ 6,864	€ 6,864	€ 6,864	€ 6,864	€ 7,002	€ 7,142	€ 7,285	€ 7,430	€ 7,579
Foreign exchange gain on sterling contributions										
External Grants	€ 913	€ 883	€ 850	€ 874	€ 890	€ 913	€ 883	€ 850	€ 874	€ 890
Other income										
Unpaid contributions										
Total Income	€ 7,777	€ 7,748	€ 7,715	€ 7,738	€ 7,755	€ 7,915	€ 8,025	€ 8,135	€ 8,304	€ 8,469

Fig. 9 Snapshot of the simplified modelling tool to present forecasted RI income (Mock Data): Member States Funding and External grants funding (including personnel cost, other direct, subcontracting, and indirect costs)—Author's elaboration

- Grants in executions that will continue or finish during the timeframe of the ELIXIR Scientific Programme 2019–23.
- Grants to be started that will be in execution or finish during the timeframe of the ELIXIR Scientific Programme 2019–23.
- Grant proposals submitted, under preparation or to be developed that will be in execution or finish during the timeframe of the ELIXIR Scientific Programme 2019–23, based on the expected success rate.

An estimation of the additional funding that the RI can expect to attract from external grants (beyond the published calls) during the lifetime of the Scientific Programme is also included, based on the success rates and funds awarded in the previous years (Fig. 8).

Both income streams (Member States and External Grants) are brought into our financial model and incorporated into each of the scenarios being considered as detailed below (Fig. 9).

Constraints

Each RI will have to incorporate a number of financial constraints that model the financial environment in which the RI is expected to operate during the timeframe of the Scientific Programme. Usual constraints to be considered are cost inflation, salaries inflation, exchange rate exposure, and support and administrative infrastructure costs (Fig. 10).

	2019	2020	2021	2022	2023
> Cash Reserve Target %	15.00%	15.00%	15.00%	15.00%	15.00%
> Cost inflation	3.00%	3.00%	3.00%	3.00%	3.00%
> Salary inflation (Hub)	3.00%	3.00%	3.00%	3.00%	3.00%
> FX impact	3.00%	3.00%	3.00%	3.00%	3.00%
> level of cost contigency	3.00%	3.00%	3.00%	3.00%	3.00%
> £/€ Fx Rate (Forecast)	0.95	0.95	0.95	0.95	0.95
> Suport and Admin Costs %	35%	33%	31%	30%	29%
> Grants Indirect Costs %	25%	25%	25%	25%	25%

Fig. 10 Examples of financial constraints modelling (Mock Data)—Author's elaboration

					Additonal Budget (Contigency):	€380,000.0	Apply to (1=yes, 0=no)				
Type	Description	Likelihood	Impact	Score	Impact €	Contingency €	2019	2020	2021	2022	2023
Risk	Disruption of RI operations.	5 - Very High	5 - Very Higt	25	€400,000.0	€400,000.0	1	1	1	1	1
Opportunity	Small-size country joining the RI	5 - Very High	1- Very Low	5	€15,000.0		1	1	1	1	1
Opportunity	Mid-size country joining the RI	5 - Very High	3 - Medium	15	€400,000.0	-€400,000.0	0	1	1	1	1
Risk	Mid-size country leaving the RI	1- Very Low	4 - High	4	€550,000.0		1	1	1	1	1
Opportunity	Large-size country joining the RI	1- Very Low	5 - Very Higt	5	€900,000.0		1	1	1	1	1
Risk	Large-size country leaving the RI	2 - Low	5 - Very Higt	10	€1,200,000.0		1	1	1	1	1
Risk	Cost claim rejected in external projects	3 - Medium	4 - High	12	€300,000.0	€300,000.0	0	1	1	0	1
Risk	ELIXIR Hub attritoin	4 - High	4 - High	16	€80,000.0	€80,000.0	1	1	1	1	1

2019	€480,000.0
2020	€380,000.0
2021	€380,000.0
2022	€80,000.0
2023	€380,000.0

Fig. 11 Examples of financial constraints modelling (Mock Data)—Author's elaboration

In the case of ELIXIR, probably the most important constraint is the need to keep a positive cash reserve at all times (by its statutes ELIXIR cannot have a negative cash reserve). To that end, ELIXIR has defined the target of keeping the cash reserve above 15% of our yearly operational cost. This constraint will provide ELIXIR with enough resilience to accommodate different situations, for example, delays associated with the payment of MS contributions, which is not unusual as they undergo complex processes in each country that can be lengthy, at times, due to a number of factors.

Contingencies

As part of the risk and opportunity management, the associated financial risks (+) and opportunities (−) are assessed and built into the financial plan, according to the likelihood and financial impact, and setting aside resources to enable the RI to operate even in case those risks are realized. In the case of ELIXIR and to ensure we keep a positive balance at all times we set a target for our cash reserve (non-allocated funds) to be 15% of our yearly operational costs (Fig. 11).

Scenarios =>	0% increase					2% Increase				
Financial Plan 2019-23	2019 €000	2020 €000	2021 €000	2022 €000	2023 €000	2019 €000	2020 €000	2021 €000	2022 €000	2023 €000
Internal Expenditure (Direct Costs)										
Technological Activities										
Salaries	€ 681	€ 665	€ 687	€ 715	€ 729	€ 681	€ 665	€ 687	€ 715	€ 729
Running Costs	€ 386	€ 398	€ 412	€ 420	€ 434	€ 386	€ 398	€ 412	€ 420	€ 434
Capital and Equipment	€ 5	€ 5	€ 5	€ 6	€ 6	€ 5	€ 5	€ 5	€ 6	€ 6
Directorate and Administrative Costs										
Salaries	€ 741	€ 786	€ 844	€ 863	€ 892	€ 741	€ 786	€ 844	€ 863	€ 892
Running Costs	€ 386	€ 398	€ 412	€ 420	€ 434	€ 386	€ 398	€ 412	€ 420	€ 434
Equipment	€ 5	€ 5	€ 5	€ 6	€ 6	€ 5	€ 5	€ 5	€ 6	€ 6
Support and Admin Infrastructure Costs	€ 708	€ 674	€ 670	€ 661	€ 655	€ 708	€ 674	€ 670	€ 661	€ 655
Grants Expenditure										
Salaries	€ 635	€ 614	€ 591	€ 608	€ 619	€ 635	€ 614	€ 591	€ 608	€ 619
Running Costs	€ 95	€ 92	€ 89	€ 91	€ 93	€ 95	€ 92	€ 89	€ 91	€ 93
Indirect Costs	€ 183	€ 177	€ 170	€ 175	€ 178	€ 183	€ 177	€ 170	€ 175	€ 178
Total Grants Expenditure	€ 913	€ 883	€ 850	€ 874	€ 890	€ 913	€ 883	€ 850	€ 874	€ 890

Fig. 12 Snapshot of simplified modelling tool used to model hub cost for the period 2019–23 (Example Data)—Author's elaboration

Funding the ELIXIR Scientific Programme

The financial plan accompanies the Scientific Programme providing the resources to fund the scientific and technical activities required to accomplish the strategic objectives set for the period. The MS pay a contribution towards the ELIXIR Hub budget which is then distributed between Directorate and Administrative Activities and Technological Activities, the latter including Commissioned Services where most of the budget is set to fund the development of technical activities at our Nodes.

Financial planning of Directorate, Administration, and Technical Activities at the ELIXIR Hub and grants.

When building the financial plan using the ELIXIR financial model, we first look at the cost associated with the ELIXIR Hub (staff cost, running cost, and equipment) that are estimated based on the staff required to manage, coordinate, and support our core activities. The support and administrative infrastructure costs are estimated based on the expected usage that ELIXIR will make of the services provided by our host EMBL (Fig. 12).

Technological Activities (Commissioned Services)

The largest part of the ELIXIR Hub budget is allocated to the implementation of our technical programme via services commissioned to our Nodes that will then carry out the technical development. The Scientific Programme defines seven different categories of Commissioned Services (Fig. 13).

To facilitate the planning and phasing of the investment in Commissioned Services, a specific tool has been developed and integrated into the financial model to allow:

- Comparison of different scenarios while checking that the main constraint—adequate cash reserve—be available at any time to avoid entering into a negative cash reserve.

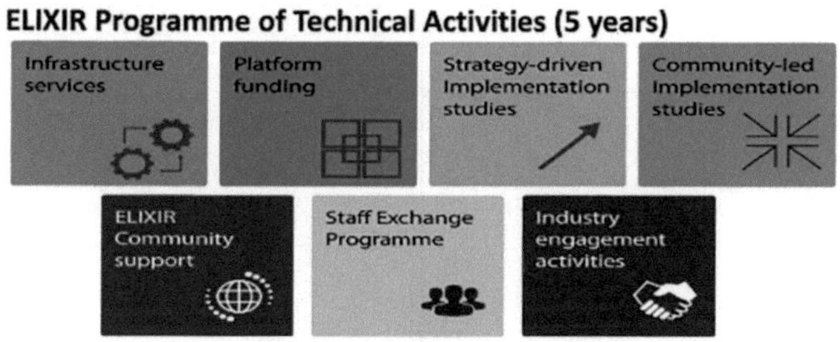

Year	2019	2020	2021	2022	2023
Committed CoS 2018	€1,953,000.00				
Platforms	€1,072,000.00	€1,072,000.00	€1,072,000.00	€1,072,000.00	€1,072,000.00
Strategy-Driven IS	€875,000.00	€1,200,000.00	€1,075,000.00	€750,000.00	€500,000.00
Community-Led IS	€500,000.00	€500,000.00	€0.00	€625,000.00	€625,000.00
Infrastructure Services	€120,000.00	€120,000.00	€480,000.00	€480,000.00	€480,000.00
Mature communities support	€690,000.00	€335,000.00	€150,000.00	€450,000.00	€450,000.00
Emerging communities support	€25,000.00	€50,000.00	€0.00	€75,000.00	€0.00
Staff Exchange Programme	€303,000.00	€306,000.00	€309,000.00	€312,000.00	€315,000.00
SME programme	€75,000.00	€75,000.00	€75,000.00	€75,000.00	€75,000.00
ToT CoS	€3,660,000.00	€3,658,000.00	€3,161,000.00	€3,839,000.00	€3,517,000.00

Fig. 13 ELIXIR 2019–23 Commissioned Services Categories—Author's elaboration

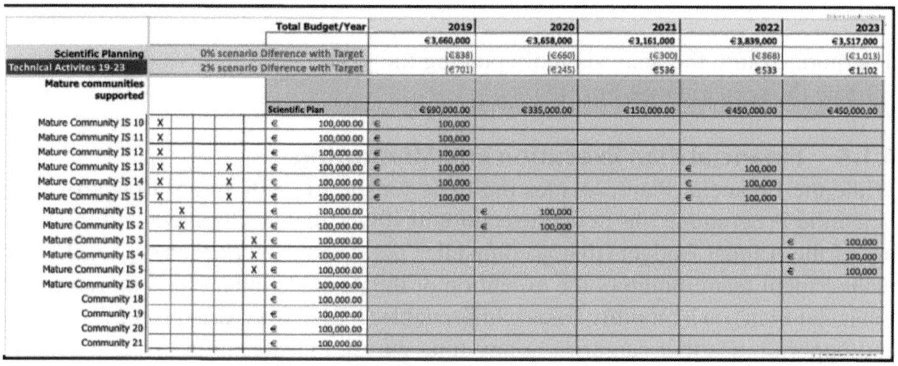

						Total Budget/Year	2019	2020	2021	2022	2023
							€3,660,000	€3,658,000	€3,161,000	€3,839,000	€3,517,000
Scientific Planning	0% scenario Diference with Target						(€838)	(€660)	(€300)	(€868)	(€1,013)
Technical Activites 19-23	2% scenario Diference with Target						(€701)	(€245)	€536	€533	€1,102
Mature communities supported						Scientific Plan	€690,000.00	€335,000.00	€150,000.00	€450,000.00	€450,000.00
Mature Community IS 10	X					€ 100,000.00	€ 100,000				
Mature Community IS 11	X					€ 100,000.00	€ 100,000				
Mature Community IS 12	X					€ 100,000.00	€ 100,000				
Mature Community IS 13	X			X		€ 100,000.00	€ 100,000			€ 100,000	
Mature Community IS 14	X			X		€ 100,000.00	€ 100,000			€ 100,000	
Mature Community IS 15	X			X		€ 100,000.00	€ 100,000			€ 100,000	
Mature Community IS 1		X				€ 100,000.00		€ 100,000			
Mature Community IS 2		X				€ 100,000.00		€ 100,000			
Mature Community IS 3					X	€ 100,000.00					€ 100,000
Mature Community IS 4					X	€ 100,000.00					€ 100,000
Mature Community IS 5					X	€ 100,000.00					€ 100,000
Mature Community IS 6						€ 100,000.00					
Community 18						€ 100,000.00					
Community 19						€ 100,000.00					
Community 20						€ 100,000.00					
Community 21						€ 100,000.00					

Fig. 14 Snapshot of the simplified modelling tool technical activities planning section (Example Data)—Author's elaboration

- Analysing how the ambition of the Scientific Programme can be better supported in the different financial scenarios, contributing to the identification of priorities and therefore the identification of the technical activities that will be supported by the Member States contributions and those that will require external funding for their implementation (Fig. 14).

4.1.4 Analysis of the Different Scenario (What If)

The financial model built for ELIXIR (simplified version) allows benchmarking of the different scenarios, because changes made in the model (income streams, constraints, contingencies, phasing of the technical activities, etc.) are automatically

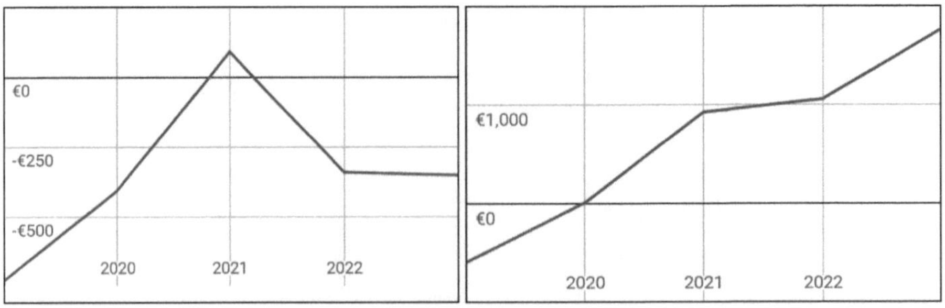

General Reserve										
Opening Balance	€2,696	€731	€752	€1,183	€866	€2,696	€869	€1,167	€2,018	€2,267
Committed Cos from 2018	€2,000					€2,000				
Movement in Year	-€1,965	€21	€ 431	-€317	-€49	-€1,827	€299	€ 851	€248	€666
Closing Balance	€731	€752	€1,183	€866	€817	€869	€1,167	€2,018	€2,267	€2,933
Yearly Target for Cash Reserve + contigency	€1,461	€1,159	€1,093	€1,208	€1,171	€1,461	€1,159	€1,093	€1,208	€1,171
Difference (Target 0)	-€730	-€407	€90	-€343	-€354	-€593	€8	€926	€1,059	€1,762

Fig. 15 Snapshot of the simplified modelling tool analysis of the different scenarios: 0% increase (left) and 2% increase (right). The 2% scenario outperforms the 0% scenario in keeping the cash reserve level above the threshold in the last 4 years. To balance the 2% scenario technical activities planned for Y1 and Y2 should be moved to Y3, Y4, or Y5 where there is still room to support additional technical activities (Example Data)—Author's elaboration

incorporated into the analysis tool updating the yearly cash reserve that is used to validate the scenario (see Fig. 15).

4.1.5 Financial Plan Execution and Monitoring

While the Financial Plan provides the basis for the ELIXIR Board to approve the Scientific Programme, the actual execution involves the development and monitoring of the Annual Budget (that accompanies the Annual Work Plan). The ELIXIR management team monitors the execution of the Annual Budget (and therefore the Financial Plan) on a monthly basis which enables ELIXIR to react promptly to risks and opportunities that can arise at any time during the execution of the Scientific Programme (Fig. 16).

5 Conclusions

This chapter has dealt with the issue of financial sustainability of Research Infrastructures and discussed the relevant strategies that RIs could rely on to overcome the main challenges that characterize their activity, specifically i) heavy dependence on public funds, usually governed by withdrawals options that do not assure long-term commitment by main funders; ii) limited diversification of sources of income; *iii*) little explored possibilities to generate new/own income; *iv*) limited role of strategic and financial planning; and *v*) increased expectations to define and demonstrate their value and impact to the wider community of stakeholders.

To address these challenges, RIs could apply the following strategies (see Fig. 3 in Sect. 2):

2019	Sep-19 Target 2019	Forecast By December-19 Total Cost (Forecast)	%	Difference (under/over)
Income				
Member State Contributions				
Ordinary Contributions	€ 7,089	€ 7,089	100.00%	€ 0
Foreign exchange gain on sterling contributions		-€ 67		€ 67
External Grants	€ 1,216	€ 1,125	92.52%	€ 91
Other income				
Unpaid contributions				
Total Income	**€ 8,305**	**€ 8,146**	**98.1%**	**€ 158**
<< Expenditure				
Hub Directorate + Hub Technical Costs				
Salaries	€ 1,464	€ 1,386	94.7%	€ 78
<< Running Costs	€ 600	€ 530	88.4%	€ 70
<< Commissioned Services	**€ 4,982**	**€ 3,470**	69.7%	**€ 1,512**
Total Hub Expenditure	**€ 7,201**	**€ 5,911**	82.1%	**€ 1,291**
Support and Admin Infrastructure Costs	€ 847	€ 920	108.6%	-€ 73
<< Grant expenditure	€ 1,216	€ 1,620	133.2%	-€ 404
Total	**€ 2,063**	**€ 2,540**	123.1%	-€ 477
Total Expenditure	**€ 9,265**	**€ 8,451**	91.2%	**€ 814**
Surplus/(Deficit)	-€ 960	-€ 304		-€ 655
General Reserve				
Opening Balance	**€ 5,220**	**€ 5,220**		
Movement in Year	-€ 960	-€ 304		-€ 655
Transfer to Depreciation Reserve				
Closing Balance	**€ 4,260**	**€ 4,916**	115.4%	-€ 655

Fig. 16 Snapshot of the annual budget monitoring tool (Exemplar Data)—Author's elaboration

(a) Foster relationships with founders/Member States on a continuous basis, for instance by providing expert advice related to the scientific field where the RI excels; it should also regularly address strategic planning where to underline its mission and revise its users' community in an ever-changing environment.

(b) Develop fundraising plans coherent to the services and products delivered and verify the possibility to use innovative fundraising techniques (like PPPs, crowdfunding, or bank loans).

(c) Develop a market and users analysis (know your customers) and a marketing plan to verify the possibility to generate new income from the markets.
(d) Use program evaluation to demonstrate value, establish high impact collaborations, and use partnership to build capacity.
(e) Invest more in the development and use of strategic and financial plan: developing costs and income forecasts for medium long-term periods, analysing income, constraints, and contingencies, and providing analysis of different scenarios.

In this context, the financial plan plays a strategic role: internally, it provides valid support for budgeting activity; externally, it represents a fundamental instrument to demonstrate to potential and existing funders the sustainability of the RI's business strategy.

Besides, an informative financial plan represents an effective tool to achieve the goal of *bankability*. It allows RI's managers to ponder on funding gap risks and potential unbalances on *capacity*. Through the financial plan, managers foster their understanding of financial stakeholders' expectations and goals; plus, through the development of scenario analysis, the financial plan allows ex ante management of risks coming from outside/market changing conditions. Finally, the financial plan is the "business card" through which RI managers can share a verifiable adequate *capacity* to meet obligations and communicate long-run vision and mission.

References

Ackoff, R. L. (1970). *A concept of corporate planning*. Wiley.

Agrawal, A. K., Catalini, C., & Goldfarb, A. (2014). Some simple economics of crowdfunding. *Innovation Policy and the Economy, 14*(1), 63–97.

Belleflamme, P., Lambert, T., & Schwienbacher, A. (2014). Crowdfunding: Tapping the right crowd. *Journal of Business Venturing, 29*(5), 585–609.

Bowman, W. (2011). Financial capacity and sustainability of ordinary nonprofits. *Nonprofit Management & Leadership, 22*(1), 37–51.

Caselli, S., Corbetta, G., & Vecchi, V. (2015). *Public private partnerships for infrastructure and business development principles, practices, and perspectives*. Palgrave Macmillan.

Dushnitsky, G., & Marom, D. (2013). Crowd monogamy. *Business Strategy Review, 24*(4), 24–26.

ESFRI. (2017). Long-Term Sustainability of Research Infrastructures, ESFRI Scripta Volume II, available at: https://www.esfri.eu/sites/default/files/u4/ESFRI_SCRIPTA_VOL2_web.pdf.

ESFRI. (2018). Roadmap and strategy report, Part 1, http://roadmap2018.esfri.eu/strategy-report/.

Florida, R., & Smith, D. F. (1993). Venture capital formation, investment, and regional industrialization. *Annals of the Associations of American Geographers, 83*(3), 434–451.

Gajdová, D., & Majdúchová, H. (2018). Financial sustainability criteria and their testing in the conditions of the Slovak non-profit sector. *Contemporary Economics, 12*(1), 33–56.

Hallberg, K. (1999). *Small and medium scale enterprises: A framework for intervention*. World Bank Publications, The World Bank and International Finance Corporation.

Helfert, E. A. (2000). *Techniques of financial analysis*. McGraw Hill.

Keating, E., Fischer, M., Gordon, T. P., & Greenlee, J. S. (2005). Assessing Financial Vulnerability in the Nonprofit Sector. *KSG Working Paper* No. RWP05-002, Hauser Center for Nonprofit Organizations Paper No. 27. January 2005.

León, P. (2001). *Four pillars of financial sustainability, resources for success series*. (Vol. 2), The nature conservancy, Arlington, Virginia, USA.

National Research Center. (2014). *5 Strategies for financial sustainability. Enhancing the value and sustainability of field stations and marine laboratories in the 21st century*. The National Academies Press.

Ng, A., & Rezaee, Z. (2018). The emergence of business sustainability: Educational, practical and research implications. In S. Boubaker, D. Cumming, & D. K. Nguyen (Eds.), *Research handbook of finance and sustainability*. Edward Elgar Publishing Ltd.

Oakey, M. P. (2003). Funding innovation and growth in UK new technology-based firms: Some observations on contributions from the public and private sectors. *Venture Capital: An International Journal of Entrepreneurial Finance, 5*(2), 161–179.

OECD. (2017). Strengthening the effectiveness and sustainability of international research infrastructures. Science, technology and industry policy papers n. 48/2017.

OECD. (2019). Reference framework for assessing the scientific and socio-economic impact of research infrastructures. Science, technology and industry policy papers n. 65/2019, available at: https://www.oecd.org/en/publications/reference-framework-for-assessing-the-scientific-and-socio-economic-impact-of-research-infrastructures_3ffee43b-en.html

RAMIRI Handbook. (2013). available on line https://www.ceric-eric.eu/project/ramiri-handbook/.

Sauermann, H., Franzoni, C., & Shafi, K. (2019). Crowdfunding scientific research: Descriptive insights and correlates of funding success. *PLoS One, 14*(1), e0208384. https://doi.org/10.1371/journal.pone.0208384

Sontag-Padilla, L. M., Staplefoote, L., & Morganti, K. G. (2012). Financial sustainability for non-profit organizations. Review of Literature, Rand Health and Rand Education.

StESFRI (2019). *Guidelines on Cost Estimation of Research Infrastructures*. StESFRI Study, https://www.esfri.eu/sites/default/files/StR-ESFRI2_STUDY_RIs_COST_ESTIMATION.pdf.

VanOmmen, G. J. B., Törnwall, O., Bréchot, C., Dagher, G., Galli, J., Hveem, K., Landegren, Luchinat, Metspalu, Nilsson, Solesvik, Perola, Litton, & Zatloukal. (2015). BBMRI-ERIC as a resource for pharmaceutical and life science industries: The development of biobank-based expert Centres. *European Journal of Human Genetics, 23*(7), 893–900.

Walsh, C. (2003). *Key management ratios*. Financial Times Prentice Hall.

Wettenhall, R. (2003). The rhetoric and reality of public-private partnerships. *Public Organization Review, 3*(1), 77–107.

Leadership and Team Management in Research Infrastructures

Francesco Paoletti, Niklas Blomberg, and Pascale Goy

Abstract

Research Infrastructures (RIs) constitute a diverse set of organisations, yet they exhibit common characteristics: they operate as complex, stakeholder-intensive environments within a rapidly evolving scientific landscape and are staffed by highly qualified personnel who both support and conduct research. These features underscore the critical role of effective leadership. However, traditional managerial models, grounded in stable structures and detailed planning, are often insufficient in scientific contexts. This chapter examines how leadership is conceived and practised in two diverse European RIs—CERN, a large single-site facility, and ELIXIR, a distributed infrastructure—to illustrate how leadership development serves as a strategic lever for organisational effectiveness. Through examining their respective approaches, the chapter identifies shared challenges as well as distinct responses, providing broader insights into leadership within RIs undergoing continual scientific and organisational change.

F. Paoletti (✉)
Department of Business and Law, University of Milano-Bicocca, Milan, Italy
e-mail: francesco.paoletti@unimib.it

N. Blomberg
ELIXIR Europe, UK (2013-2023) – Innovative Health Initiative JU, Brussels, Belgium
e-mail: Niklas.Blomberg@ihi.europa.eu

P. Goy
Learning and Development Group Human Resources, CERN, Geneva, Switzerland

E. Guarini et al. (eds.), *Research Infrastructure Management*, Management for Professionals, https://doi.org/10.1007/978-3-032-20373-1_6

1 Introduction

From an organisational perspectiveResearch Infrastructures (RIs) are highly diverse, ranging from large, international single-site facilities such as particle accelerators and telescopes to distributed networks of instruments, samples resources, and data resources. Moreover, they can vary a lot in terms of size, longevity, financial endowments, yearly budgets, human resources profiles, degree of structuring and formalisation, and so forth.

However, there are also commonalities. First, all RIs are complex organisations that have to balance the needs of many different stakeholders within the unifying goal of enabling their user community to perform excellent research by providing access to scientific resources that no single laboratory—or single country—can support. Second, they have to deal with the ever changing and unpredictable environment of science. Finally, all RIs are staffed by people with qualified scientific backgrounds who ultimately work to support other scientists, and oftentimes are themselves engaged in research projects.

It is well proven that leadership matters for every organisation (e.g. Barrick et al., 1991; Bass et al., 2003; Bertrand & Schoar, 2003; Koene et al., 2002): capable leaders are needed when it comes to challenging the status quo, creating visions of the future, and inspiring organisational members to work hard and effectively to make these visions a reality. Then, we should expect leadership to be even more important for RIs, as these organisations are oriented towards the future and innovation and, in the meantime, they must quickly adapt in response to the environmental challenges posed by their reference sciences. In this context, it is hard to manage by formulating detailed plans and designing stable, formalised, and efficient structures for their execution. Organisations are rather to be thought as adhocracies: dynamic and fluid team-based structures where people collaborate by joining or leaving the single teams according to their skills and expertise as required by the task to be performed (Mintzberg & McHugh, 1985).

In this chapter, we aim to illustrate leadership in RIs by drawing on our experiences from developments in two European cases: CERN, a large single-site facility that has been in operation for decades, and ELIXIR, a more recently established distributed infrastructure. By comparing these very different organisations, we will make some general observations on RI leadership before illustrating how its development can be used to drive organisational strategies.

In the case of CERN, the development of leadership competencies is entrusted to formal processes: a competency model has been designed to provide a coherent criterion throughout every HR practice to drive the organisational performance as well as the staff's continuous development. Human resources management tools and processes are grounded in this framework and aimed at identifying and growing the next generation of leaders, and at preparing the organisation for planned future transitions in instrumentation and scientific direction.

In the case of ELIXIR, a focus on community-building drives the alignment of technology platforms and the establishment of a European community of experts across the national nodes spread in every Member State.

2 Leadership and Team Management

Many definitions of leadership have been proposed in management theory (for a review: Northouse, 2007; Bass & Bass, 2008), but in the end, all refer to an individual's ability to exert influence over a group's members by motivating and directing their efforts towards the attainment of a vision or a common set of goals (Yukl, 1989). As a consequence, we might posit that effective leadership can be inferred only from followers' acquiescence behaviour, and that this will come when the leader provides the team with what the members need, and when it is needed for successful collective action (Hackman & Wageman, 2005).

Researchers first tried to identify where leadership comes from by focusing on individual traits, i.e. personal qualities and characteristics that might predict effective leadership. The most substantial results in this stream were achieved in studies aimed at understanding whether and how personality measured through the dimensions of the well-established Five Factor Model (Costa & McCrae, 1985)—emotional stability, extraversion, agreeableness, conscientiousness, and openness to experience—can be related to leadership. Evidence was found that extraversion is the best predictor, even though it might be more related to the emergence of leaders rather than to their effectiveness (Judge et al., 2002): extroverted people are indeed sociable and dominant, dispositions that make them more likely to be identified as prospective leaders, yet their leadership performance might be poor should they override their teams.

Other studies proved that leadership effectiveness is more likely when extraversion is combined with other traits, namely conscientiousness and openness to experience. Conscientiousness is related to an individual's ability to keep commitments and, when combined with extraversion, it is positively related to leaders' self-efficacy: people are more likely to follow someone who is seen as confident in moving the team in the right direction (Colbert et al., 2014). Openness to experience would predict cognitive flexibility and the ability to actively listen to the team members and leverage their competencies to find innovative solutions or strategies.

However, the predictive power of traits might vary depending on a specific style of leadership: for example, a study of leaders from over 200 organisations revealed that extraversion and agreeableness positively predicted transformational leadership, whereas openness only initially correlated – as its effects disappeared after controlling for the influence of the first two traits – and conscientiousness came out irrelevant (Judge & Bono, 2000). Moreover, the effects are moderated by the situation and the job context that might activate or not a specific trait (Judge & Zapata, 2015), for example requiring a different style of leadership.

In summary, trait theories certainly help in predicting leadership—particularly its emergence—and eventually in assessing the best candidate for a leading position, but they do not ensure that a subject exhibiting all the proper personality attributes will actually be followed by a given team in a particular situation. On the other hand, a person who does not reveal all those traits could still prove an effective leader by becoming more aware of her/his strength and weaknesses, and learning how to perform leading behaviours that fit the team composition and the situation.

Behavioural theories address these issues and suggest that leaders can be trained by focusing on the actual behaviours that will make them effective in a given situation. Many different models have been proposed (e.g. Fiedler, 1967; House, 1996; Bass & Bass, 2008; Graen & Uhl-Bien, 1995), and a full discussion of all of them is not in the purpose and the span of this chapter. Here we might simply try to synthetise the main results from this body of research by highlighting three major processes that followers expect from their leaders, and must be addressed to the whole team rather than to a single member: first, followers need to see that their leaders are able to envision a possible and positive future for their organisation and themselves; second, they must feel guided towards the execution of that vision by a clarification of their roles, goals, and task requirements; finally, they can better contribute if they are empowered being trusted and supported by their leaders.

Envisioning involves visualising and communicating a long-term strategy to achieve a series of captivating, credible, and challenging set of goals by linking the present to a better future for the organisation. The vision has to fit with the times and the circumstances—the ongoing environmental scenarios—and has to reflect the uniqueness of the organisation by leveraging internal resources to face external threats and seize incoming opportunities. A vision statement, declaring an organisation's mission and a set of values may be used to inspire the followers on an overarching purpose and mobilise their energy. It is not just a matter of ability and passionate communication, however. This will certainly not hurt, but the team members are more interested in assessing the vision's credibility, so they will carefully watch the leaders' actions more than their words. For that reason, a leader may want to engage in emotion-inducing behaviour to demonstrate courage and conviction about the vision, build the followers' self-esteem and confidence, and set a tone of cooperation and mutual support. These processes ultimately build a leader's charisma in the eyes of the team (Conger & Kanungo, 1998).

To engage the team members in facing the challenges related to the vision's attainment, a leader has to define and structure roles and expectations, assign tasks, set goals or other performance standards, and emphasise deadlines. By these actions, the team members feel guided in the vision's execution, and this drives and sustains their motivation enhancing their willingness to cooperate and coordinate their efforts towards the achievement of the organisation's goals. A reward strategy can boost the effects of these processes, but it will not work unless they are already put in place.

Finally, empowering means giving employees the authority, skills, and self-control to perform their tasks by making them responsible for the expected results. (Kirkman & Rosen, 1999). Oftentimes, this process is analysed more in the structural issues, i.e. considering the degree of delegation to employees of decisions formerly reserved to managers or staff specialist: these may include the freedom to set schedules, determine work methods, adapt the quality of the work, assign priorities, seek solutions to problems rather than calling immediately for the manager, and so on. However, the effects on leadership are strongly affected by the psychological dimensions of empowerment: individuals and team members are motivated to perform and willing to follow a leader when they not only have some formal autonomy but also perceive themselves as competent and able to accomplish the task (potency), to achieve important and valuable outcomes (meaningfulness), and to actually positively influence their organisation performance (impact). For that to happen, they need to feel that they are trusted and not constantly micromanaged by their leaders, that their ideas are respected and taken into serious consideration, and that their growth in competencies is supported by frank, clear, and reliable feedback.

To summarise, behavioural theories posit that to be effective a leader must be able to perform envisioning, engaging, and empowering behaviours that would motivate the team members to follow. These behaviours are not innate, nor are related to some traits of personality; on the opposite, they can be learnt from training and experience (e.g. the chance of working in close contact with a very effective leader), even though with the proper personality traits this learning might occur more easily. In any case, leaders have to find their unique style that fits with their personality to perform these behaviours and be credible in the eyes of their followers. In other words, they need to work on the best possible version of themselves.

3 Organisational Features of Research Infrastructures

As we have already stated, RIs can be very diverse, yet they share three features that certainly determine the importance of leadership and team management processes.

First, all RIs are complex organisations that have to balance the needs of many different stakeholders within a common goal. In this facet, most RIs have to be seen as "meta-organisations" since they are formed of other organisations rather than individuals in an employment relationship and subject to formal authority (Ahrne & Brunsson, 2008; Gulati et al., 2012). They are basically open communities of legally autonomous and peer actors who associate in collaboration to achieve a system-level set of goals: each agent has its own motivations, incentives, and cognitions, and some individuals might even belong to multiple structures, e.g. being assigned temporarily and part-time as an in-kind contribution to the central hub organisation, and still keeping a position at a national node.

The defining feature of meta-organisations is the weakness of formal authority between the constituent entities: authority is the legitimate power to dictate actions, but in these contexts it can exist only within the boundaries of a member organisation, and does not extend to the ties that connect them. As a consequence, the management principles of control, hierarchy, role formalisation, and rewards have less traction and leadership processes—a key issue for every organisation—become crucial since central actors need to fill the authority gap with informal influence by leveraging on their expertise, reputation, status, gatekeeping, and/or privileges of regulation and control over organisational processes, such as planning and budgeting.

A second point is the fact that RIs have to deal with the highly volatile and unpredictable environment of science. As a consequence, they need to adopt an adaptive and flexible organisational form which looks more like a loosely coupled system network of interactions (Orton & Weick, 1990) than a bureaucratic structure. In this form that had been labelled "adhocracy" (Mintzberg, 1979) people are brought together in project teams, usually short-lived, and coordination occurs mainly informally by means of a constant exchange of information between the team members. Adhocracies have few formal rules and regulations or standardised routines, and a very flat structure with a high degree of horizontal differentiation since they are staffed mainly by professionals, each with their own expertise and specialisation. Moreover, they oftentimes employ a significant proportion of staff who work on a temporary basis, or are in a joint assignment from other organisations to which they open their boundaries by signing an agreement of cooperation to speed up the innovation process (Chesbrough, 2003). The structure then works as a double network connecting internal and external teams (Perrone, 1997), and the only way to drive people who are so diverse towards a common goal is to go beyond management and exert leadership by building a shared identity that can inspire every team member.

Finally, all RIs are staffed with qualified scientists and professionals who ultimately work to support other researchers, and oftentimes carry on their own research agenda. These people usually have a great passion and motivation for their work which can be leveraged on, yet they might be self-centred, narcissistic, and hard to integrate in a common effort as it is needed to avoid risks of low productivity and failures (Hackett & Parker, 2012). Transformational leadership competencies based on the processes of idealised influence, inspirational motivation, individualised consideration, and intellectual stimulation can better achieve a balance between creativity and coordination in a research context (Eggleton, 2017).

4 Leadership in a Centralised Network: The Case of CERN

CERN— the European Organization for Nuclear Research is the world's leading laboratory for particle physics. Its origin can be traced in 1946 after the Second World War: a group of visionary scientists and diplomats imagined using science to unite Europe and created the European particle, physics laboratory to share the increasing cost of nuclear physics facilities, and stop the brain drain to the United States. The European Council for Nuclear Research (CERN) was then established as an interim organisation by 12 founding States in 1952, and disbanded on 29 September 1954 upon ratification of the convention that brought into existence the European Organization for Nuclear Research - which maintained the original acronym CERN.

CERN's convention states: "The Organisation shall have no concern with work for military requirements and the results of its experimental and theoretical work shall be published or otherwise made generally available." CERN's mission then is "to provide a unique range of particle accelerator facilities that enable research at the forefront of human knowledge, perform world-class research in fundamental physics and unite people from all over the world to push the frontiers of science and technology, for the benefit of all".

This mission has been accomplished with a long history of great discoveries that actually lead to radical advancements and even paradigm shifts in the field of physics. Three CERN scientists have won the Nobel: Charpak, Rubbia and van der Meer.

Englert and Higgs won it after the existence of the Higgs boson had been demonstrated. Knowledge dissemination was impressive also in other fields. The most notable example here is probably the invention of the HTML language, the HTTP protocol, and the WWW server, which were used to collect and share all the information that was generated in internal project. These inventions were later made publicly available making possible the development of Internet, thus giving life to the principle of disseminating the knowledge in "open access" that is embedded in CERN's culture since its foundation.

In its site situated both in Switzerland and France CERN has installed a Large Hadron Collider (LHC), the world's most powerful particle accelerator: an underground tunnel at a depth of 100 m covers a 27-kilometre ring of superconducting magnets making it the biggest cryogenic system in the world. About 2,750 staff, 800 fellows, and 800 students, and approximately 13,500 visiting scientist (called users) work in this infrastructure every year. Users are people that belong to different organisations but stably work on projects in cooperation with CERN staff. In 2026 CERN has 25 Member States. Some other non-European states (e.g. Pakistan, Russia, China…) are associates, observers or are in the accessing process, making CERN a truly global organisation with a budget of about one billion CHF (about 940 million EUR).

Even though CERN is a single-sited infrastructure, this features make it not so dissimilar in governance from other distributed RIs: being a Member State-funded organisation, CERN must keep all the members satisfied and engaged by proving its benefit and value to them. Furthermore, attracting new members to enlarge the scope of its activities and get the resources needed to perform the best scientific research is part of its mandate. So, CERN's governance is managed through a quite complex structure. The Council is the highest authority of the Organisation, and has responsibility for all key decisions in scientific, technical, and administrative matters (including the budget approval). The Director General (DG), who is the Chief Executive Officer, manages the CERN Laboratory and is supported by a Directorate of four Directors, as well as by the Enlarged Directorate and a departmental structure (however, this may change from DG to DG). Also, to be counted as part of CERN's governance is the Tripartite Employment Conditions Forum (TREF) which is a large assembly where Staff Association, Management, and the Member States are all represented.

In this governance model, strategy definition is driven by the "apical" Management vision, yet the Staff Association which is a statutory organ for staff representation is involved and is critical to get through its development and implementation. Member States are obviously very important too, therefore, the agreement and support of every component of the TREF have to be reached before a decision gets to the Council, which aims for a consensus as close as possible to unanimity. As we anticipated in paragraph 3, this process of consensus-building is typical of meta-organisations and requires a great leadership effort from the Director General, its Directorate, and all the management When CERN people address the Member States representatives, they need to understand their expectations and their challenges to convince them to support the long-term vision running to 2035, e.g. the

LHC infrastructure evolution towards the building of a much more powerful collider (the Future Circular Collider – FCC) and other future projects.

Once the consensus on a given strategy is reached, its effective execution implies the goals to be deployed across the whole Organisation, making every staff member involved in their achievement. In single-sited RIs, this process might apparently come easier than in distributed, still it requires great coordination work. Until 2026, CERN's structure was divided into four large Sectors and two Units related to the DG office (Fig. 1). In each Sector, there were several Departments, some of them counting up to 400 people.

Authority lines are well defined, and formal management and planning tools can certainly be used to achieve effective coordination. However, CERN is a hierarchical organisation for staff and fellows only. The case is different for external collaborators and users who belong to other organisations and have only a part-time project commitment inside. Those people participate in CERN activities in a ratio of about 4:1 with the inside members, and all of them work in project teams which they

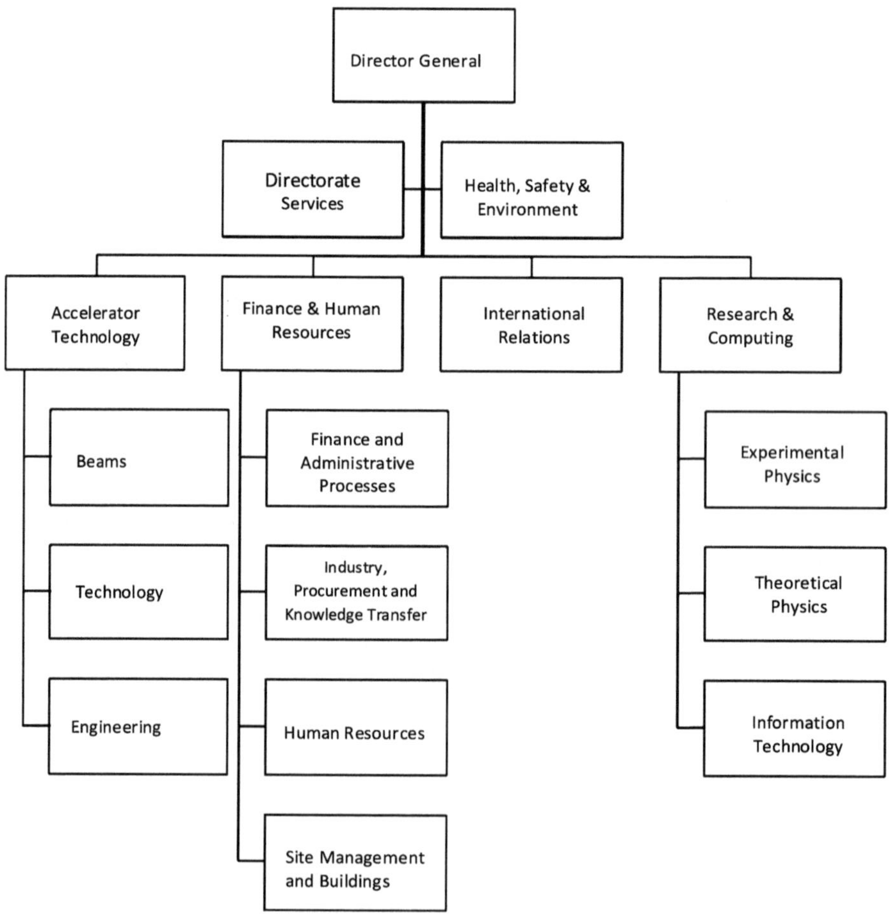

Fig. 1 CERN Organisation—Authors' elaboration

dynamically join or leave according to their research goals as well as the skills and expertise required to perform the tasks.

CERN then can be considered as a distributed adhocracy organised more as double-network of internal and external interactions than as a bureaucratic structure managed through formalised processes. About 90 Group Leaders (GL) constitute the senior management. Their responsibility is to lead and coordinate more than 270 Section Leaders (SL) and more than 700 supervisors who perform the middle management functions, and who actually run the organisational units and the project teams. Overall, leaders and supervisors account for about 41% of CERN staff (Table 1).

A big challenge for them is to make these different populations that are not under the same hierarchy to work together towards the same goals. For this to happen, management competencies (such as planning, directing, monitoring, controlling, and so forth) are not sufficient. To move forward and achieve results, leadership and team management competencies must be developed broadly in the entire staff population, which is composed of physicists, engineers, technicians and office workers. Many of them have no prior experience in people and team management, as they were initially recruited for a specific scientific or technical expertise. When the day comes to take on responsibilities as supervisors, team leaders or even senior leaders the pool for selection is sometimes limited. This is why developing future leaders needs to be strategically prepared and channelled through leadership training.

In a large and structured organisation such as CERN the development of a leadership capability has to be carefully planned. Between 2012 and 2018, several surveys and focus groups were run to collect data and analyse why leadership competence was needed, taking into account specific features required at CERN. The data was complemented with information drawn in the grapevine and through informal discussions with the apical leaders. A people vision based on several dimensions was then elaborated to drive all the Human Resources Management practices.

The first dimension is about the need to drive the alignment of the Organisation with the Member States' objectives by spreading political sensitivity in every CERN leader. When addressing Member States representatives, it is of utmost importance to understand their interests, contraints and challenges in order to find appropriate arguments, be convincing and persuasive, thus contributing to CERN's mission. Such competence is essential to sustain the goal of affiliating new

Table 1 CERN population breakdown (August 2019)

Staff population	Headcount	%
DG + directors	5	
Department Heads and Units (DH)	13	
Group leaders (GL)	93	3,5%
Section leaders (SL)	273	10,3%
Supervisors	733	27,6%
Total	1.099	41,4%

countries Member States and persuading all the members to support and fund the future strategic projects for the post-LHC era.

The second dimension is to recognize that CERN is an organisation primarily composed of extraordinary scientific experts who will most probably have to learn management on the job. To this end, they will need training to understand and develop the required and agile leadership culture needed to drive the Organisation in an external fast-changing global environment.

This leads to the third dimension: the need to create appropriate and relevant opportunities for future leaders to enhance their skillset beyond technical and scientific expertise.

Finally, the identification of high potential individuals who will develop their path towards senior management/leadership positions is the ultimate goal. As explained earlier, this represents a challenge as people are primarily hired at CERN for their strong scientific or technical background.

To support good leadership practice, CERN developed a set of organisational guidelines. The main one is the Code of Conduct, which is the blueprint for CERN culture. It is composed of five organisational values: integrity, commitment, professionalism, creativity, and diversity. They pave the way towards excellence and are a bold statement of the organisational identity that each employee is expected to share.

Indeed the Code of Conduct—that can be publicly accessed on CERN's website—describes for the core values the proper standards of behaviour that every person (staff member, student, user, or collaborator) must follow and is entitled to expect from every other colleague in the workplace.

The CERN's Competency Model (CCM) is another useful tool, rooted in the CERN values, which provides a pragmatic approach for employees. Two main types of competencies characterize the way of making work at CERN: technical and behavioural. Technical competencies are identified from the main domains of expertise that CERN needs (physics, electrical, mechanical engineering and information technology). Behavioural competencies describe how work is carried out. Thus, the CCM is a reference document aimed at achieving consistency and coherence throughout all organisational HR-related processes. Its elaboration lasted 2 years, and was based on surveys and focus groups to classify leadership functions as viewed by representative samples of CERN's staff. The enlisted behaviours are neither a duplication or an extension of existing legal rights or obligations, nor an exhaustive list of "dos and don'ts", but rather a tool intended to facilitate the understanding and practice of the core values.

In more details, the technical competencies are organised in fourteen domains of expertise, each of them further divided into sub-domains with a corresponding list of attached competencies that is constantly updated upon the needs of the Departments. As for the fifteen behavioural competencies, they are divided into ten core competencies that are needed for every organisational role, and five leadership competencies, which are required only for leading positions. All these competencies are embedded in the CERN learning offer and are used to organise the different training portfolios.

A summary of this framework is provided in Table 2.

Table 2 CERN competency model (CCM)—summary

Values	Core competencies	Leadership competencies
Integrity	• Demonstrating accountability • Managing self	Leading with strength and credibility
Commitment	• Working in the interest of the organisation • Demonstrating flexibility	Creating vision and strategic partnership
Professionalism	• Achieving results • Communicating effectively	Optimising resources
Creativity	• Solving problems • Learning and sharing knowledge	Setting direction
Diversity	• Building relationships • Working in teams	Bringing out the best in people

Table 3 CERN leadership program pipeline

All supervisors
1. "Introduction to CERN Internal Processes" (E-learning modules) 2. "Essential of People Management" (workshop, 5 days) • *180 degree feedback and coaching* 3. "Getting the Most Out of the Annual Review" (1 day) 4. "Communicating with Impact" (2 days)
Mid management and above
1. "Corporate Development Package for Group Leaders & Deputy Group Leaders" • *360 degree feedback (using CCM).* Module 1: "Creating an Engaging Leadership" (2 days) • *Coaching session* Module 2: "Interpersonal Leadership" (2 days) • *Coaching session* Module 3: "Delivering with Others" (2 days)

The CCM has an impact not only on the performance appraisal (managers/leaders are encouraged to use the CCM when providing regular feedback and also in the year-end annual interview) but also on many other HR activities, such as recruitment processes, indefinite contract awards, promotions, internal mobility, succession planning, manpower planning not to forget learning and development. Indeed, this model helps employees to understand what is expected from them as well as how they can enhance their motivation at any level and role.

CERN is committed to the continuous development of all its employees through a systematic and sustained learning culture. As such, the learning and development policy is the official document providing the underlying principles for development. Investments in education at CERN are very substantial: every year, each staff member can spend up to ten days in training (including in-class training, on-line training, on-the-job training and conferences). People who are identified as potential leaders are offered to participate to a "Leadership Program Pipeline" (LPP), a pathway of courses moving from fundamentals to advanced leadership competencies. This mandatory suite, described in Table 3, is designed according to the CCM, and it is conceived as a journey towards leadership excellence that lasts several years exposing the candidate to a mix of in-class and beyond class activities: these include multisource feedbacks and coaching, and provide opportunities for individual consideration while giving continuity to future leaders' growth.

The LPP starts with the "Introduction to CERN Internal Processes" e-learning preparatory module offered when a person is going to achieve a supervisor position. The next and more substantial step is the "Essential of People Management" workshop, which includes several face-to face modules, as well as 180 degrees feedback and leadership coaching support over several months. Two more short courses on performance management annual interviews and impact communication competencies complete this training. Candidates for mid-management positions will then attend a second program designed around Group Leaders' key competencies, and including several modules, different resources, a 360 degrees feedback based on the CCM, as well as executive coaching.

Of course, other leadership courses are proposed in the global learning offer and can be attended on a voluntary basis to develop further specific performance competencies related to personal or team development and impact (e.g. "Developing a High Performing Team"; "Driving for Impact and Influence"; "Challenging Discussions"; "Leading for Success") Other learning solutions focusing on more advanced competencies (e.g. "Emotional intelligence", "Resilience", "Strategic and emotional agility"...) are proposed and can be customised for senior leaders. Experience at CERN proves that at a certain hierarchical level, leadership or executive coaching is actually the most appropriate and effective form for development.

Based on participants' feedback, all the training programmes are regularly evaluated and fine-tuned to meet the organisation needs. This is a key aspect for a continuous and qualitative learning offer. Every year, about 300 managers/leaders (about 30 courses) take part in the LPP. The figures are very stable from one year to the next and prove the commitment of the HR Direction.

5 The Building of a Community in a Dispersed RI Network: ELIXIR

ELIXIR is a distributed Research Infrastructure: this model is widely diffused in the European landscape (ESFRI, 2018) in response to the political challenge of relocating a large amount of national research funding internationally, and to the scientific need of bringing together facilities that cover many different ecosystems (e.g. EMBRC's access to coastal stations) or distributed arrays of instruments (e.g. ICOS/ENVRI).

In distributed models, most of the people working within the RI are not employed directly by the central hub, but rather via national centres. Thus, a distributed RI represents a very unusual, non-hierarchical, organisation, and the model leads to a diversity in conditions for employees and organisational cultures. A key leadership challenge is to align the work of many people, located in different organisations across Europe, who contribute with only a fraction of their worktime. For this reason, many corporate management tools (e.g. mandatory policies, standards, and performance management mechanisms for all the employees) are not directly applicable. While the organisational form is unusual—and no leadership tools were specifically proposed for it in the management literature—the development of leadership competencies can be based on the adaptation of some more general models as well as draw on the experience of volunteer-based organisations and large open-source software projects, in particular on the frame of community-building processes (Bacon, 2012).

ELIXIR's organisation is similar to most European distributed research infrastructures, with a central hub and national nodes—sometimes formed by bringing together all the relevant resources into a single national (networked) facility. Many of the points raised in this paragraph should then be applicable to both European and nationally distributed scientific organisations.

ELIXIR's mission is to coordinate life science-related data resources, including databases, software tools, training material, cloud storage, and supercomputers making it easier for scientists to store, find, and share data; exchange expertise; and agree upon best practices. The infrastructure was launched in 2013, after several years of preparation, and brings together 25 countries and one international organisation, EMBL (The European Molecularly Biology Laboratory), conveying over 220 research organisations. The central hub is located in the UK and is funded via Member State contributions; it coordinates the national nodes that are funded from national programs, produce and manage the data, and aggregate the local users requiring services from the network.

In ELIXIR, the scientific and technical activities are run by five "Platforms" which bring together experts from every node to define the strategy and provide services in a particular area; for example, the "Data Platform" drives the sharing of life science data by identifying key data resources across Europe and providing users with access to robust, long-term sustainable, coordinated, and scalable data ecosystem. These services are produced and funded via national schemes with ELIXIR providing technical coordination, integration, and standards development to help connect, scale, and sustain bioinformatics resources across its Member States.

Moreover, there are currently 11 "Communities" that aggregate experts to develop standards, services, and training within specific domains, for example, "Marine metagenomics", "Metabolomics", "Proteomics", and so forth. Again, the services are offered by the national nodes, and the infrastructure technically only coordinates their development and sharing.

Ultimately, ELIXIR rests on bringing together a strong and well-organised scientific base from each of the Member States. As a consequence, leadership needs to be exerted in many directions, and all of them are almost equally important. For example, the Director needs to:

- Deal with every national node to build a strong and organised scientific base in each country, and support all of them in developing their own "business case" to get consensus from the national funders.
- Interface with and achieve the consensus of the Board representing the national funders, which approves the annual plan and provides the required financial resources.
- Work on common projects and standards within the community of the service providers, since services are not delivered by the centre but rather produced by the nodes.
- Relate with the end-users community that aggregates more organisations with sometimes different needs in every country.
- Lead the team of people at the hub that constitutes his direct or indirect reports and can be of great support in the management of all these relationships.

Ultimately, all these activities can be seen as a community-building effort that requires the leader's ability to adopt different behavioural styles to effectively gain consensus from all these diverse subjects and in different situations.

As in every distributed RI, this effort in community-building is first aimed at obtaining the commitment of national scientists, which is essential to get resources and make available the quality services that might support their researches: the people who can "open the door" to the national funders in every country are scientists working there, but their commitment ultimately will come only if they find it useful, worthwhile, interesting, and helpful for their research to be part of the infrastructure.

Then, perhaps the harder thing is to work with every national community to support the development of its "business case" with the national funders and demonstrate the added value to their investments from participating in the infrastructure. Unfortunately, each node will need to build a distinct case in response to the country-specific funding structure. It is not just about hard data, such as financial metrics: sometimes qualitative issues might be even more important, but this requires a full understanding of the national funders' perspectives in valuing their being part of such an international network.

Since it is very hard at the centre to actually understand what is going on in every nation, a collaborative effort based on an open and transparent, constant dialogue is needed; it is very important to listen to the nodes, collect factual information, and get a picture of their reality before advancing any suggestions.

Formal agreement on budget, funding allocation and scientific priorities must be reached by the participant Member States. This happens at the Board level. To reach consensus, ELIXIR has adopted a quite formalised and structured governance process: decisions are analysed in written documents which are elaborated through interactions; consensus is built through discussions prior to the final release of the Board documents for formal approval. The purpose is to ensure that the programs complement the national roadmaps, which usually move from different priorities in investments and constraints.

This is a demanding process, which generates a workload of about 50 Board Papers made every year; nonetheless, it is probably the most effective way of managing agreements, build confidence in the decisions, and maintain trust among all the actors. That trust is a capital that can be drawn on to achieve consensus in difficult situations: for example, a country might step back about a non-immediate and compelling necessity to favour a solution that satisfies other countries' needs provided it trusts that they will benefit from the overall program.

Operational coordination among the nodes is achieved through "lateral management" processes aimed at building consensus and commitment in such a community of peers. There is a committee, the ELIXIR's Head-of-Nodes group, composed of the Directors of all the national infrastructures who meet 4 or 5 times a year. This committee is positioned as a sort of ELIXIR's "faculty": it is the senior body that agrees on strategy, priorities, and objectives by setting out the Annual work plan and the distribution of the resources between the nodes. More importantly, they agree on scientific approaches and recommendations that are backed up by all the national centres. The group produces papers on "standards" that are finally endorsed to be implemented across all the countries. For example, the training community has brought forward recommendations on how to benchmark courses and define quality indicators and metrics for feedback that progressively were applied in the same way in all the nodes, making it easier for the comparison of results.

In a distributed RI, the adherence to standards cannot be hierarchically enforced with binding and prescriptive guidelines since the partner's organisations are legally independent units, and each has a local institutional policy that it is bound by. Achieving coordination then is more a matter of sharing a vision and common values: when the members are aligned on themes that they feel crucial they became self-determined to execute strategies that were agreed on to pursue the organisation's mission. This community spirit is what ultimately keeps a distributed infrastructure such as ELIXIR delivering by connecting its best assets: about 350 people belonging to many different organisations who work together on common projects to deliver the expected outcome.

However, a collaborative community of equals move in the same direction by chance. It is the result of the effort of many people: mainly, the Heads of Nodes, as well as the Platforms and Community Leaders and the Training and Technical coordinators; these people are spending many hours after their working time to build and develop the infrastructure by teaming with colleagues and peers from other countries to collectively set the direction. It is an exercise in distributed leadership which rests on the scientific program defined by the Head-of-Nodes Group: a document that sets out ELIXIR's scientific and technical ambition in a 5 years horizon, defines the structure with the different groups, gives top-level objectives and goals for each group, and then is used to drill down those goals into individual tasks and projects.

Many activities are aimed at community-building. For example, budgets are invested in providing space to the community by bringing people together in workshops, key meetings, hackathons, and so forth, sometimes even using some central funds to help key people coming to important meetings when their nodes don't have travel budgets. In this way, they have the possibility of knowing each other, sharing knowledge and experience, developing mutual trust, and feeling the spirit of the community.

For people working in technical infrastructures, the career paths in academia are often challenging. The groups in ELIXIR offer a development path by providing the opportunity to engage in interesting projects at a scale they couldn't reach in their structures as well as the occasion to work into peer groups with other experts that might not even exist in their countries, especially for those who come from small countries. Resources are also invested in staff exchange and capacity-building programs to move people between the nodes building up and spreading key capabilities.

Finally, the last exercise in leadership is about the people working at the hub. They are essentially a group of experts organised into two tiers: a senior team supporting the Director and a junior team of professionals who joined more recently and work primarily with them. To get the most from these people a leader has to leverage their competence by defining a clear delegation of responsibility and leaving them the freedom to operate to reach their goals.

As we stated in paragraph 3, three processes are required to achieve consensus from the followers: envisioning, engaging, and empowering.

The first process in ELIXIR is naturally supported by the fact that the hub experts are themselves part of the community and contribute to its development by participating to the groups. They are also engaged in managing daily the relationship with many members. So, they strive to be responsive towards the national nodes: direct contacts avoid barriers with the hub, and quick responses keep an ongoing dialogue that helps understanding the issues they are facing. This is the major benefit of being approachable: if something comes up in a country, people will let the hub know and this allows them to respond to that. Responsiveness ultimately fosters the sense of belongingness, and it is then one of the organisational core values.

Engaging in ELIXIR is entrusted on a Performance Management System, which is part of the overall planning process (Fig. 2).

The vision and the mission drive the strategy and the setting of long-term goals. Then, every year, annual objectives are set; they are deployed in an annual plan analysing who is working on what, what are the resources and the skills needed in the team, and what are the expected outcomes following a methodology that has been defined at Intel (Grove, 2015) to ensure clarity objectives are expressed in very short sentences, and defined in terms of key results that must be achieved. It is a conventional approach and the ELIXIR case demonstrates it can work in a distributed RI.

As for the empowering, to be effective people must have all the information and competence required by the tasks they have to accomplish. Training here is the key, and it is based on the well-known 10-20-70 model: an effective combination of 10% learning events (conventional "classroom" activities such as workshops, seminars, and e-learning), 20% learning momentums (mostly occurring in the communities and the platforms), and 70% learning workplace integration through one-to-one coaching and action learning (Bloom, 1984). Training is not only planned through formal systems but comes out from the ongoing activities, and leaders are expected to invest some time in developing and applying coaching competencies to sustain the on-the-job growth of junior people.

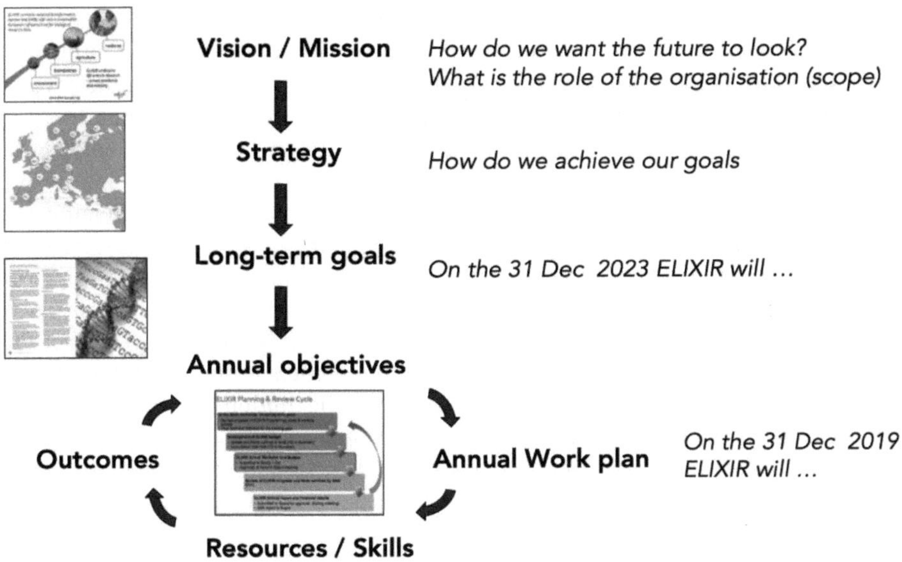

Fig. 2 ELIXIR Planning process—Author's elaboration

6 Discussion and Concluding Remarks

CERN and ELIXIR cases draw on our experiences from two different infrastructures: one single sited and lasting for decades, and the other one very distributed and more recently started up. Our initial aim was to compare and contrast these organisations looking for features of leadership we expected to be specific and differentiated among them.

The more we wrote, the more it became clear that contrasting is to some extent artificial: leadership processes in such organisations have more things in common than we would have initially expected.

First, both RIs are actually meta-organisations: then the two Directors—and, in the case of CERN, the whole Directorate—have to spend great effort in organising the consensus of the constituting entities in the Board, and in the other senior committees from which they need to get approval. In both organisations, decisions are based on agreements that are reached with long and formalised discussions that accompany the production of written documents until final approval: this process, while demanding, allows to integrate issues that might come from the diverse interest of each Member State with the purpose of maintaining their long-term commitment.

Leadership is also essential because both organisations need to manage the performance of many people who collaborate but are not their staff members: this is evident in the case of ELIXIR that—as a distributed structure—only coordinates the service data production from the national nodes node, but it also happens at CERN which is single sited and directly possesses the infrastructure physical resources, yet it is open to a net of about 30,000 external collaborators who participate temporarily in various roles in the projects.

Furthermore, these people are qualified experts and scientists who, paraphrasing the famous Karl Marx's statement, "own the means of production" that ultimately correspond to their knowledge. They are usually very passionate about their work, yet tend to be somewhat individualistic in pursuing their goals; their commitment is essential to fully leverage their competence, and it can be obtained only in an empowering working environment.

As a consequence, hierarchical management based only on formal planning and control mechanisms wouldn't be effective. So, both organisations invest significant effort, time, and resources to build and maintain a community that keeps together scientists spread across many independent organisations and based in different countries. We explored more deeply how this practices work at ELIXIR, but the same connectivity with an external network of researchers is pursued at CERN that has achieved focality and legitimacy as an anchor institution hub in fundamental physics since decades: an enduring scientific reputation, recurrent global seminars and conferences, and a light approach in integrating international collaborative partners and staff into its multidisciplinary projects teams make researchers from everywhere willing to collaborate with it.

Internal culture-driven coordination mechanisms are essential for both organisations: key values need to be identified, and every effort has to be made to ensure that they drive coherent people behaviours. At CERN, given the organisation's size and longevity, this process has been structured through a participative internal research study leading to the identification of the organisation's core values and the development of a competency model that guides the design of human resources management practices; at ELIXIR this process is more implicit, and it is managed through continuous conversations between the Director and the Senior Managers who somewhat shaped together the core values in practising the expected behaviours, and are now diffusing them by example and communication to junior staff who joined more recently.

Both organisations finally rely on extensive training investments to support the development of the staff competencies. At CERN they are planned and partially mandatory, including leadership training for the people who are going to manage the double net of internal and external collaborators; at ELIXIR they are more emergent and linked to the ongoing activities of the community, which they support and contribute to building.

References

Ahrne, G., & Brunsson, N. (2008). *Meta-organisations*. Edward Elgar.

Bacon, J. (2012). *The art of community* (2nd ed.). O'Reilly Media.

Barrick, M. R., Day, D. V., Lord, R. G., & Alexander, R. A. (1991). Assessing the utility of executive leadership. *Leadership Quarterly, 2*(1), 9–22.

Bass, B. M., Avolio, B. J., Jung, D. I., & Berson, Y. (2003). Predicting unit performance by assessing transformational and transactional leadership. *Journal of Applied Psychology, 88*(2), 207–218.

Bass, B. M., & Bass, R. (2008). *The Bass handbook of leadership: Theory, research, and managerial applications* (4th ed.). Free Press.

Bertrand, M., & Schoar, A. (2003). Managing with style: The effect of managers on firm polices. *Quarterly Journal of Economics, 118*(4), 1169–1208.
Bloom, B. S. (1984). The 2 sigma problem: The search for methods of group instruction as effective one-to-one tutoring. *Educational Researcher, 13*(6), 4–16.
Chesbrough, H. (2003). *Open innovation: The new imperative for creating and profiting from technology*. Harvard Business School Press.
Colbert, A. E., Barrick, M. R., & Bradley, B. H. (2014). Personality and leadership composition in top management teams: Implications for organisational effectiveness. *Personnel Psychology, 67*(2), 351–387.
Conger, J. A., & Kanungo, R. N. (1998). *Charismatic leadership in organizations*. Sage.
Costa, P. T., Jr., & McCrae, R. R. (1985). The NEO personality inventory manual. Psychological Assessment Resources.
Eggleton, D. E. (2017). Examining the relationship between leadership and megascience projects. (Unpublished doctoral dissertation). University of Sussex. Brighton, UK.
ESFRI. (2018). Strategy report on research infrastructures. Roadmap 2018 http://roadmap2018.esfri.eu/media/1066/esfri-roadmap-2018.pdf. Accessed May 27, 2020.
Fiedler, F. E. (1967). *A theory of leadership effectiveness*. McGraw-Hill.
Graen, G. B., & Uhl-Bien, M. (1995). The relationship-based approach to leadership: Development of LMX theory of leadership over 25 years: Applying a multi-level, multi-domain perspective. *Leadership Quarterly, 6*(2), 219–247.
Grove, A. S. (2015). *High output management* (3rd ed.). Vintage Books.
Gulati, R., Puranam, P., & Tushman, M. (2012). Meta-organisations design: Rethinking design in interorganisational and community contexts. *Strategic Management Journal, 33*(6), 571–586.
Hackett, E., & Parker, J. (2012). Research groups. In W. Bainbridge (Ed.), *Leadership in science and technology: A reference handbook* (pp. 165–174). Sage.
Hackman, J. R., & Wageman, R. (2005). A theory of team coaching. *Academy of Management Review, 30*(2), 269–287.
House, R. J. (1996). Path-goal theory of leadership: Lessons, legacy, and a reformulated theory. *Leadership Quarterly, 7*(3), 323–352.
Judge, T. A., & Bono, J. E. (2000). Five-factor model of personality and transformational leadership. *Journal of Applied Psychology., 85*(5), 751–765.
Judge, T. A., Bono, J. E., Ilies, R., & Gerhardt, M. W. (2002). Personality and leadership: A qualitative and quantitative review. *Journal of Applied Psychology, 87*(4), 765–780.
Judge, T. A., & Zapata, C. P. (2015). The person-situation debate revisited: Effect of the situation strength and trait activation on the validity of the big five personality traits in predicting job performance. *Academy of Management Journal, 58*(4), 1149–1170.
Koene, B. A., Vogelaar, A. L., & Soeters, J. L. (2002). Leadership effects on organizational climate and financial performance: Local leadership effects in chain organizations. *Leadership Quarterly, 13*(3), 193–215.
Kirkman, B. L., & Rosen, B. (1999). Beyond self-management: Antecedents and consequences of team empowerment. *Academy of Management Journal, 42*(1), 58–74.
Mintzberg, H. (1979). *The structuring of the organisations. A synthesis of the research*. Prentice-Hall.
Mintzberg, H., & McHugh, A. (1985). Strategy formation in an adhocracy. *Administrative Science Quarterly, 30*(2), 160–197.
Northouse, P. G. (2007). *Leadership: Theory and practice* (4th ed.). Sage.
Orton, J. D., & Weick, K. (1990). Loosely coupled systems: A reconceptualization. *Academy of Management Review, 15*(2), 203–223.
Perrone, V. (1997). The co-evolution of contexts and forms: The N-form. In T. Clark (Ed.), *Advances in Organisational behaviour. A festschrift to honour Derek Pugh*. Ashgate Publishing Company.
Yukl, G. (1989). Managerial leadership: A review of theory and research. *Journal of Management, 15*(2), 251–289.

European Research Infrastructures' Compliance with International and European Law

Carla Gulotta and Ohad Graber-Soudry

Abstract

This chapter provides a practical introduction to the legal environment governing European Research Infrastructures (RIs), aimed at readers with predominantly scientific backgrounds. It outlines the core features of the national, European, and international normative systems that shape the legal and organizational structures of RIs, highlighting how these frameworks influence strategic decisions. Through two empirical cases, the chapter illustrates the significant impact of public procurement regimes on the choice of legal model, clarifying when motivations—such as VAT advantages or exemptions from EU procurement rules—are appropriate or misguided. The discussion then shifts to the internal legal tools that RIs require for their daily operations, including contracts that regulate access, employment, data protection, intellectual property, and ethical considerations. The international dimension of RIs adds further complexity by raising questions about applicable law and jurisdiction in cross-border contractual relationships.

The original version of the chapter has been revised. A correction to this chapter can be found at https://doi.org/10.1007/978-3-032-20373-1_11

This chapter has been developed jointly. However, Ohad Graber-Soudry has drafted paragraphs 2 and 4, Carla Gulotta has drafted paragraphs 1, 3, and 5.

C. Gulotta (✉)
Department of Business and Law, University of Milano-Bicocca, Milan, Italy
e-mail: carla.gulotta@unimib.it

O. Graber-Soudry
X-Officio, Lund, Sweden
e-mail: ohad.graber-soudry@xofficio.eu

E. Guarini et al. (eds.), *Research Infrastructure Management*, Management for Professionals, https://doi.org/10.1007/978-3-032-20373-1_7

1 RIs' (Complex) Legal Environment

1.1 Introductory Notes

European research infrastructures (RIs) operate within a complex legal framework in which different legal systems (national, international, and European) concur in terms of setting the rules with which they must comply. The aim of this chapter is to help readers with a mainly scientific background to identify legal criticalities when they arise, anticipate necessary compliance steps and procedures, sketch out possible solutions, and identify situations where specialized legal counsel may be required. This initiatory path into the realm of the law will start with a survey of the main features of the normative systems that apply to RIs. A basic understanding of this subject is necessary to carefully choose an RI's legal and organizational structure (Sect. 1 of the chapter).

1.2 RIs Must Comply with a Multi-Layered Legal Framework

Let us consider the legal environment in which European RIs operate. For an RI in the European Union, prescriptions coming from different legal orders may become relevant to regulate different aspects of their activities. For example, an RI in Italy must comply with the Italian Unified Code on Health and Safety at Work (legislative decree No. 81/2008) If it is established as a European Research Infrastructure Consortium (ERIC), it must also comply with the ERIC Regulation. In addition, the scientific community expects it to adhere the access principles set out in the European Charter for Access to RIs (2016, revised in 2024).[1] Thus, compliance with national, European, and international law will usually be required, while contracts (private law) and "soft law" (guidelines, charters of principles, codes of conduct, etc.) may also be of relevance.

In reference to global law, Italian scholar Sabino Cassese (2009) has compared the resulting interrelation of rules to a marble cake to underline the intermingling of different layers of norms that sometimes overlap without a clear hierarchical structure. Therefore, to find one's bearings in the global legal environment, it is essential to have some foundation of knowledge of the main features of the concurring systems, considering first the specific scope of application of each one of them and ending with a brief overview of the methods and rules designed to connect them all to one another.

[1] European Commission: Directorate-General for Research and Innovation, European Charter for Access to Research Infrastructures – Principles and guidelines for access and related services, Publications Office of the European Union, 2024, . https://data.europa.eu/doi/10.2777/8299402. Last accessed on 26 March 2026.

1.2.1 International Law

Starting with international law, the first thing to note is that it only applies to states and intergovernmental organizations.[2] International law sources include customs and general principles, which are binding for all members of the international community; treaties, which are comparable to contracts and only bind the signatory parties; and acts of international organizations, which usually have a recommendatory nature but can sometimes produce binding effects, as is the case for the acts of EU institutions (see *infra* Sect. 1.2.2).

While treaties can derogate from international customs due to the principle of speciality (*lex specialis derogat generali*), a few principles[3] are deemed so essential that they are mandatory with no exceptions (*jus cogens*).

Constitutions set the link between international and national legal systems (e.g. in Italy, Article 10 of the Constitution states that the Italian legal system automatically conforms to international customs, while a ratification law gives legal effect to treaties in the country).

1.2.2 European Law

The laws of the EU create a legal order of a new type, differing both from international and municipal law. European law applies not only to EU member states but also to its citizens (both individuals and legal entities). This may be considered the most striking innovation of the former European Community in comparison to all other international organizations.

EU provisions can have *direct effect*, which means that they can create individual rights that national courts must protect.[4] In *Costa v ENEL* (1964), case 6/64, the European Court of Justice drew up the *supremacy doctrine* of EU law over the domestic laws of its member states.

The links between national legal orders and the EU's legal order are found in the ratification of the establishing treaties. The sources of EU law consist of the EU treaties and the Charter of Fundamental Rights of the European Union (primary sources); regulations, directives, and decisions (secondary legislation); and recommendations and opinions (non mandatory). They have different scopes of application and effects.

The Treaty of the European Union (TEU) outlines the objectives and structure of the Union, and the Treaty on the Functioning of the EU (TFEU) provides details on its institutions, acts, and policies. Since 2009 and the Treaty of Lisbon, the Charter of Fundamental Rights of the European Union has acquired the same legal force as the establishing treaties. Regulations are binding on member states and their

[2] The majority of scholars, in fact, still deny international subjectivity to new actors such as multinational enterprises, nongovernmental organizations, or individuals. It is true, however, that sometimes individuals may draw benefits from international law (through principles or treaties ratified by their country, e.g. human rights treaties).

[3] For instance, the one prohibiting gross violations of human rights.

[4] Court of Justice of the European Communities, judgement of 5 February 1963, Van Gend en Loos, Case 26/62, European Court Reports (1963), 1.

citizens. They directly produce legal effects in the national legal systems of the EU member states, whereas directives require a national act in order to be implemented. As an exception, detailed directives may produce effects directly on individuals. Decisions are immediately binding for the subjects they are addressed to, but may also have general application.

1.2.3 National Law

As for national law, its most salient feature from our perspective is its territorial scope of application (within the state's boundaries). Domestic legal sources are hierarchically organized, with the constitution at the top, while a judicial system provides for the application of the law.

In EU member states, domestic law is constantly integrating European law, and national legal orders encompass provisions that aim to regulate international situations; here, we refer to *private international law* and *international procedural law.*[5]

1.2.4 Soft Law

Other rules that RIs might be expected to comply with are those belonging to the so-called soft law. Although such rules are neither binding nor enforceable, they are capable of producing effects. How this happens can be explained by the fact that these rules—often coming from a community of people operating in a given field—can meet the needs of the subjects that are expected to apply them. Another reason why soft law rules tend to be carried out is that often their content goes beyond the law in asking for ethical behaviour; thus, disregarding them would possibly be viewed disfavourably (e.g. the European Charter for Access to Research Infrastructures of the EU Commission[6]).

1.3 Legal Structure and Applicable Rules of RIs

Research infrastructures are structures, facilities, resources, or services that significantly increase research capability and scientific reach, foster innovation, and have a positive impact on society. They are used by the research community to achieve excellence, and their establishment or operation requires large-scale investment and collaborative effort, which is often interdisciplinary, by way of pooling resources on a national or international level. According to the Commission, their operations are to be integrated "as a continuum of complementary services" in the emerging landscape of technology infrastructures, which are "required to develop, test, upscale and validate technology" in order to accelerate its societal and market readiness.[7] RIs may take the form of a single-sited infrastructure, a distributed infrastructure, or

[5] How these rules work shall be briefly explained in the following sections.

[6] *Supra*, note 1.

[7] COMMUNICATION FROM THE COMMISSION, A EUROPEAN STRATEGY ON RESEARCH AND TECHNOLOGY INFRASTRUCTURES, COM(2025) 497 final/2, Brussels, 30.9.2025, 3.

an e-infrastructure and enable a shared research capability to address state-of-the-art or fundamental questions (Graber-Soudry, 2019). (See Chap. 1 "The Concept of Research Infrastructure")

In the above definition, two features of RIs stand out as being particularly relevant. The first is that by having the function of being able to boost innovation, the public interest of RIs is paramount: that is why governments are traditionally involved in their creation and funding. The second feature is that—from an organizational viewpoint—their function can be carried out by adopting a centralized structure (single-sited RIs) or choosing a decentralized structure (distributed RIs) with a central hub and interlinked national nodes. In legal terms, the latter would resemble a "group structure", with decentralized nodes that are not juridical persons themselves but in most cases will be part of another legal entity, such as a university or a research institution.

Single-sited RIs are perhaps the best format for facilitating researchers' shared use of major scientific equipment (e.g. the Large Hadron Collider at the European Council for Nuclear Research—in French Conseil Européen pour la Recherche Nucléaire—CERN); by contrast, a distributed structure, with a central hub and a number of affiliated entities, can better allow for the sharing of collections, archives, and equipment. Almost no physical structures are needed for e-infrastructures such as data and computing systems or communication networks (the so-called virtual RIs).

Considering the geographic scope of their operations, we can distinguish European RIs from global RIs. European RIs are intended to operate in the European market, but this does not mean that non-EU countries cannot participate. Global RIs were conceived at the G7 level as a tool to boost international cooperation in scientific research.

The same polymorphism connotes RIs from a legal viewpoint as well: if we ask what legal form an RI must assume, the answer is that no particular form is required by law. This opens up a number of different possibilities that must be carefully considered.

1.3.1 Memorandum of Understanding (MoU) or Cooperation Agreement

Research infrastructures could be formed as the result of agreements made by researchers from universities and medical or other institutions in different countries to cooperate for the fulfilment of common research needs; a simple non-binding commitment (e.g. an MoU) could be enough to set in motion such cooperation. However, signing a cooperation agreement in the legal form of an international treaty (if signatories are states or intergovernmental organizations) or that of a contract (if signatories are private entities) instead would confer legal enforceability upon the document.

Both formats appear at first glance to be quite flexible—unless states are directly involved as signatories—because they are equally viable for private and public parties and can be easily entered into and amended. However, they also present some drawbacks. For example, they do not seem fit for long-lasting cooperation, as any of the parties could easily decide to put an end to their commitment at any time, while major problems arising from the international character of the deal could remain unresolved. For instance, such instruments would be inadequate to set up a special regime for the place where RI facilities are being built that modify the power of the territorial state therein, dispose of the substantial funds that states parties must guarantee, introduce a special regulation for the RI's personnel (scientists and high-ranking and clerical staff) or for the fiscal treatment of the RI. That is why different legal tools have been used over time to consent to more stable and better organized cooperation.

1.3.2 International Consortia

International research has been carried out through "international consortia" in which each partner retains their legal personality although a common organization is set up to manage their activities of common interest, including setting aside dedicated funds and having separate responsibilities. In the case of the European Life-Science Infrastructure (ELIXIR), landmark RI for biological data, the founding consortium agreement relies on the European Molecular Biology Laboratory (EMBL), an international organization, for its institutional/administrative structure.

1.3.3 The Case for Legal Personality

The European Strategy Forum on Research Infrastructures (ESFRI) has long outlined the steps necessary to construct fully operational European RIs.[8] Upstream, however, a basic decision on the legal structure of the future RI still has to be taken. Although we have already seen that alternatives are possible (ELIXIR), the ESFRI explicitly considers only the three different models it favours most: an international organization, a national legal entity, or an ERIC.

Let us consider the main elements of each of these models and highlight the reasons why one model might be preferred to the others.

International Organizations

Because scientific research and development are sensitive issues strictly connected with state sovereignty, in the past governments have generally chosen to regulate any international cooperation in this area by treaties establishing intergovernmental organizations. This is not at all surprising if we remember that as early as the second half of the nineteenth century,[9] intergovernmental organizations were established precisely in order to create stable cooperation among states in technical matters. After World War II, international organizations spread as the main instrument of international cooperation.

---

[8] ESFRI ROADMAP 2006, updated in 2021; the ongoing process of updating the Roadmap is expected to be finalised by December 2026. https://www.esfri.eu/esfri-roadmap. Last accessed 26 March 2026.

[9] In 1865, in the form of the International Telegraph Union, which is now the International Telecommunication Union in Geneva, and in 1874, in the form of the Universal Postal Union, which still has its seat in Bern.

International organizations are created by states and intergovernmental organizations and are themselves subject to public international law. In the fields of science and technology, this legal format has been chosen to establish organizations such as CERN, ESO, EMBL and more recently, the Square Kilometre Array (SKA).

When an RI ois structured as an international organization, its agents have privileges and immunities. Staff regulations may provide for equal treatment of personnel with regard to wages and taxes, regardless of nationality or place of work. The founding treaty can also provide for the exemption of most taxes and duties.

Among the strengths of this model are the fact that i) it fosters a more stable cooperation among the parties; ii) states are directly involved and can dispose of their normative power to respond to any arising needs; and iii) a treaty may prove to be the best tool with which to negotiate delicate issues (e.g. facilities of great economic value; issues of territoriality).

On the other hand, this model does not allow non-state parties (such as research institutions or universities) to be members; there will be a need for ministries or public agencies acting on behalf of the state (sometimes more than one for each state) to take part in the preparatory phase, which is time consuming; and there is the need to garner political support from governments and national parliaments, which makes the process of establishing an international organization long and complex.

National Entities

The alternative to an international organization that still grants an RI legal personality is to set it up as a national company, foundation, or association. Every country offers different legal tools with which to achieve this, such as through a not-for-profit or a private limited company in the UK (e.g. EMEC—European Marine Energy Centre Ltd); a limited liability company in Germany (e.g. CTAO GmbH, which evolved into an ERIC in January 2025; an Association sans but lucratif in Belgium (e.g. PRACE—Partnership for Advanced Computing in Europe AISBL); a société civile in France (ESRF in Grenoble); or a società per azioni (Spa) or società a responsabilità limitata (Srl) in Italy.

These entities appear to be more viable legal tools: they can usually be set up in a short amount of time, are regulated under national law (with clear legal rules already tested in their application), and their membership is open to both private and public entities. A strong point in favour of this model is its flexibility: different company models are available in different legal systems, so it is possible to pick up a structure that aligns with the needs of the RI that is going to be established. The limited liability regime that underlies most national entities' legal structures also appeals to many RIs.

If the RI takes the form of a national company, then the direct involvement or support from states is ruled out, as are privileges and immunities for its agents, tax and excise exemptions, and special treatment in public procurement.[10] Even worse

[10] See *infra*, Sect. 2.

is that a company might also not be recognized as a legal entity in a state other than the one in which it was incorporated.[11]

European Research Infrastructure Consortium (ERIC)

To overcome the criticalities featured in both the international organization and national entity models, the European Union decided to exercise its competence in the areas of research, technological development, and space through Article 4(3) TFEU[12] and set up a new legal structure that it deemed necessary for the efficient execution of Union research. Acting under Article 187 TFEU[13] and giving effect to what had been established in the Seventh Framework Programme of the EC for Research, the EU adopted Council Regulation No. 723/2009,[14] then amended it in 2013,[15] on the Community legal framework for a European Research Infrastructure Consortium ("ERIC Regulation").

As for the institutional structure, the ERIC Regulation provides for an assembly of members and a director or board of directors, which is the executive body and legal representative of the ERIC. Other bodies can be created according to the statutes of each ERIC. In the template for the statutes of an ERIC provided by the EU Commission,[16] the setting up of one or more advisory bodies is suggested. These might be vested with functions related to scientific or ethical issues.[17] Other bodies could also be created, according to the same template, to assist the director in the implementation of his or her tasks or to represent and coordinate the different entities involved in the activities of the ERIC at the national level.

Membership in the new structure is open to EU member states, associate countries, and third countries. Intergovernmental organizations may also become members, but the majority of votes in the assembly must belong jointly to member states of the Union or associated countries.

Among the strengths of the ERIC model, we can list the fact that it has a legal personality which is recognized in all EU member states and that it benefits from

---

[11] This statement does not apply in the European Union, where a principle of mutual recognition grants legal personality to member states' companies.

[12] It has been called "a hybrid shared competence": the EU can take actions in these areas without excluding a similar right by the member states.

[13] Article 187 TFEU (e.g. Article 171 TEC) states that the Union may set up joint undertakings or any other structure necessary for the efficient execution of Union research, technological development, and demonstration programmes.

[14] Council Regulation (EC) No. 723/2009 of 25 June 2009 on the Community legal framework for a European Research Infrastructure Consortium (ERIC) (2009) OJ L206, 1–8.

[15] Council Regulation (EU) No. 1261/2013 of 2 December 2013, (2013) OJ L326, 1.

[16] EU Commission, ERIC practical guidelines: Legal framework for a European Research Infrastructure Consortium, second edition, 2025, 26 ff.

[17] In the BBMRI-ERIC statutes, we find both a scientific and ethical advisory board and two committees—one to assist the assembly of members (this is the finance committee) and the other to assist the director general. The latter, called the management committee, comprises the coordinators of national/organizational nodes and common services and can be of the utmost importance in facilitating the smooth functioning of a complex distributed RI like BBMRI-ERIC.

exemptions from value added tax (VAT) and excise duties, which allows ERICs to concentrate funds on substantial research. ERICs also benefit from an exemption from the EU procurement directives.[18]

The ERIC model allows states to finance and manage RIs together following a procedure that is set but also flexible; doing so does not require the approval of national parliaments (except Finland) but of ministries or national research authorities/other bodies, depending on national legislation. The EU Commission's control of the ERIC, with the assistance of a committee formed with representatives of all member states, allows for news on the current status and needs of European research to be circulated across the entire Union. Also important to add is that the ERIC can constitute a platform for the creation and testing of common rules that may later on be accepted by the wider scientific community.

The other side of the coin is that, unfortunately, because of the limited EU competence in the area of scientific research, the ERIC cannot play a harmonizing role in member states' legislations. A drawback with the establishment of ERICs is the divergence in the implementation and practical procedures that the different countries follow, e.g. to register the ERIC or to recognize its legal independence or how the VAT rules are applied.

Moreover, the fact that only states and intergovernmental organizations can become members reduces the possibility of adopting this model when private institutions are among the constituent parties. Finally, the process to establish an ERIC could still be simplified.

1.3.4 Legal Form of RIs and Applicable Rules

The choice of an RI's legal model includes deciding on the rules that will apply to its establishment and operations. An international organization will be regulated under the founding treaty (international law), and treaty provisions may prevail over national law (e.g. regarding fiscal rules, staff regulation, privileges, and immunities). Any disputes should be subject to international jurisdiction (International Court of Justice or international arbitration).

RIs created as national companies shall be regulated under the law of the state where the company has its statutory seat or has been incorporated. For companies incorporated in a European Union member state, European law also applies, together with international law that has become part of the national legal system.

If the RI has been set up under the ERIC Regulation, the applicable law and jurisdiction are determined by Article 15, as follows:

1. The setting-up and internal functioning of an ERIC shall be governed:
    (a) by Community law[19], in particular this Regulation, and the decisions referred to in Articles 6(1)(a) and 11(1)

[18] For a comment on the scope of the exemption and the related advantages, see *infra* Sect. 2.

[19] Following the Treaty of Lisbon (2009), all references to the European Communities or Community law should be understood as referring to the Union.

(b) by the law of the State where the ERIC has its statutory seat in the case of matters not, or only partly, regulated by acts referred to in point (a)
(c) by the Statutes and their implementing rules.

2. The Court of Justice of the European Communities shall have jurisdiction over litigation among the members in relation to the ERIC, between the members and the ERIC, and over any litigation to which the Community is a party.
3. Community legislation on jurisdiction shall apply to disputes between an ERIC and third parties. In cases not covered by Community legislation, the law of the State where the ERIC has its statutory seat shall determine the competent jurisdiction for the resolution of such disputes.

What deserves particular mention in this provision is paragraph 1(b). The regulation prescribes that apart from its own provisions and the decisions of the EU Commission in setting up the ERIC and amending its statutes, the applicable law shall be that of the country where the ERIC has its statutory seat. This provision has an important implication: deciding the state where the ERIC shall have its seat also means deciding the laws to which it will be subject.

Whatever model is chosen, RIs will be expected to apply international soft law pertaining to their activities. If we had to draw an initial conclusion on the legal dimension of RIs, it would be that before the creation/transformation of an RI, a strong knowledge of the main features of each of the described models is necessary and an accurate assessment of the characteristics of the specific infrastructure must be made. Political aspects must be considered as relevant as legal ones. Eventually, it can also be considered that giving the RI a formal legal structure may enable it to broaden its horizons to assume a global form of scientific cooperation.[20]

2 Public Procurement Rules and Policy

Two empirical cases are used here to illustrate the relevance of public procurement considerations to the choice of the legal model. In the first case, two big RIs in the construction phase engage in significant procurement activity under a demanding project schedule. All other things being equal, one of the RIs spends 30% more on tender and procurement compliance costs when compared to the other RI. What led to such a difference?

[20] The opportunity to boost international cooperation in scientific research on a global scale was underlined at the first G8 Science and Technology Ministers Meeting held in Okinawa on 15 June 2008. A group of senior officials (GSO) was created, and in September 2017, it presented in Turin the so-called GSO Framework. In this document, the GSO recognizes the vital role of global RIs in addressing worldwide science and technology challenges and the benefits of coordinating investments in global RIs to efficiently use the available resources and achieve their potential.

The GSO Framework contains a number of criteria that global RIs should meet. For an EU RI, being a legal entity would greatly help it to take part in such enlarged global projects.

In the second case, another early-stage distributed RI with a small central hub is considering the most appropriate legal entity for its operations phase. The project coordinators suggest the ERIC as the most suitable legal vehicle due to the unique advantages it offers in terms of VAT relief and the exemption from EU public procurement directives. The general assembly accepts the recommendation and opts for the ERIC. Was this the correct motivation for choosing the ERIC as a legal vehicle for that specific RI?

In order to answer these questions, we need to examine the relationship between the procurement regime applicable to the RI, the scope of the procurement activity envisaged for the RI, and the choice of legal entity for the RI.

2.1 Legal Framework

The relevant legal framework for public procurement in the EU is based on the TFEU and, more specifically, on EU Directive 2014/24/EU ("the Directive").[21] EU public procurement law imposes obligations upon "contracting authorities" when they award contracts for the provision of goods, services, and works. The Directive specifies the means by which contract opportunities must be advertised, the process that the contracting authority can use to select contractors, and the remedies that are available to unsuccessful bidders.

In particular, if the value of a contract meets certain financial thresholds, the contracting authority is obliged to advertise the contract opportunity in the *Official Journal of the European Union* (OJEU) and to use a specific procurement procedure set out in the Directive. If a contract is not subject to the Directive, either because its value is below the relevant threshold or because a specific exemption applies, then the contracting authority will not be required to advertise the contract in the OJEU and there will be no need to follow a regulated procurement procedure. However, depending on its legal status, the contracting authority may (or may not) need to observe certain fundamental principles of EU law when it awards a contract that is of "cross-border interest", meaning that a supplier in another member state may be interested in bidding for it. These principles include, for example, non-discrimination on grounds of nationality, equal treatment, transparency, competition, and proportionality, to name but a few.

To illustrate, the Court of Justice of the European Union (CJEU) has established that, based on these principles, contracting authorities should advertise any contract of "cross-border interest" to a sufficient degree to inform potential suppliers in other EU member states. They must also treat all offers fairly and impartially, set proportionate deadlines, and evaluate proposals using transparent and objective criteria. In some cases, therefore, even if a contract falls outside the scope of the Directive, the contracting authority may still need to run a competition and not award the contract directly to a preferred supplier without prior advertisement.

[21] Directive 2014/24/EU of the European Parliament and of the Council of 26 February 2014 on public procurement and repealing Directive 2004/18/EC (2014) OJ L94/65.

2.2 RIs as "Contracting Authorities" Within the Meaning of the EU Public Procurement Directives

In order to understand why the choice of the legal entity for the RI could be decisive in terms of applicable regulatory obligations and procurement compliance costs, it is important to first understand the concept of a "contracting authority" under the Directive. A "contracting authority" is defined by the Directive as "the State, regional or local authorities, bodies governed by public law or associations formed by one or more such authorities or one or more such bodies governed by public law".[22]

Since RIs do not usually form a part of state, regional, or local authorities, consideration needs to be given to whether or not the RI is a "body governed by public law". The relevant definition under the Directive provides that an entity will be a "body governed by public law" if the following criteria are met:

1. It is established for the specific purpose of meeting needs in the general interest, not having an industrial or commercial character
2. It has legal personality and
3. It has any of the following characteristics:
   (a) It is financed, for the most part, by state, regional, or local authorities or by other bodies governed by public law
   (b) It is subject to management supervision by those authorities or bodies or
   (c) It has an administrative, managerial, or supervisory board, more than half of whose members are appointed by the state, regional, or local authorities or by other bodies governed by public law

The test is such that the criteria in (1) and (2) must be met, and any one (though not necessarily all) of the characteristics in (3) must be met.

2.3 Mapping RIs According to Their Legal Status

Earlier in this chapter, three main models of legal vehicles for RIs were identified[23]: 1) national vehicle (such as a limited liability company, GmbH, AISBL, a foundation, etc.); 2) ERIC; and 3) international organizations. Many of the existing RIs, particularly national RIs, are likely to fall under the first category.[24] There are

[22] Article 2.1(1), Directive 2014/24/EU of the European Parliament and of the Council of 26 February 2014 on public procurement and repealing Directive 2004/18/EC (2014) OJ L94/65.

[23] While this classification covers the vast majority of RIs, it is by no means comprehensive, for example, the European Economic Interest Grouping (EEIG) does not neatly fit into any of these models and could instead be classified as a non-ERIC European entity.

[24] Examples include, DESY, XFEL, and MAX IV.

currently 32 established ERICs[25] falling under the second category, and a number of RIs have been formed as international organizations,[26] hence falling under the third category.

While the test for whether a particular RI meets the definition of a "body governed by public law" will be applied in the same way to all RIs regardless of their legal form, the choice of the legal form for the RI could be decisive in terms of any specific exemptions from the EU legal framework on procurement that are granted to some legal forms. Such exemptions, in turn, are likely to reduce the cost of compliance with EU rules applicable to procurement activity.

2.4 Procurement by National Vehicles

Determining whether a specific RI falls within the scope of the Directive and the TFEU is a matter of case-by-case analysis. However, given their composition, objectives, non-commercial character, and financing sources, most RIs incorporated under a national vehicle are likely to fall within the definition of a "body governed by public law"; hence, they will be considered "contracting authorities" as per the Directive.[27]

This means that capital-intensive or "big science" RIs incorporated under a national vehicle are likely to incur significant procurement compliance costs and face higher legal risks when performing their procurement activities. Early-stage big science RIs would therefore need to consider whether the benefits associated with incorporation under a national vehicle outweigh the costs that they will expect to incur for their regulated procurement compliance. Similarly, big science RIs in upgrade phases should earmark larger margins (contingencies) to cover the legal risks associated with potential challenges to their procurement procedures by aggrieved bidders seeking to enforce their rights under the EU public procurement regime.

In contrast, for RIs with low-capital investment or distributed RIs with limited procurement activity by the ERIC, the choice to incorporate under a national vehicle is unlikely to incur significant procurement compliance costs, particularly if the value of their envisaged purchases is likely to fall below the relevant EU and national thresholds.

[25] For a full list of existing ERICs, see https://eur-lex.europa.eu/EN/legal-content/summary/european-research-infrastructure-consortium-eric.html#:~:text=Regulation%20(EU)%20No%20723/,a%20member%20of%20an%20ERIC. Last accessed 26 March 2026.

[26] Most notably CERN.

[27] See the definition of a "body governed by public law" above.

2.5 Procurement by ERICs

In recent years, a growing number of European-based RIs have chosen to organize themselves under the ERIC Regulation.[28] As a relatively new legal form, the intention behind the ERIC Regulation is to provide for a legal framework that is tailored to the needs of setting up and operating European RIs. The ERIC Regulation provides European RIs with a separate legal entity with "the most extensive legal capacity" recognized in all EU member states. It also includes certain provisions on exemption from taxation, staff rules, derogations from national laws, limitation of liability, and an exemption from the EU public procurement directives.

Article 7(3) of the ERIC Regulation provides that an ERIC is an "international organisation" within the meaning of EU public procurement directives.[29] The Directive[30] provides that "this directive shall not apply to public contracts and design contests which the contracting authority is obliged to award or organise in accordance with procurement procedures different from those laid down in this directive established by any of the following: (…) an international organisation". Thus, ERICs fall outside the scope of the EU public procurement directives[31] and will not be subject to the same scope of obligations as other non-exempt bodies governed by public law.

However, ERICs' exemption from the EU public procurement directives does not mean that they are also exempt from the obligations stemming from TFEU's general principles (Graber-Soudry, 2019). As mentioned earlier, these principles have been consistently used by the CJEU to clarify and expand the scope of EU public procurement law to contracts that are not fully subject to the EU public procurement directives. This in turn imposes considerable limits on the level of freedom that ERICs may enjoy while developing their own procurement policies and limits the scope of their choice when compared to "genuine" international organizations. In practice, it means that ERICs will have to consider EU law, as interpreted by the CJEU, when deciding on the procurement policy they propose to adopt and for the level of remedies that must be made available for aggrieved bidders—at least those that are established in one or more EU member states.

2.6 Procurement by International Organizations

As has been mentioned, the Directive does not apply to contracts in which the contracting authority is obliged to award or organize in accordance with the procurement procedures established by an international organization.[32] The term

---

[28] Council Regulation (EC) No. 723/2009 of 25 June 2009, *supra*, note 13.

[29] Reference in the ERIC Regulation is made to Article 15(c) of Directive 2004/18/EC, but this is now transformed into Article 9(1)(b) of Directive 2014/24/EU.

[30] As per the above comment, it is now Article 9(1)(b) of Directive 2014/24/EU.

[31] Provided all relevant conditions in Article 9(1)(b) of Directive 2014/24/EU are fulfilled.

[32] Article 9(1)(b) of Directive 24/2014/EU.

"international organization" is not defined in the Directive but it generally covers any treaty-based organization having a separate legal personality in which only states and/or other international organizations are members.

International organizations are usually granted some form of privileges and immunities, which means that the international organization is released from certain legal obligations and is not subject to the adjudication and enforcement of applicable laws against it by a court of law that would otherwise have jurisdiction.

In contrast to ERICs, which are subject to the TFEU even if they are exempt from the EU Directive, international organizations are not subject to any of them. Therefore, RIs that have been established as international organizations have the complete freedom to develop their procurement policies in the manner they deem fit, free from any restrictions derived from EU law.

It follows from the discussion above that the choice of an appropriate legal entity for big science RIs is important, particularly during construction or upgrade phases, and should be considered carefully. In contrast, the advantages that legal forms such as ERIC and international organizations bring about in terms of exemptions from the EU public procurement regime are limited for ERICs with a limited scope of procurement activity, and such benefits should not be overestimated.

3 Contractual and Ethical Issues in RIs

3.1 Introductory Notes

In the first two sections, we focused on the alternative legal models that European RIs adopt for their external structure and on the implications of such choices for public procurement. Now, our glance will turn inward to the legal tools that RIs need in the performance of their day-to-day tasks.

While RIs cover different sectors of the European Research Area, they perform a common function, which is mainly to allow a shared use of research devices or to provide services. They also have in common the international character of their activities. From this, it follows that although the legal tools of interest for a specific infrastructure may vary according to the particular field of science to which it contributes, there are legal issues that are common to them all. For example, every European RI will need to regulate its relationships with researchers and employees, their access to its facilities or collections, and the protection of privacy and personal data. It will also have to handle intellectual property rights. Being at the forefront of scientific and technological innovation, RIs are also constantly confronted with ethical issues.

Most of the legal issues just mentioned are to be handled through contractual instruments, but the international dimension of RIs stipulates the necessity of international contracts, which raises two basic legal problems regarding how to determine the law applicable to the contract and which court will have jurisdiction should a dispute arise.

3.2 Employment Contracts in International Settings

Under which law are contracts of employment in the RI regulated? To answer this question, the legal form of the RI is the first variable to consider.

Whereas in a treaty-based RI formed as an international organization, one will have to look to the establishing treaty and at the staff regulations, in the other two models (national vehicle and ERIC), it will be national law that applies.

Even in the case of an ERIC, the application of EU law and of the statutes of the organization does not rule out the need to respect national laws (similarly, local environmental laws and administrative procedures shall have to be respected). That is why familiarity with the legal system of the country where the RI has its seat and/or conducts its operations may be required. But it is not only the fear of violating norms that calls for strong legal expertise. As Article 8 of the Rome Regulation on individual employment contracts shows,[33] there is often a range of legal possibilities among which one must be able to choose:

1. An individual employment contract shall be governed by the law chosen by the parties in accordance with Article 3. Such a choice of law may not, however, have the result of depriving the employee of the protection afforded to him by provisions that cannot be derogated from by agreement under the law that, in the absence of choice, would have been applicable pursuant to paragraphs 2, 3, and 4 of this Article.
2. To the extent that the law applicable to the individual employment contract has not been chosen by the parties, the contract shall be governed by the law of the country in which or, failing that, from which the employee habitually carries out his work in performance of the contract. The country where the work is habitually carried out shall not be deemed to have changed if he is temporarily employed in another country.
3. Where the law applicable cannot be determined pursuant to paragraph 2, the contract shall be governed by the law of the country where the place of business through which the employee was engaged is situated.
4. Where it appears from the circumstances as a whole that the contract is more closely connected with a country other than that indicated in paragraphs 2 or 3, the law of that other country shall apply.

Reading the text of Article 8 of the Rome Regulation offers an excellent sample of the level of complexity that legal issues in an RI present: given the state where the RI has its seat, will it be better to add a choice-of-law clause in the employment contract or will the law described in Article 8(2) do? (That would be the law of the country where the job is habitually performed.)

Article 8 of the Rome Regulation applies the EU's "conflict of law rules" to contractual obligations. These are special rules that aim to provide criteria that lead to

[33] Regulation (EC) No. 593/2008 of the European Parliament and of the Council of 17 June 2008 on the law applicable to contractual obligations (Rome I) (2008) OJ L177, 6–16.

the application of the most suitable law in cases that involve multiple jurisdictions, such as: What law applies to a contract stipulated in Paris between an Austrian service provider and a German citizen?

A similar set of rules (the rules on conflict of jurisdiction) helps us to identify the competent court in the event that a contract is breached. Traditionally, every European state has had its own rules on conflicting laws and jurisdictions. But the differences between national rules governing the law applicable to international contracts, jurisdiction, and the recognition of judgments could hamper the sound operation of the internal market—that is why common rules have been made in the EU, giving way to the "Europeanization of private international law".

The so-called Rome I Regulation provides for uniform conflict-of-law rules in contractual matters, which designate the same national law irrespective of the country of the court in which an action is brought. Provisions to unify the rules of jurisdictional conflict in civil and commercial matters and to ensure the rapid recognition and enforcement of judgments given in a member state are provided instead by the Brussels I Recast Regulation of 2012.[34]

Looking a little deeper into the Rome Regulation scheme, we find that one of the cornerstones of the system of conflict-of-law rules in matters of contractual obligation is parties' freedom to choose the applicable law. But if there is no choice of law by the parties, the Regulation provides for other criteria for typical contracts; and if these are not applicable, relevance could be given to the law of the country where the party required to effect the characteristic performance habitually resides or to the law of the country with which the contract is most closely connected.[35] Special conflict-of-law rules, then, afford protection to weaker contractual parties, like workers and consumers.

3.3 Access Policy

Model contracts on material and data transfer can serve to guarantee the effective implementation of an RI's access policy, considering that access policies can render the stipulation of such contracts compulsory (this happens in BBMRI-ERIC) and that their content reflects an RI's decisions on access to materials and data.

[34] Regulation (EU) No. 1215/2012 of the European Parliament and of the Council of 12 December 2012 on jurisdiction and the recognition and enforcement of judgments in civil and commercial matters (2012) OJ L351, 1–32.

[35] Article 4: Applicable law in the absence of choice

1. To the extent that the law applicable to the contract has not been chosen in accordance with Article 3 and without prejudice to Articles 5 to 8, the law governing the contract shall be determined as follows:

(a) A contract for the sale of goods shall be governed by the law of the country where the seller has his habitual residence;

(b) A contract for the provision of services shall be governed by the law of the country where the service provider has his habitual residence [...]

The access policy is at the core of RI activity, so it is worthwhile to examine how it has to be regulated. We find guidance in EU treaties—particularly in Title XIX TFEU. Based on its provisions as a whole, it is possible to deduce that the approach taken by European RIs to determining access policies pertaining to scientific and technological research in the Union is informed by the principles of the free movement of researchers, free movement of knowledge, openness to market operators (especially SMEs), and cooperation with third countries and international organizations.

Access to infrastructure must then comply with the law, especially with human rights law. To avoid being confronted with the difficulty of drawing up potentially tricky contract clauses governing the performance of their daily tasks, RIs could resort to model contracts. Templates for recurring types of contractual relationships, e.g., a contract for the transfer of materials and data, can be prepared with the assistance of legal experts and published on the RI's webpage, thereby positively affecting legal certainty, transparency, and the speed of transactions.[36]

The importance of a European RI clearly setting out the rules governing access to its facility or collection is confirmed by the ERIC Regulation, which prescribes including the framework of ERIC's access policy in statutes. While in this way the main elements of the policy acquire a rigid formal nature, more detailed requirements and rules on access shall preferably be developed in a separate document to outline all relevant criteria and procedures.

As for the legal nature of an access policy, certainly it shall be binding for ERIC's members, the partners in their relationships and users. It could also serve as a template for BBMRI-ERIC's individual biobanks and third parties' access policies, for example. A strong point in favour of adopting the ERIC legal structure is that it may work as a platform where common criteria and standards may be established and spread throughout the scientific community.

3.4 Ethical Issues

The collection and stewardship of biological materials of human origin and of personal data entail evident regulatory and ethical issues, but bioethical questions may also appear in any RI within the social science and humanities fields. For example, under what conditions should researchers be allowed to ask for and to store samples of biological materials? Should using biospecimens in research projects other than the ones they were collected for be permitted? Under what conditions should the sharing of sensitive personal data be allowed within the scientific community collections?

---

[36] I.e., material or data transfer agreements. Article 12 of the BBMRI-ERIC Material Transfer Agreement template is a good example of a choice of law and jurisdiction clause, providing for the application of Belgian law and for mediation according to World Intellectual Property Organization mediation rules in case of dispute.

Hard law, both at the international and national level, has not always been able to keep up with the enormous progress being made in medical research in the last decades, and many of these issues are now being dealt with by turning to soft law. Here, soft law plays a sort of "institutionalized role"; legislators themselves seem to recognize the inadequacy of traditional legal orders to catch up with medical research innovations. Not wanting to leave the new sensitive problems arising from this sudden development in science unresolved, they tend to devolve the responsibility to decide on ethical issues to special bodies (ethics committees) composed not only of scientists but also of scholars of philosophy, sociology, and law so as to tackle all the different facets of the new decisions to be made in the best interests of society. So, the importance of establishing an ethics committee and involving it in all of the RI's sensitive decision-making is the first rule. This may not be easy to enact, however, as distributed RIs may find themselves in the position to dispose of such bodies for each of their partners (hospital, biobanks, or other entities). A quite advanced approach in this field is that which was taken by BBMRI-ERIC, which has set up a highly innovative service in the form of ELSI (Ethical, Legal and Societal Issues in Biobanking) to provide support to researchers and to the biomedical science community as a whole, which can constitute an inspirational model for other infrastructures to replicate.[37]

As for the legal rules that European RIs must comply with when dealing with ethical issues, at the level of international law sources, primary reference has to be made to the Additional Protocol to the Convention on Human Rights and Biomedicine, concerning biomedical research[38] and the Nagoya Protocol on access and benefit sharing.

The Additional Protocol on biomedical research was stipulated in 2005 by the Council of Europe and entered into force in September 2007. It affirms important principles and rules that signatory states are bound to introduce in their domestic legal orders, among them: the protection of the dignity, and of the identity, of the human beings involved in research (Article 1); the primacy of the interests and welfare of the human being over the interests of society and research (Article 3); the need for an ethics committee to approve of research projects in advance (Article 9); the "informed, free, express, specific and documented consent" that participants in the research must give after receiving adequate information about it (Article 14); and the protection of the confidentiality of any information of a personal nature (Article 25).

Signed by 23 states, the Additional Protocol is currently enforced in only 12 of them, including Norway, Portugal, Hungary, Slovak Republic, and Slovenia. Eleven other countries (among them Italy, Sweden, and Denmark) signed the Additional Protocol but have not yet ratified it.

What is the legal value of the Additional Protocol for European RIs? Of course, it is binding for the states that signed and ratified it. Hence, if one of those countries

[37] https://www.bbmri-eric.eu/services/common-service-elsi. Last accessed 26 March 2026.

[38] This is an international treaty connected to the Convention on Human Rights and biomedicine (the Oviedo Convention of 1997).

(like Portugal or Norway, as an EU associate country) is a member of an RI, it will have to see that its activities comply with it. Nonetheless, not even RIs operating in such countries could be expected to apply prescriptions that are in the Additional Protocol but that require state intervention to be applicable in the domestic legal order.[39] Article 29 imposes on researchers from countries that signed the Additional Protocol to see that its requirements are met even in projects in non-party states. Independent of ratification, the Additional Protocol is an authoritative source of principles for all interested subjects.

The Nagoya Protocol elaborates on one of the main goals of the 1992 UN Convention on Biological Diversity: assuring the fair and equitable sharing of benefits arising from the utilization of genetic resources and of associated traditional knowledge. Adopted in 2010, the Nagoya Protocol is currently in force in 142 countries.[40] The aim of the Nagoya Protocol is to provide legal certainty on the international regime for the exploitation of genetic resources based on prior informed consent and requires the sharing of the benefits obtained by researchers with the original owner country/community of said resources or knowledge. However, the implementation of these principles has proven extremely tricky. The discretion left to each signatory on how to ensure compliance with the several substantial as well as procedural duties introduced by the Nagoya Protocol has created a slippery terrain into which researchers/users may lack the confidence to venture.

In the EU, a further layer of complexity is added by the need to distinguish between the subjects of Union competence and those of national competence. Regulation No. 511/2014, which has implemented the Nagoya Protocol in the EU, has placed on the users of genetic resources and/or traditional knowledge a duty of due diligence (Article 4).[41] This implies that they should "seek, keep and transfer to subsequent users" an internationally recognized certificate of compliance or, if not available, gather information/documents that allow the legal acquisition of the resources to be ascertained.

Compliance with these duties may render the management of genetic resources quite challenging and create a fear of checks and penalties (Articles 7, 9 and 11) for making any mistakes; this might even induce researchers to shift to non-EU countries for genetic sources. Significant help in abiding by the Nagoya Protocol rules comes from the Access and Benefit-Sharing Clearing House, a platform where users

---

[39] For example, consider Article 24: parties to the Additional Protocol are asked to take measures to ensure that research projects are re-examined if this is justified in the light of scientific developments. This provision sets an obligation upon the state. If such measures are not taken by the state party, RIs operating in its territory will not be bound by the law to set a re-examination of the projects. It must be considered, though, that the major part of the Additional Protocol's provisions—affirming general principles—could be judged to be self-executing (meaning that it does not need to be turned into a domestic act but may produce legal effects before the courts by itself).

[40] https://www.cbd.int/abs/doc/protocol/nagoya-protocol-en.pdf.

[41] Regulation (EU) No. 511/2014 of the European Parliament and of the Council of 16 April 2014 (2014) OJ L150, 59 ff. on compliance measures for users from the Nagoya Protocol on Access to Genetic Resources and the Fair and Equitable Sharing of Benefits Arising from their Utilization in the Union.

of genetic resources can find information on—among others—competent national authorities and legislative, administrative, and policy measures adopted to implement the rules in national legal orders.[42] A survey mandated by the EU Commission has nonetheless detected that this tool is not always abreast of all relevant information and has called for a reform of the implementation procedure of the Protocol, at least at the European level.[43]

Even European law provides for rules that RIs must comply with and principles that can offer them guidance in tackling issues that have sensitive ethical implications. A basic provision is Article 19 of the Horizon Europe Regulation of 2021, which states that all research and innovation activities carried out under Horizon 2020 must comply with ethical principles and relevant national, Union, and international legislation. The Charter of Fundamental Rights of the European Union and the European Convention on Human Rights and its supplementary protocols are expressly mentioned. They are, in more general terms, also outside the scope of application of said regulation, the benchmark for the protection of human rights in the Union.

According to Article 19 of the Horizon Europe Regulation, particular attention must be paid to the principle of proportionality, the right to privacy, the right to the protection of personal data, the right to the physical and mental integrity of a person, the right to non-discrimination, and the need to ensure high levels of human health protection. Ethical guidance can also be drawn from the fields of research that are excluded from financing or deemed financeable only under given conditions.[44]

Another EU law source that is undoubtedly relevant to RIs is Directive 2010/63/EU of 22 September 2010, which sets the rules of the European Union on the protection of animals used for scientific purposes.[45] This directive is the EU's transposi-

[42] https://absch.cbd.int/.

[43] Milieu Law and Policy Consulting, Analysis of implications of compliance with the EU ABS Regulation for research organizations and private sector companies, May 2020, 33 ff.

[44] "3. The following fields of research shall not be financed:

(a) activities aiming at human cloning for reproductive purposes;

(b) activities intended to modify the genetic heritage of human beings which could make such modifications heritable(28);

(c) activities intended to create human embryos solely for the purpose of research or for the purpose of stem cell procurement, including by means of somatic cell nuclear transfer.

4. Research on human stem cells, both adult and embryonic, may be financed depending both on the contents of the scientific proposal and the legal framework of the Member States involved. No funding shall be provided within or outside the Union for research activities that are prohibited in all Member States. No funding shall be provided in a Member State for a research activity which is forbidden in that Member State." (Article 18, Regulation (EU) 2021/695 of the European Parliament and of the Council of 28 April 2021 establishing Horizon Europe – the Framework Programme for Research and Innovation, laying down its rules for participation and dissemination, and repealing Regulations (EU) No 1290/2013 and (EU) No 1291/2013, Text with EEA relevance (2021) OJ L170, 1-68).

[45] Directive 2010/63/EU of the European Parliament and of the Council of 22 September 2010 on the protection of animals used for scientific purposes, OJ L276, 20.10.2010, 33 ff. The directive has been amended by regulation (EU) 2019/1010 of 5 June 2019: see the current consolidated version at https://eur-lex.europa.eu/legal-content/EN/TXT/?uri=CELEX:02010L0063-20190626.

tion of the Council of Europe Convention on the same topic[46] and is based on the triple principle of the "replacement, reduction and refinement" of the use of living animals in research (Article 4). The favour for animal welfare that is the *ratio* of the act is well expressed by Article 2, which allows member states to maintain provisions ensuring a more extensive protection of animals, which were already in force on 9 November 2010; this qualifies the common rules as a minimum floor rather than a full harmonization.

The directive, which member states had to implement by 10 November 2012,[47] provides for a triple level of animal protection: duties are set directly on breeders, suppliers, and users of animals for scientific purposes and on member countries, while at the Union level, the Commission oversees the correct implementation of the rules.

Accordingly, member state governments have set up competent authorities and national committees in charge of the authorization and inspection procedures and are responsible for the application of penalties in case of infringement. The final users of animals for research purposes are required to follow a procedure encompassing the submission of a project proposal justifying the use of animals that must be evaluated and approved; an application for authorization from the national competent authority; and the setting up of an animal-welfare body.[48] They are also bound to keep records for at least five years of all relevant information pertaining to their behaviour towards the animals covered by the directive.

EU member states can have different legislation on ethical topics linked to biomedical research (shared competence with the EU). Even an EU regulation can leave to member states margins of discretion which hamper uniformity. Recently, Regulation 2024/1938 was introduced to establish high quality and safety standards for all substances of human origin (SoHO) intended for human use. This regulation does not interfere with ethical decisions made by Member States, such as those concerning the use or limitation of the use of reproductive SoHO and embryonic stem cells, provided these decisions adhere to the Charter.[49] It shall be necessary, then, to acquire deep knowledge of the national legislation of any countries where projects are going to be developed, even within the boundaries of the EU.

Soft law also plays a special role in dealing with issues that are at the boundary between law and ethics. Many documents have been drawn up at the international and national level to guide scientists and researchers and also to help public authorities called to take decisions with sensitive ethical implications (think of judges

[46] Council of Europe, European Convention for the Protection of Vertebrate Animals used for Experimental and Other Scientific Purposes, Strasbourg, 18.III.1986, https://rm.coe.int/168007a67b.

[47] For updated news on the directive's implementing legislation and the list of member states' national authorities, see: https://ec.europa.eu/environment/chemicals/lab_animals/legislation_en.htm.

[48] According to Article 26(3), member countries can allow small breeders, suppliers, and users to replace this last requirement with alternative means of protection.

[49] 47See Wheras (28), Art. 2(3) and Art. 4 of the regulation: https://eur-lex.europa.eu/legal-content/EN/TXT/PDF/?uri=OJ:L_202401938.

dealing with cases where the rights of a person to donate their body to science come into play).

The correct approach to these soft law instruments is to use them as guidance whenever the law leaves a gap to be filled. It will be necessary to assess if any such charters or guidelines have acquired a binding nature for an RI in terms of a contractual obligation to respect them, which may be included in the RI's statutes or ethical policy.

3.5 Privacy Issues: Compliance with the EU Regime on Personal Data

The protection of natural persons in relation to the processing of personal data is, in the EU legal order, a fundamental right. Article 8(1) of the Charter of Fundamental Rights of the European Union ("the Charter") and TFEU Article 16(1) provide that everyone has the right to the protection of their personal data.

A strong tradition of emphasizing individual rights has led the EU to pass extremely advanced legislation for the protection of personal data. At the same time, the EU is well aware of the fact that big data and artificial intelligence (AI) are fundamental tools that may advance innovation, scientific development, and societal progress and that "in order to release that potential we have to find our European way, balancing the flow and wide use of data while preserving high privacy, security, safety and ethical standards" (von der Leyen, 2019, 13).

The General Data Protection Regulation (GDPR), which came into force on 25 May 2018, aims at balancing these interests and is certainly a relevant piece of legislation with which European RIs have to comply.[50] Key points of the GDPR are the following: privacy policies must be written in a clear, straightforward language; the data subject needs to give their expressed consent before their data can be used (silence is not consent); data collectors/businesses can process data only for a well-defined purpose[51] and they need to clearly inform the data subject when their data are transferred outside the EU and in the event of any harmful data breach; the data subject has the right to access and get a copy of the data that collectors/businesses keep about them; they also have the "right to be forgotten" (right to erasure) with clear safeguards.

While the GDPR staunchly defends privacy and creates a cogent set of rules for data collection and processing which prohibits the processing of genetic data or data concerning health (Article 9(1)), it also introduces *exceptions* related to scientific research. The processing of data for scientific research purposes is allowed when it is necessary, proportional to the aim pursued, and it respects the essence of the right

[50] Regulation (EU) 2016/679 of the European Parliament and of the Council of 27 April 2016 on the protection of natural persons with regard to the processing of personal data and on the free movement of such data, and repealing Directive 95/46/EC (General Data Protection Regulation) (2016) OJ L119, 1–88.

[51] They will have to inform the data subject about the new purposes for the processing of their data.

to data protection, provides for suitable and specific measures to safeguard the fundamental rights and the interests of the data subject, ensuring that technical and organizational measures are put in place to respect the principle of data minimization,[52] and is in accordance with EU and member states' laws[53] (Article 9(2)(j) and Article 89). The latter may introduce further conditions, including limitations to the processing of genetic data and data concerning health, as well as derogations of some of the rights of data subjects (Article 9(4) and Article 89(2)), so it is important for RIs to be well aware of the legislation of the countries where they operate and that applies to their research activities.

Another level of complexity in ensuring the legal compliance and ethics of data use is due to the proliferation of AI systems, which are now regulated in the EU under Regulation 2024/1689 (the AI Act). Although Article 2(6) of the regulation exempts AI systems and models "specifically developed and put into service for the sole purpose of scientific research and development" from its scope, RIs should develop a policy to prevent their use of such systems from having a negative impact on human rights and the values of a democratic society.

It is also worth noting that derogations that may be lawful according to the GDPR and municipal law may not necessarily be compliant with ethical principles introduced by authoritative soft law instruments.[54] It is therefore of the utmost importance for European RIs to adopt clear procedural rules and straightforward policies to deal with the ethical issues related to the use of data for research purposes. Governance choices, such as whether to establish a general ethics committee for the whole RI, may depend on several elements related to the municipal legislations involved and will have to be considered case by case, but what is certain is that experts' recourse to such bodies is today unavoidable given the growing sensitivity of the ethical problems that the scientific community is going to face in the coming years.

4 Intellectual Property Issues

4.1 Intellectual Property

The term "intellectual property" is a legal concept that refers to creations of the mind for which exclusive rights are recognized. Under intellectual property law, owners are granted certain exclusive property rights to a variety of intangible assets.

[52] Besides data minimization, the other principles that must apply to the processing of data in the EU, according to Article 5 of the GDPR, are lawfulness, fairness and transparency, purpose limitation, accuracy, storage limitation, integrity, and confidentiality.

[53] In Italy, see the Italian Data Protection Authority, Provvedimento n. 146, 5 June 2019, https://www.garanteprivacy.it/web/guest/home/docweb/-/docweb-display/docweb/9124510. Last accessed 26 March 2026.

[54] Such as the Council of Europe 2016 Recommendation, the Taipei Declaration, the Declaration of Helsinki, and the UNESCO Declaration on Human Genetic Data. For a complete survey of the main instruments, see Staunton et al. (2019).

In the absence of one agreed-upon definition of the term intellectual property, most RIs include in their statutes or governing documents a reference to the definition provided in Article 2 of the Convention Establishing the World Intellectual Property Organization 1967. The definition provides that "intellectual property" shall include rights relating to:

- Linguistic, artistic, and scientific works
- Performances of performing artists, phonograms, and broadcasts
- Inventions in all fields of human endeavour
- Scientific discoveries
- Industrial designs
- Trademarks, service marks and commercial names, and designations
- Protection against unfair competition and all other rights resulting from intellectual activity in the industrial, scientific, literary, or artistic fields

For the majority of RIs, the most relevant forms of intellectual property include patents (protecting inventions), copyright (protecting works of art), trademarks (protecting marks used in trade), and registered designs (protecting design and form). Other forms of intellectual property, such as trade secrets, plant breeders' rights, and semiconductor chip protection, appear to be less relevant for the majority of RIs and will not be discussed here.

4.2 Patents

Patents protect an invention, meaning a technical solution to a specific problem that relates to a product or a process. Patents grant exclusive rights to an inventor which restricts others from commercially using the invention. Patents are given for a defined geographical area and for a set protection period; they are accompanied by a public disclosure of the invention.

Not every invention is patentable. To qualify for patent protection, the invention must fulfil four basic conditions:

- Patentable subject matter: All kinds of inventions may be patented but there are some exceptions, for example, mere discoveries (e.g. a previously unknown substance), scientific formulas, mathematical methods and inventions contrary to public order or morality. These would not have patentable subject matter.
- Novelty: This requires that the invention does not form part of the "state of the art" and has not been disclosed or made available to the public previously (including, for example, during an oral presentation at a conference).
- Inventive step (non-obviousness): In legal terms, this means that the invention must not be "obvious to a person skilled in the art".
- Industrial applicability (utility): The invention must have some functional purpose.

4.3 Copyright

Copyright protects both the moral and economic rights of creators over their literary, scientific, and artistic works. No exhaustive list of the works that can be covered by copyright exists, but common examples include musical compositions (songs, operas, musicals, etc.), motion pictures (movies, broadcasting, cartoons, etc.), writings (novels, short stories, poems, drama, etc.), artistic works (drawings, paintings, sculptures, architectural and technical drawings, etc.), photographic and visual arts works, and probably most relevant for RIs: computer programs, databases, source code, and software.

The copyrightable work must be an original creation (not the idea, but the form in which it is expressed). In contrast to patents, no registration is needed, as copyright comes into existence merely by creating a copyrightable work. However, in some countries, there is the possibility to voluntarily register works protected by copyright, which may be useful in some situations.

4.4 Trademarks

A trademark is an exclusive right over the use of the sign for which it is registered. It consists of signs capable of distinguishing the goods or services of one trader from those of others. Trademarks may include logos, names, brands, catchphrases, images, and other categories and types of signs such as sounds and 3D models. A trademark is subject to registration and forms a valuable part of the goodwill of the business with which it is associated; it also serves as an indication of origin.

4.5 Registered Designs

Design refers to the appearance of a product, such as the shape or ornamentation of commodities (layout, graphic symbols, packaging, etc.), and it satisfies the need for the commodity to appeal visually to consumers while allowing it to perform its intended function. A registered design refers to the right granted to the design features of a product (and not the product itself). It allows the owners to exclude others from making, importing, selling, hiring, or offering products for sale that embody the registered design. Granting legal protection to designs provides an incentive to invest in the design element of production. In order to qualify for protection, the conditions of novelty and individual character must be fulfilled.

5 Concluding Remarks

To conclude this overview of the legal issues most relevant to European RIs, it might be useful to sum up the criteria that RI leaders should consider in their decision-making processes when choosing the most suitable form for/location of their infrastructure.

A starting point is of course the funds that can be disposed of and that are deemed necessary to run the infrastructure: initial capital requirements are prescribed by national company laws for specific types of companies (e.g. 50,000 euros for an spa in Italy but only 1 euro for a sarl in France), but no specific requirements are set for ERICs or international organizations. It should be considered, however, that a direct involvement of governments through the international organization form could induce them to contribute more generously to the construction and management of facilities of great economic value.

As a second step, the nature of the partners involved in the initiative should be considered: the presence of private parties will necessarily rule out the international organization form and ERICs, but national vehicles do not have such limitations.

Closely related to the first economic criterion is that of the administrative costs that can be anticipated: the different national legal environments should be compared in terms of the complexity/time needed to register a national vehicle, the amount of corporation and other taxes, the burden of red tape in the daily management of the infrastructure (e.g. in some countries, it may be difficult to open a bank account for the ERIC, even if its legal personality is a matter of fact), and employment and social security laws. These elements will also be relevant in the choice of the country most suitable to host the statutory seat of the RI.

Another element to be carefully considered is that of the governance structure of the RI: as a rule, a single-sited structure is advisable for RIs focused on the management of a specific physical facility (e.g. particle accelerators, telescopes, etc.); by contrast, the "net structure" of a distributed RI may better facilitate the common sharing of resources hosted in different hospitals, universities, or research centres.

Lastly, the rules on public procurement are also relevant for deciding on the legal form of an RI. The exemption of ERICs from the application of the EU public procurement directives (explained earlier in Sect. 2) may be of major importance if the RI requires the construction and maintenance of facilities or buildings or it may be less relevant for those RIs which essentially provide the service of networking existing units for the sharing of resources or data.

References

Cassese, S. (2009). *Il diritto globale. Giustizia e democrazia oltre lo Stato*. Einaudi.

Graber-Soudry, O. (2019). Regulating procurement by European Research Infrastructure Consortia (ERICs) and the exemption for international organisations. In X. Groussot, S. Bogojevic, & J. Hettne (Eds.), *Discretion in EU Public Procurement Law* (pp. 249–264). Hart Publishing.

Staunton, C., Slokenberga, S., & Mascalzoni, D. (2019). The GDPR and the research exemption: Considerations on the necessary safeguards for research biobanks. *European Journal of Human Genetics, 27*, 1159–1167.

von der Leyen, U. (2019). A union that strives for more: My agenda for Europe, Political guidelines for the next European Commission 2019–2024, https://ec.europa.eu/commission/sites/beta-political/files/political-guidelines-next-commission_en.pdf. Last Accessed December 14, 2025.

Service Design in Research Infrastructures

Benedetta Trivellato and Laura Mariani

Abstract

This chapter explores how Research Infrastructures (RIs) can improve the design and delivery of services they offer to diverse user communities. Adopting a service management perspective, it outlines a structured approach for analysing service processes, identifying weaknesses, and implementing effective redesign strategies. Drawing on examples from RI services, the chapter illustrates how gaps emerge in service provision and how redesign strategies can address them. Emphasizing user-centred design, it highlights the importance of understanding user needs and managing interactions across both standardized and customized services.

1 Research Infrastructures as Service Providers

Research infrastructures (RIs) are often complex organizations that provide services to a variety of external as well as internal users. As we focus on how such services may be subject to evaluation and redesign, we rely on a definition of services that sees them as economic activities embedding an exchange of value between two parties, and which from the perspective of the customer/user/purchaser can be seen as 'benefits without ownership' (Lovelock & Wirtz, 2016). In a service transaction, a payment is made for using or accessing something—usually for a defined period of time—instead of buying it outright and/or to allow participation in network systems

B. Trivellato (✉)
Department of Sociology and Social Research, University of Milano-Bicocca, Milan, Italy
e-mail: benedetta.trivellato@unimib.it

L. Mariani
Department of Management, University of Bergamo, Bergamo, Italy
e-mail: laura.mariani@unibg.it

E. Guarini et al. (eds.), *Research Infrastructure Management*, Management for Professionals, https://doi.org/10.1007/978-3-032-20373-1_8

that individuals and organizations cannot afford. In this perspective, services are seen as forms of rentals of a physical good (a car, a fancy dress costume), of a defined place or space (a seat in an aircraft, storage space in a warehouse), or labour and expertise (house cleaning, management consulting), or they are seen as forms of access to shared physical environments (theme parks, toll roads) or forms of access to and usage of systems and networks (telecommunications, utilities, banking). RIs provide services that fall in all these categories, sometimes even integrating several categories into a bundle of services. For instance, a service that includes access to an e-infrastructure together with training and expert support for its use combines labour and expertise rental with access and usage of networks. The analysis of an ancient monument or a fragile artefact through a mobile laboratory performed by an employee of the RI involves again rental of labour and expertise, with that of the tools that are part of the mobile laboratory. Most services provided by RIs are supplied to users that are external to the organization, but this is not always necessarily the case. For instance, a European RI that provides high performance computing resources to life science researchers over a platform allows access to both external users and researchers within the RI itself.

Because of changes in technology, customer needs, and regulation, the services provided by RIs can—like those of any other organization—become obsolete, inefficient, or irrelevant over time. There are two main reasons why service processes deteriorate (Lovelock & Wirtz, 2016). First, the changes in the external environment make existing practices obsolete. This means that the organization must redesign the underlying processes and sometimes create new processes to remain relevant and responsive. The second reason is organizational and reflects a natural weakening of internal processes or the development of unofficial standards. Symptoms that the processes are not working properly include the following: (1) the increase in the number of information exchanges with the customer and between organizational units, since available data are not useful; (2) an increase in the ratio between control activities and those with high added value; (3) higher demand for better exception handling; and (4) an increasing number of customer complaints about procedures that are deemed inconvenient or unnecessary.

By adopting a service management perspective, the aim of this chapter is to propose a set of tools that can be useful to support service redesign in RIs, so as to improve quality, efficiency, and effectiveness in service provision both for external and internal users. We propose a four-step approach where services are described as a sequence of interrelated phases, which also allows to identify possible weaknesses along the process, the causes of such gaps, and potential solutions to improve service quality in terms of both efficiency and effectiveness.

2 Service Redesign as a Process

Services may be seen from a process perspective, that is, as a sequence of phases where people perform certain activities as they interact with artefacts and their surrounding environment. These phases do not need to remain the same over time, nor does their sequence, their actors, or their defining features. However, seeing the service as a process may be extremely helpful when approaching its design, and eventually its redesign.

In very general terms, the service process may be seen as a recurrent sequence of phases, beginning with the choice of process type. Here the main distinction is among the categories that have been identified by Lovelock and Wirtz (2016) as they propose a categorization based on two dimensions: the nature of the service act and the recipient of the service (see below for further details). Whether the service under consideration falls into one or another of these categories is relevant, as each has specific implications for the factors to focus on during process design. The subsequent macrophases then involve the design and then the implementation of the service process. This is to be complemented by a system for monitoring and evaluating the service process itself, so as to check that it remains effective and does not become obsolete. Whenever such monitoring and evaluation highlight an opportunity or a need for change, the next step involves a redesign of the process. This may be so radical as to lead to a different choice of process type, or to a redesign of the process while the type remains the same.

As mentioned above, the two dimensions along which services may be classified are (1) the nature of the service act, consisting of tangible or intangible actions, and (2) the recipient of the service, that is, whether the direct recipients of the service are people as opposed to their possessions. Combining these two dimensions yields four categories: people processing, possession processing, mental stimulus processing, and information processing.

Services that fall in the category of 'people processing' are those that are directed at people's bodies, i.e. the nature of the service act is tangible, and the recipient is a person usually in a way that involves their body. This category of services is rarely provided by RIs; examples of such services rather include the following: transport of people, medical care, hotels, restaurants, gyms, hairdressers, funeral parlours, etc. Factors that need to be taken into account in the design of the service process include the fact that customers must physically enter the service factory, with the related attention to be given to its functionality and aesthetics, although sometimes the supplier is willing to move with his tools (as in the case of the hairdresser or the medical doctor who visits the client/patient at their homes). Also, appropriate procedures need to be built into the process that ensure that the clients/users cooperate actively with the service operation—for instance, they need to express their wish in relation to their desired haircut, or the symptoms of a disease. Also, the length of stay in the service factory may vary, as shown by the difference between a few minutes' bus ride and a months-long stay in the hospital. This implies that physical and functional features of the environment need to be planned appropriately in the case of extended lengths, but also that a certain degree of discomfort is likely to be accepted by users when such length is short (e.g. in the case of standing places in the bus). The more general implication is that designers and managers should think about the service process and output from the customer's perspective, so as to clarify as much as possible the benefits and the non-financial costs that are generated in terms of time, and also in terms of mental and physical effort.

Services that fall in the category of 'possession processing' are those that are directed at people's possessions, i.e. the nature of the service act is tangible, and the recipient is a person's possession, which may include an inanimate object, but also an animal or a plant. Examples of such services include semi-manufacturing operations in which there is no simultaneity, such as cleaning, maintenance, storage or repair of physical objects; transport, storage, wholesale or retail distribution of goods; etc. Here the involvement of the person as the possession's owner is much more limited than in the previous case, as it is mostly limited to the delivery and the collection of the possession. The interaction usually involves the request for a service that is often relatively standardized, and the payment. The fact that the client's physical involvement is much lower than in the previous case has significant implications when planning the physical appearance of the service factory. Moreover, its functionality and layout should be based on the needs and the convenience of the service provider rather than those of the client. Contrary to what happens in case of several services, including those in the previous category where service production and consumption are simultaneous, in this case, the two actions are separable, i.e. they take place at different times and places. The production phase can then be timed and structured in a more flexible way relative to the case when the customer is directly involved in the production process, either physically or mentally. On the other hand, in certain cases, the customer may want to participate in the production process or at least supervise it (e.g. in the mowing of a lawn or the bathing of a dog).

Services that fall in the category of 'mental stimulus processing' are those that are directed at people's mind, i.e. the nature of the service act is intangible, and the recipient is the person him/herself. Examples of such services include advertising, entertainment, consulting, education, news and information, psychotherapy, etc. A critical issue here from the perspective of process design is the fact that what touches the mind has the power to shape attitudes and influence behaviour, and therefore ethical standards are required because customers might be manipulated. The physical presence of the recipients is often not required, as opposed to people-processing services; however, the physical presence can make the difference in terms of quality of the customer's experience. This is the case, for instance, of a lecture or a concert, which can be attended in person but also at a distance, e.g., through television or a computer. Moreover, the core content of the services is information-based: the service can therefore, to a certain extent, be stocked and 'inventoried', e.g. saved as a video file and then stored or transferred to other users.

Services that fall in the category of 'information processing' are those that are directed at people's possession, but where the nature of the service act is intangible. Examples of such services include banking services, accounting, marketing services, management consulting, legal services, and medical diagnosis services. In fact, this is the most intangible form of service, because it usually involves the processing and/or transformation of information; at the same time, the results of such actions may be transformed into enduring forms of output, such as reports, books, videos—which are not only tangible (when not implemented in electronic form), but can be stocked to be consumed at different times.

Services provided by RIs fall mostly into the last three categories, and often span across their boundaries. For instance, specimens that are sent on loan to researchers belong to possession processing but also to information processing in all those cases where specimens are available in digital form. The analysis of an ancient monument or a fragile artefact through a mobile laboratory also corresponds to possession processing. On the other hand, access to an e-infrastructure together with Helpdesk support and training may be seen as information processing as far as data treatment is concerned, and as mental stimulus processing when support and training are provided for the handling, interpretation, or analysis of the data. Or again, a service that allows scientists to screen large collections of chemicals, so as to identify those with the specific features that are useful for them, falls into the category of information processing.

2.1 Service Description: Flowcharting the Process

The above-described classification is useful to see the implications for process design of certain features of services, but also to focus on certain characteristics of the service process when using a specific tool: the service process flowchart. The flowchart is a technique to represent the nature and sequence of the different steps that constitute the service process. It helps clarify what the constituent elements of the product/service are, and it offers a way to understand the overall customer service experience, and to identify potential failure points. It shows how customer engagement varies according to service categories (people, possession, mental stimulus, and information processing), with the related implications in terms of physical artefact and actions that need to be planned and implemented around the customer.

An example is provided by an RI which constitutes the national-level node of a EU-wide organization that is active in the provision of life-science resources, including databases, software tools, training materials, cloud storage, and supercomputers. Users vary from inexperienced clinical PhD students requiring help on how to analyse or upload data to the e-infrastructure, to experienced bioinformaticians needing assistance with sensitive data or with the technical details of a certain analysis. Among their services is a ‘bioinformatics user support’ service which includes both expert advice by the RI’s Helpdesk and technical solutions and tools provided through their e-infrastructure.

Figure 1 exemplifies the depiction of a flowchart for this service. The shaded box on the right shows the actions that allow the customer’s need to be fulfilled; the upper boxes represent the phases of the process as the customer goes through them, whereas the lower boxes with the dotted boundaries represent actions that need to be taken by the service providers, often in the back-end of the service process. These actions, however, are crucial for the customer’s need to be fulfilled. The arrows depict the flow of action or information from one step to another.

The process begins when a user experiences the need for bioinformatics support, and learns about the services provided by the RI. In most cases, the user contacts the RI after the experiment has been performed and the raw data has been generated,

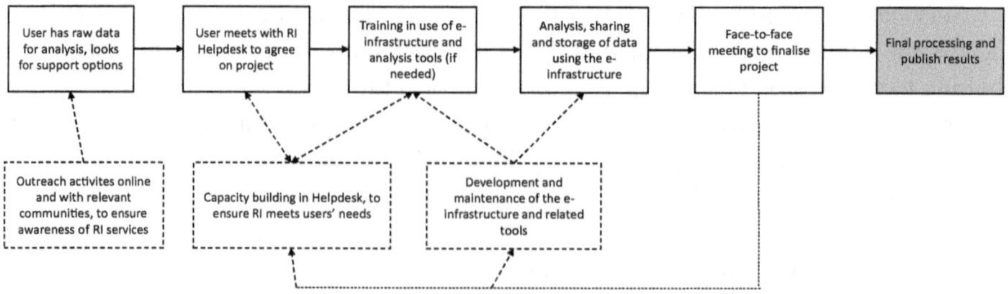

Fig. 1 Flowchart of a 'bioinformatics user support' service. Authors' elaboration

though the RI prefers to have the first meeting prior to data generation, so that the experiment may be optimally designed together with the user (this would imply a switch between the first two boxes). In order for users to identify the RI as service provider, the RI needs to perform outreach activities online and with relevant communities and data-generating core facilities, as shown in the lower box on the left. The second step in the user's journey involves a face-to-face meeting between the user and members of the Helpdesk, in order to define the project, discuss options for the analysis, and give advice. At this point, the user may be satisfied with the advice and proceed to analyse the data herself, or she may realize that she does not have the necessary expertise, and will take advantage of 2 days of service that are provided free of charge by the RI; or, the user may realize that she needs more extensive support, and therefore purchases a service contract from the Helpdesk. Back-end activities for this step include capacity building internally in the Helpdesk, to ensure the RI has the expertise that the users need. The third step may or may not occur, depending on whether the user needs training in the use of the e-infrastructure. The back-end activities that are required to support this step are, as depicted in the lower part of the figure, capacity building within the Helpdesk, and development and maintenance of the e-infrastructure. This latter activity is also crucial for the fourth step of the user's journey, where she analyses, shares, and stores her data using the e-infrastructure. The fifth step involves another face-to-face meeting between the Helpdesk staff and the user, so as to discuss the results of the analysis and the possible ways forward. Any feedback given by the user together with the results of this phase is used to improve the back-end activities of Helpdesk capacity building and e-infrastructure development, as shown by the dotted arrows which link the fifth phase to the back-end activities. Finally, in the last step of the process, the user performs the final processing of the data and publishes her results.

2.2 Identifying Weaknesses in the Service Process: The Service Quality Gaps

Quality can mean different things to people depending on the context (Lovelock & Wirtz, 2016). For instance, the *transcendent approach* views quality as excellence, and is often applied in the case of visual and performing arts. It is based on the assumption that people learn to recognize quality as they are repeatedly exposed to it; however, this approach is not particularly useful from a management point of view. The *manufacturing-based approach*, on the other hand, focuses especially on engineering and manufacturing practices, and therefore sees quality as delivery against standards that are measurable, with certain levels of tolerance. In the case of services, it focuses on how a service conforms to certain specifications, which are usually aligned with goals related to productivity and cost containment. A third, *user-based approach* highlights the idea that quality lies in the eyes of the beholder: it is a subjective perspective, acknowledging that people have different needs. Finally, the *value-based approach* defines quality in terms of trade-off between price paid and the value that is offered.

In the case of services, their nature makes it more difficult to assess quality than in the case of a physical good. Also, clients are often involved in the production of a service. This implies that it is useful to distinguish between the service provision process and its outcome. Moreover, perceived quality in the case of services tends to be the result of an evaluation process where clients compare their perceptions of the actual service provision with their expectations. The main dimensions of service quality have been categorized by a number of scholars as follows (Parasuraman et al., 1985):

- Tangible aspects have to do with the appearance of physical elements (Is the outlook of the restaurant pleasant? Is the consultant dressed appropriately?)
- Reliability has to do with the capacity to provide what has been promised in an accurate manner (Does the lawyer call back as she promised? Has the computer been repaired correctly and definitely?)
- Responsiveness has to do with the capacity to respond promptly (When there's a problem, do service employees address it rapidly? Is the plumber communicating the timing of his arrival?)
- Assurance includes various dimensions such as competence, courtesy, credibility, and security (Is the operator of the call centre polite? Is the ATM designed so as to ensure the client's security when he withdraws money?)
- Empathy deals with easy access, good communication, and understanding of the customer (Is there an email or phone contact when something goes wrong? Does the hotel manager recognize returning clients?)

Once the main dimensions of service quality have been introduced, we may consider a model that allows to identify and correct service quality problems at the overall firm level. The Gap model (see Fig. 2) identifies 5 potential gaps within the service organization, and these may lead to the sixth and most serious final gap: that is the difference between what customers expected and what they perceive was delivered (Parasuraman et al., 1985).

The figure shows the gaps that can occur at different points during the design and delivery of a service performance. The first is the *knowledge gap*, that is, the difference between what senior management believes that the customer expects, and what the customer actually needs and expects. The second is the *standards gap*, which is

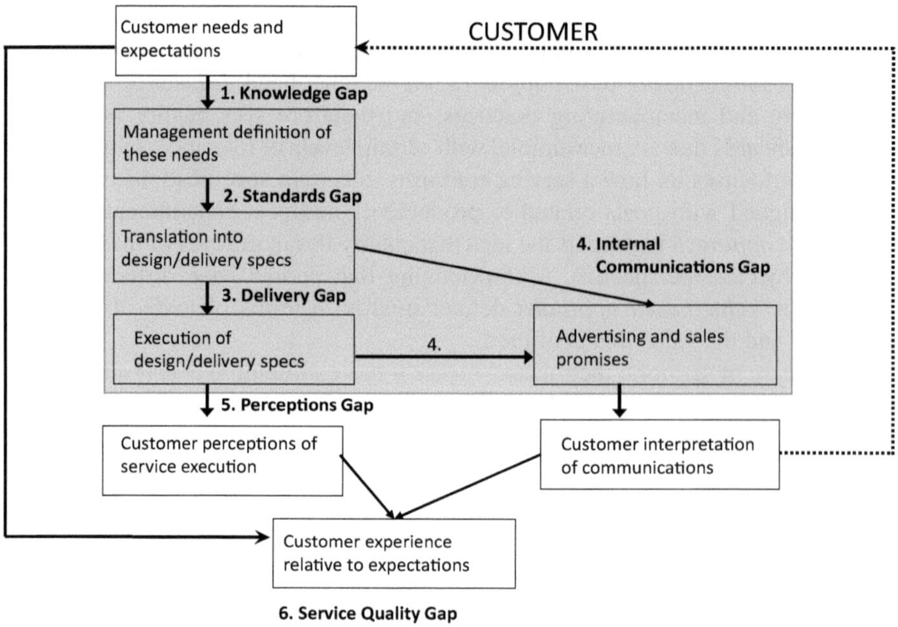

Fig. 2 The Gap Model. Adapted from Parasuraman et al. (1985), Lovelock and Wirtz (2016)

the difference between the management's understanding of the expectations of the customers, and the service standards that they set for service delivery. It is also sometimes called 'policy gap' because it tends to reflect a policy to set standards below customer expectations, because of cost and feasibility considerations. Next is the *delivery gap*, that is, the difference between specified service standards and the actual performance of the delivery team on these standards. The fourth is the *communications gap*, that is, the difference between what the company communicates, and what the customer understands and then experiences. This is followed by the *perceptions gap*, that is, the difference between what is actually delivered and what customers feel they have received, because they are unable to judge service quality accurately. The sixth—the *service quality gap—is* the difference between what customers expect to receive and their perception of the service that is actually delivered. In this model, gaps 1, 5, and 6 represent external gaps between the customer and the organization, whereas gaps 2, 3, and 4 are internal gaps occurring between various functions and departments within the organization.

These gaps may occur in various forms in the case of RIs. As an example, we can consider the case of one European RI that provides access to specimens that are held by more than 100 institutions across Europe: the transnational access service allows researchers to request a specimen to be sent to them, retain it for a certain period of time for research purposes, and then to return it.

A knowledge gap occurs because most natural scientific collections are not yet digitized, with the implication that researchers need to get in contact with individual collection experts to find out which specimens are available. As institutes often do not have defined procedures on response time, a request may remain unanswered for a certain time if the person in charge is on holiday; or it may not be clear who is the relevant person in charge, or what is the policy for approving or rejecting a loan request. There is no clear indication of how a complaint (if any) may be submitted, or to whom.

A standards/policy gap, on the other hand, occurs because the policy for granting loans is not always clear, nor is the national legislation that applies. The website may specify that certain specimens—e.g. those that are fragile, rare, or very large—may not be sent, but other unofficial procedures may apply: for instance, a researcher may see his request rejected if he already has a high number of objects on loan, or if he has damaged objects during previous loans, or if similar specimens are available in his own country. Moreover, given that loans are registered in different systems, a comprehensive and precise overview of the state of the loans at any moment is lacking. It follows that requests for objects that are already on loan may be approved by a person who is not aware of this.

A delivery gap sometimes occurs when an institute sets certain standards, but then does not meet or monitor them. For instance, they may declare that they do not lend a certain specimen, while in practice they do. A request may be forgotten or directed to a person who does not work at the institute anymore; information on loans may be stored in a registry that cannot be accessed by the person in charge of the decision on a certain loan. Alternatively, that person may not have the technical skills to access the system and generate a report.

A communication gap may occur if an institute declares that it accepts loan requests at a global level, but then its employees only speak the local language well, and are not very familiar with the regulations applying to specimens being sent to certain countries.

A perception gap may occur when a request for a loan is met and approved, but the researcher does not receive communications regularly and does not have opportunities to give feedback once the loan is completed.

Overall, the extent of the difference between what customers expect to receive and their perception of the service that is actually delivered—i.e. the overall service quality gap—depends on the extent and magnitude of the above-mentioned intermediate gaps.

2.3 Identifying the Sources of Quality Gaps Using the Fishbone Diagram

Once certain quality gaps have been acknowledged, the next step is to identify their causes. By understanding the nature of the misalignments in the service delivery process, it is possible to find possible solutions during the redesign phase. Table 1 exemplifies the connections between the three phases through the case of a RI that provides facilities for the production and analysis of the metabolism data of the whole cell in a given time.

Table 1 Gaps' causes and proposed solutions in the case of an RI providing metabolism-related services

No	Quality gap	Cause	Solution
1	Knowledge gap	Market is mostly unexplored	Perform market research about the market. Each service request should become a source of information about clients' requirements
2	Policy gap	There are no official policies concerning communication towards users	Specific policies for each step of the service pipeline should be detailed
3	Delivery gap	Users often use the service to validate theory. Mismatch between expectations and actual results causes disbelief	Users should be trained and given proper information. Informal training sessions to explain how the analysis is carried out and which outcomes are to be expected

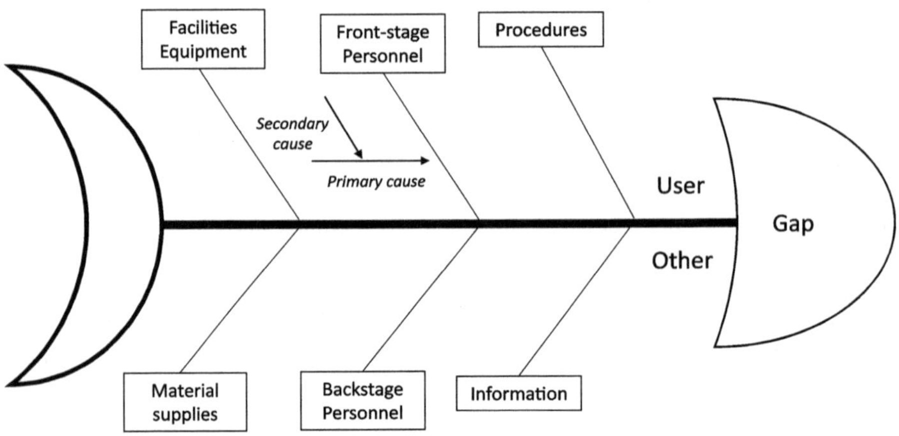

Fig. 3 The fishbone diagram. Authors' elaboration on the basis of Lovelock and Wirtz (2016)

A tool that can be used to identify the sources of quality gaps is the 'fishbone diagram' (see Fig. 3), a cause-and-effect diagram that was first developed for manufacturing and then extended to services (Lovelock & Wirtz, 2016). Groups of managers and staff brainstorm all the possible reasons that might cause a specific problem, with the resulting reasons then grouped into one of the following 8 groupings: procedures, information, frontstage personnel, backstage personnel, facilities equipment, material supplies, customers, and, lastly, other causes. Certain categories are especially important in the case of services, as opposed to manufacturing. For instance, the possible causes related to employees' behaviours need to be distinguished between frontstage personnel, where problems are experienced directly by customers, and backstage personnel, where failures tend to emerge indirectly. Information needs to be separated from procedures, to recognize the fact that many service failures are due to information failures. For instance, they happen because frontstage personnel do not have readily the required information, or do not tell customers what to do and when to do it. Lastly, an important source of root causes is represented by customers in the case of services (while this is generally not the case for manufacturing). Customers are very often involved in frontstage operations in various ways. If they don't play their role correctly, they may reduce productivity and may cause quality problems for themselves and other customers.

The already mentioned RI that supplies specimens may be used once again as an example. Here the quality gaps may result in delays affecting one or more phases of the service process, when not in the request being lost or rejected despite being eligible for the loan. Possible sources of problems that are identified through the fishbone diagram include the following. In terms of *procedures*, as there are no clear guidelines in relation to international regulations, and as specimens are often difficult to be given a value, they are often shipped with a 'no value' label, with the related risk of being destroyed by customs or subject to other problems. As for the *information* category, reliance on outdated forms may lead to redundant or poor communication that can cause delays in responding to a request, or a missed opportunity to receive valuable customer feedback. As for sources related to *frontstage personnel* behaviour or their characteristics, language barriers may affect the quality of communication, lack of capacity may lead to late reactions, and finally poor alignment with backstage personnel may lead to confusion in communication if the user happens to receive information also from backstage personnel. The latter, *backstage personnel*, may be hindered by not having the necessary authorization to make decisions, or may suffer from resource constraints (e.g. limited number of personnel involved in the task and/or shared with other tasks and therefore may not be always available). *Facilities equipment* may be a source of service quality problems if no specific helpdesk tool is available to effectively register the requests, assign them to the relevant personnel, and/or monitor their progress. If no system is available to provide a comprehensive view of the collections, additional time may be needed to verify whether a certain request can be accepted. *Material supplies*, on the other hand, may be a source of problems whenever different systems are used depending on the purpose of the loan—e.g. for research or for exhibitions—with the related late discovery that a certain object is already on loan. A poor collection management system may not properly highlight the fact that a certain specimen needs additional administration, digitization, or preparation before it can be shipped, thereby causing further delays. Finally, *customers* may also be a source of service quality problems if they do not express their needs or requests effectively, which may also be the consequence of insufficient guidance on how to make a request. Other external causes refer to all those events that may negatively impact on the shipping of the specimen, including delays or disruptions in the postal service, or the unavailability of a tracking system.

In addition to the fishbone diagram, the flowchart described above can also be used to identify potential fail points where failures are most likely to occur, and also how failures at one point may have a ripple effect on the later stages of the process. Once the fail points are identified, frequency counts can be added to check which failures happen most frequently, and therefore need urgent attention. The best solution would be to design fail points out of the system. When this is not possible—for instance, when problems are related to delays in the postal services in the previous example—managers should develop adequate contingency plans and service recovery guidelines. In the case of the RI supplying specimens, potential fail points include the following: wrong institute contacted; loan not approved; high number of people involved in communication and information transmission leading to misunderstandings; dependency on external delivery service for the specimen to reach the final user. Once these potential fail points have been identified, options for service recovery actions may be explored and subsequently planned. For instance, it may be planned that a non-approval decision requires double-check of a list of possible motives, and that a structured explanation be sent to the requester.

2.4 Guidelines for Effective Service Redesign

As mentioned in the first section, even when service processes are effective at the time they are designed and implemented, they are likely to become outdated over time because of changes in technology, in customer needs, new service offerings, or even because changes in legislation make existing processes inefficient or irrelevant. Service process redesign may then become appropriate, when not necessary, and can be carried out by reliance on one or more of the following approaches.

A first approach relates to eliminating non-value-adding steps in the service delivery process. Consider the request form that is usually a critical tool for most RIs, and the related knowledge management system: often the form can be redesigned so that certain sections do not need to be filled by all users, or so that certain information is supplied by the user only at the time of his/her first request, in case of repeated interaction with the same RI. A similar approach may be adopted to eliminate steps in the decision-making process, for instance, when the frontline personnel is empowered with tasks such as checking the eligibility of a request and making the related decisions. This approach improves users' experience insofar as they avoid unnecessary steps and are less likely to experience delays; it may also help improve efficiency and productivity, as intermediate steps that require the use of internal resources (human or physical) are eliminated or reduced.

A second approach relates to adopting self-service technologies that allow customers to perform certain steps (or the entire service process) on their own. In the case of RIs, this may include web-based systems which allow the prospective user to check whether a certain specimen or data analysis system is available, and at what conditions and user requirements, with a related estimate of the total service provision time once all the relevant information has been supplied. The prospective users may then assess by themselves whether the service is indeed available at that point in time and whether they are eligible to access it—thereby relieving the RI's personnel from performing these tasks—and may benefit from improved user experience due to greater awareness of what they are to expect. Benefits for the RI relate to increases in productivity, because a number of steps that were carried out by the service provider are now carried out directly by the customer, but also increases in service quality because the customer is not required to wait until certain tasks are performed by the RI's personnel. Self-service technologies imply lower costs for the service provider and therefore possibly also lower prices for customers. The use of self-service may also enhance the technology reputation of the company, which then becomes another point of differentiation and attraction especially with certain targets of customers. Still, companies that decide to follow this path need to remember that customers appreciate self-service technologies when they work as expected. Service providers should ensure that they are user-friendly, that instructions are clear and not too long and complicated, and that they make clear what the customer can do and who she can contact (and how) if something doesn't work as expected.

A third approach has to do with redesigning the service delivery process so that the provider goes to the customer, and not vice versa. This may improve quality for the customer because of higher convenience. Productivity can be improved by eliminating the costs related to establishment and maintenance of physical locations where the service is supplied, and can also translate into lower costs for the user. This solution may also increase the customer base in terms of reaching groups of consumers who could not be otherwise reached, as they would not visit the service provider. In the case of RIs this may involve, for instance, the RI's personnel being able to visit the user to provide training or support in the use of a tool, a database, or a technology, especially if the user's need requires close integration between her own (or her institution's) resources and the expertise provided by the RI's personnel. In other cases, the object of the analysis cannot be moved from its location, as in the case of ancient monuments or buildings, or would be too costly or risky to move, as in the case of a fragile artefact. The RI's personnel, equipped with a mobile laboratory, may then visit the user and provide the relevant service on site.

A fourth approach relates to the bundling of services. This involves grouping multiple services into one offer, focusing on a well-defined customer group. When they are well designed, these bundles increase satisfaction as they are customized to the needs of that particular target. They also increase per capita service use, as they often include services that specific target client may not have chosen if they were left to their free choice. Another benefit relates to the increase in productivity with customized service: customization is usually appreciated by customers as it fits their specific needs, but it can become costly for the service provider if it's too widespread and left to the initiative of the customer. With bundling, the customization is designed into the delivery process so that it can be offered in the most efficient and productive way. In the case of RIs, this may include offering bundles based on typical profiles of users, e.g. PhDs or inexperienced users who may need research support and training in the use of an e-infrastructure in addition to the 'basic' service that consists of just accessing the e-infrastructure to perform a certain data analysis.

Lastly, providers may redesign physical aspects of service processes, including facilities and equipment. These solutions may increase convenience for customers because they make certain aspects of the service easier to use or to access, or waiting times less burdensome. These solutions may also positively affect the satisfaction and productivity of the frontline staff, which in turn affects customer satisfaction. They may cultivate interest in customers because physical aspects are visible and tangible, which is often not the case with several dimensions of service processes. This means that they contribute to attracting potential customers, and reduce the risk and reluctance that are linked to what cannot be seen. In the case of RIs, this approach includes the redesign of tools that are used for research so as to make them more user-friendly, effective, or efficient (for instance, in terms of the time needed to reach a certain result, or in terms of the data to be supplied as input for the analysis). In those cases where the researcher needs to visit the RI's premises to get access to a physical good or to an e-infrastructure, the spaces devoted to these activities may be redesigned in their shape, availability of individual cubicles or workstations, flexibility and modularity of tables and seating, lighting, etc., so as to improve the user's experience in terms of maximizing the effectiveness and/or efficiency of the time spent.

3 Designing User-Centred Services: Challenges for Research Infrastructures

Research infrastructures provide a variety of services that to different extents require face-to-face and/or remote interaction. Remote interactions are more easily and usefully standardized, with a relatively lower level of customization, whereas face-to-face interactions are more likely to be characterized by a certain level of customization, and relatively low standardization. As we focus on these specific aspects, the managerial implications that can be drawn by reflecting on the experience of a number of European RIs are different in the two instances.

In the case of relatively standardized services that are provided mainly through remote interaction, a good practice for RIs who are designing or redesigning such services is to involve users in the definition of the standards and in the identification of possible alternative paths in the fruition of the service. This is recommended in order to minimize the risk of exceptions that would make the standardization fruitless. Secondly, intermediate and final users should be trained in the use of the service: this implies setting comprehensible and user-friendly directions, suited to users with different levels of expertise if needed, and also clear instructions on what to do and who can be contacted should anything go wrong along the process. At the same time, those involved in the design of relatively standardized services should keep in mind that users are located in different parts of Europe and possibly spread at a wider international scale, with the implication that a certain level of adaptation to local needs and/or regulations may be appropriate.

Customized services should rely on a flexible use of internal resources, both human and material to the extent possible, so that the service process does not experience delays or interruptions if the person in charge of a certain step is unavailable. Technology, including databases or customer relationship management systems, may to some extent substitute for human actions—for instance, to track the specimen loan history of the researchers belonging to a certain organization—but they need to be maintained and updated in order to be effective. A second insight relates to the convenience of developing network relations with other organizations, both service users and providers. These networks can be relied upon to increase the above-mentioned flexibility as needed, and to access additional resources that the organization may not consider possible or convenient to hold directly.

Within the various steps of the analysis and redesign of the service process, the role of the user is of critical importance. Thus, redefining a service requires managing the relationship with the user in the perspective of customer experience management, where the frontline staff becomes particularly important relative to the middle and top management. In this context, the RI is called to study the user's experience whenever there is an interaction with the RI itself, and to design its offer of services with a particular focus on the user's viewpoint. In fact, adopting a user-centred design approach implies trying to understand not only the users' needs and wishes, but also the constraints they face, the factors that support their motivation, and more generally what is important to them. A further key element relates to the emotional dimension, which is also influenced by the tangible components of the service. Users may be upset by the results of a data analysis service that does not return the expected outcome: this cannot be changed, but the RI can supply expertise or a support service to direct the researchers' efforts. A physical environment that is structured in a certain way influences users' behaviour as well as their sensations: redesigning a laboratory in one way rather than another creates different possibilities for interaction and user experience. User-centred design, therefore, allows one to remember that the functional characteristics of a space are as important as those that are related to emotions. At the same time, this approach also implies recognizing that there may be different solutions to a problem or need, that they should be taken into consideration—at least in a certain number—and then compared. One or more of the solutions that are more promising can thus be translated into a prototype, which can be put to the test of users in their environments, so as to check possible changes or improvements. This triggers an iterative process which, through continuous transformations, ultimately leads to a configuration of the service that represents the most effective response to a certain need, within the inevitable constraints, until the changes inherent in the passage of time will suggest the opportunity for a new redesign.

References

Lovelock, J., & Wirtz, C. (2016). *Services marketing. People, technology, strategy* (8th ed.). World Scientific.

Parasuraman, A., Valarie A. Zeithaml, & Leonard L. Berry. (1985). A conceptual model of service quality and its implications for future research. *The Journal of Marketing, 49*(4), 41–50.

Sustainable Funding in EMPHASIS as a Distributed Research Infrastructure

Sven Fahrner and Roland Pieruschka

Abstract

This chapter outlines the development of an initial sustainable business and funding framework for EMPHASIS, a distributed ESFRI Research Infrastructure dedicated to multi-scale plant phenotyping, at the end of its Preparatory Phase. The developed framework is intended to provide decision-making support for ministries representing potential members of EMPHASIS in its Operational Phase. Responding to global challenges such as population growth, climate change, and increasing demands for food and renewable resources, EMPHASIS aims to enhance access to advanced phenotyping facilities, data resources, and modelling tools across Europe. A comprehensive landscape analysis—drawing on previous EU projects, national initiatives, workshops, and stakeholder consultations—identified major user groups and nearly 200 potential installations, forming the basis for a demand-driven service portfolio. Towards the end of the Preparatory Phase, seven Functional Units have been proposed to structure these services, addressing access, quality standards, data management, innovation support, communication, training, and coordination. To ensure long-term viability, the chapter presents a methodology for constructing funding scenarios for the Operational Phase. Three models are proposed for EMPHASIS, ranging from full to minimal service coverage, each based on explicit assumptions regarding personnel, overheads, service costs, and Member State contributions.

S. Fahrner (✉) · R. Pieruschka
Institute of Plant Sciences (IBG-2), Forschungszentrum Jülich, Jülich, Germany
e-mail: s.fahrner@fz-juelich.de; r.pieruschka@fz-juelich.de

E. Guarini et al. (eds.), *Research Infrastructure Management*, Management for Professionals, https://doi.org/10.1007/978-3-032-20373-1_9

1 Introduction

EMPHASIS (European Infrastructure for Multi-scale Plant Phenomics and Simulation)[1] is a distributed Research Infrastructure (RI) that was listed on the ESFRI Roadmap in 2016 (ESFRI Roadmap, 2016[2]) and started the Preparatory Phase in 2017 with one of the key goals to develop a business plan for implementation and future operations. A distributed RI such as EMPHASIS has dedicated characteristics driven by Central Service providers and interlinked National Nodes with key elements such as: i) legal status and a governance structure; ii) coordination competences and resources to the Central Service providers; iii) access policy; iv) dedicated user strategy; v) measurable key performance indicators (KPI) addressing the effectiveness; vi) human resources policy; vii) joint investment strategy aimed at strengthening the RI (for more details, see: ESFRI Roadmap, 2018[3]). These key elements of an RI need to be outlined in a business plan including a sound and sustainable funding framework to enable excellent and innovative services highly demanded by different stakeholders. Additionally, it is rather essential to take the specific requirements and characteristics of an RI into account, in case of EMPHASIS to enable utilisation of services related to plant phenotyping that requires access to physical and virtual infrastructures and harness innovation. In this chapter, we will outline the approach of EMPHASIS to identify strategic options of the key elements of a business plan for excellence-driven operation of a distributed infrastructure, and as key part of it a sustainable business framework supporting implementation and operation. These business plan options are supposed to be a decision-making support for potential future legal owners of the infrastructure, i.e. national ministries.

The strategic options presented here depict a very preliminary first draft that illustrates the potential EMPHASIS business and has been developed long before negotiations with ministries started. It is worth stressing that the presented funding framework scenarios are intended to illustrate the methodology of its development, being based on a large number of assumptions that will need to be modified once entering discussions with national ministries or funding bodies. The presented concrete monetary values thus need to be interpreted as very preliminary and as a very first starting point for discussions with funders, expected to be strongly adapted according to the expectations of the future EMPHASIS member countries.

2 Demand for Plant Phenotyping

Several complex and interconnected megatrends raise the requirement for enhancements in the quantity and quality of crop production contributing to a sustainable bioeconomy: increased demand for high-quality food and feed production, demand for an increase in green energy production, demand for natural resources, while

[1] https://emphasis.plant-phenotyping.eu/ project and RI website.

[2] https://www.esfri.eu/roadmap-2016 Strategy Report on RIs.

[3] http://roadmap2018.esfri.eu/.

there is no additional arable land and climate change posing additional pressure (Serraj et al., 2019). With the world population steadily growing and reaching an estimated 9 billion by 2050, food production will have to double for major crops while enabling nutritious diet for all. At the same time, climate change will have severe impacts on resource availability for crop production in Europe and beyond. Regions that already suffer from resource limitation often depend on agricultural production for economic and social stability. A sustainable intensification of crop production is one of the central aims to address these grand challenges (FAO, 2017). However, no major land reserves remain available for farming, raising the requirement to increase agricultural production by yield increases. This requires innovations and advancements in breeding to generate new crop varieties.

Creating new varieties in plant breeding is a long-term process, as developing and bringing new varieties to the markets may take up 15 years or even more. Breeding and genetic crop improvements in Europe have already generated an additional social welfare gain of almost EUR 9 billion in the agricultural sector alone and further benefits of plant breeding next to sustainable yield increases are the improvement of conditions on international markets, increasing the potential world food supply, reducing CO_2 emissions, etc. (Noleppa, 2016). However, further effort is needed and one major bottleneck in speeding up this process is the quantitative assessment of a plant phenotype (Furbank & Tester, 2011). The phenotype of an organism develops from the interaction of this organism with its environment from its very early stages until the end of its life (Houle et al., 2010). The phenotype of a plant determines the structural and functional processes of a plant that develops dynamically in an environment defining the yield, biomass quality, efficient use of water and nutrients, resistance to diseases and pests, etc. This poses challenges to record a multitude of spatial and temporal dimensions of plant traits that are necessary to understand the development of a specific phenotype. Additionally, plant phenotyping needs to take into account that there are many species that have a very diverse habitus, design in contrast to, e.g., medicine, which "only" considers a single species with very limited variability (Pieruschka & Schurr, 2019). Therefore, establishment and application of phenotyping technologies and protocols are urgently needed for quantitative assessment of a plant phenotype with the required throughput (Furbank & Tester, 2011).

Novel opportunities to address these challenges have been developed specifically during the last nearly two decades or so through novel sensors, automation, and quantitative data analysis (e.g. Fiorani & Schurr, 2013). First plant phenotyping installations that allowed a high-throughput assessment of relevant plant characteristics started with the model plant *Arabidopsis* over a decade ago with a sufficient number of genotypes providing the opportunity to associate traits to the genetic make-up of a plant in a variety of environmental cues. Further demand to address a diversity of plants has led to the development of first companies providing plant phenotyping equipment as well national infrastructures in a number of countries. For instance, the pioneering national facilities were established in Germany (German

Plant Phenotyping Network, DPPN[4]), France (PHENOME[5]) followed by development in a number of other counties. First integration of these activities was performed within the RIA projects EPPN[6] and EPPN2020,[7] providing access to key plant phenotyping installations in Europe. However, these projects focused on a limited aspect of plant phenotyping, namely assessment of plant properties under controlled environment. Thus, there was a need for a coordinated development of plant phenotyping in Europe with a comprehensive infrastructure concept demanded by the user community leading to the establishment of the Research Infrastructure EMPHASIS.[8]

3 EMPHASIS: Key Business Plan Elements

EMPHASIS builds on national infrastructures of plant phenotyping with facilities in both field and controlled conditions as well as data and computational systems and modelling platforms. The key value proposition comprises enabling demand-driven access to plant phenotyping infrastructure, data, and services to ensure excellence in basic and applied plant science. The services are the main instruments to turn the value proposition into reality, based on an intensive landscape analysis outlining among others stakeholder demands.

3.1 Landscape Analysis

The current plant phenotyping landscape in Europe has been both developed and mapped by previous and ongoing plant phenotyping projects, e.g. the RIA projects EPPN and EPPN2020, the COST Action "The quest for tolerant varieties—Phenotyping at plant and cellular level,[9]" a range of activities during the Preparatory Phase of EMPHASIS such as a series of regional conferences, dedicated thematic workshops addressing scientific communities, input by the advisory groups (Ministry, Funder, Industry, Support Group), as well as dedicated surveys and interviews and published reports. The analysis resulted in a very intense interaction with different stakeholders, which resulted in the definition of highly demanded infrastructure pillars of EMPHASIS infrastructure as: i) phenotyping installations in (semicontrolled conditions), ii) intensive field experimental sites, iii) network of field sites with minimal equipment, iv) modelling infrastructure to support plant phenotyping data analysis, and v) data and computational systems (for more details, see: https://emphasis.plant-phenotyping.eu). Nearly 200 different installations

[4] https://dppn.plant-phenotyping-network.de/.

[5] https://www.phenome-emphasis.fr/.

[6] https://www.plant-phenotyping-network.eu/.

[7] https://eppn2020.plant-phenotyping.eu/.

[8] https://emphasis.plant-phenotyping.eu/.

[9] https://www.plant-phenotyping.org/home_costfa1306.

potentially participating in EMPHASIS have been identified up to now, representing a sound basis for the provision of high-quality pan-European services, including an integrated data management system for storing and analysing (meta)data, and modelling platforms associated with the phenotyping platforms. The landscape analysis is a constantly ongoing activity throughout preparation, implementation, and operation, allowing to adapt EMPHASIS strategy according to the latest developments and to address the latest user demands.

The landscaping analysis included an interaction with the user community to identify different users and to specify their particular demand for services. Four major groups with very specific demand for services have been identified:

I. Users from academia and industry: Demand for access to the EMPHASIS installations data and modelling platforms to address specific scientific questions related to very diverse crops and biotic and abiotic plant–environment interactions under controlled and field conditions. They are interested in understanding the plant–environment interaction and the translation of this understanding into application, e.g. in breeding.
II. Technology developers: Demand for access to EMPHASIS installations and expertise to develop and validate new technology under realistic scenarios in a way that the technology can be used to address the relevant questions for the users and operators of installations.
III. Scientists and managerial staff operating the infrastructure: Demand for EMPHASIS services related to management of the infrastructure and quality management including experimental and data standards. High-quality standards at phenotyping installations are the basis for excellent science and data reusability.
IV. Policymakers and funders: Demand for expert advice based on recurrent analysis of the plant phenotyping infrastructure and landscape in Europe. This will represent an important tool for the development of a cutting-edge research strategy agenda that will further advance the leading role in Europe in agricultural and plant sciences.

3.2 Service Portfolio

A number of services were evaluated and grouped in Functional Units focusing on very specific aspects of service provision based on the evaluation of the current status of plant phenotyping infrastructure and the user community in Europe as described above (landscape analysis). The Functional Units focus on specific areas of services related to:

I. ACCESS: Access provision for user community to the phenotyping installations incl.: controlled environment installations, field installations, networks of field sites, modelling.
II. QUALITY: Measures to implement quality criteria at research infrastructure, specifically experimental design, standards, sensor calibration, etc.

III. DATA MANAGEMENT: Approaches enabling data reusability embedded in a relevant data policy.
IV. INNOVATION: Dissemination and utilisation of technology and results from access and use of the phenotyping installations.
V. COMMUNICATION and expert advice: Engaging all relevant stakeholders and providing expert advice related to plant phenotyping.
VI. TRAINING: Supporting the next generation of plant scientists.
VII. SUPPORT AND COORDINATION: Coordination of all functional units and utilisation of the synergies.

Each of the functional units includes a large set of specific services, which should be operated synergistically to maximise the return on investment. Dedicated key performance indicators (KPIs) were defined to evaluate the performance of the services and adapt them to the dynamic needs of the users. EMPHASIS will as such throughout implementation and operation readjust the services according to user demand towards optimising benefits generation and improved service provision. This re-evaluation process may include realigning and adopting ongoing services as well as setting up new services that are demanded, but also terminating services that are not required anymore or do not deliver any relevant benefit (Dodgson et al., 2014). Additionally, services that might be offered to the community commercially, e.g., by a start-up initiated by EMPHASIS, will not be provided by the EMPHASIS RI itself. The implementation phase is also complemented by piloting selected services that were chosen based on the most significant demands expressed by the community during the landscaping analysis. The pilot services will illustrate i) the potential to generate benefits in concrete terms, ii) the potential to increase the return on investments for ministries and funders, and iii) the feasibility of service provision and optimising the underlying processes, e.g. identification and application of KPIs.

3.3 Business Model

The landscape analysis and service portfolio lead to a first business model draft, summarised in a business model canvas (Fig. 1). The core element therein defines the value proposition with the focus on demand-driven access to plant phenotyping infrastructure, data, and services to ensure excellence in basic and applied plant science. To support this value proposition, activities with key partners have been defined and required key resources identified. Key beneficiaries and the underlying stakeholder engagement approaches and instruments have been set. The underlying cost structure includes costs for the operation of service centres and funding for the implementation, operation, and decommissioning is outlined.

<table>
<tr>
<td rowspan="2">Key partners
• European Commission
• National plant phenotyping infrastructures and communities
• National governments and funding agencies
• ESFRI Forum</td>
<td>Key activities (Functional Units)
• User access
• Infrastructure quality
• Data management
• Innovation
• Communication and integration
• Support and coordination
• Training & education</td>
<td rowspan="2">Value propositions (Strategic aims)
• Global leadership of European plant phenotyping
• Facilitating innovation
• Knowledge transfer and education
• Decision-making support for policy towards food security in changing climate conditions
• FAIR phenotyping data contributing to digital life sciences in Europe
• Societal progress towards a sustainable bioeconomy</td>
<td>Stakeholder engagement
• Communication strategy with a diversity of targeted instruments
• Demand assessment of diverse user groups
• Annual stakeholder meetings
• Reports and recommendations
• Expert opinion/consulting</td>
<td rowspan="2">Beneficiaries
• Investors in plant phenotyping infrastructure in Europe (national ministries, funding organisations, EC)
• Operators of plant phenotyping infrastructures in Europe
• Academic users of phenotyping infrastructure
• Industry users of phenotyping infrastructure, especially in the field of breeding and technology development
• Society in general</td>
</tr>
<tr>
<td>Key resources
• Members of staff
• Funding for service centres and national nodes</td>
<td>Channels
• Online Catalogue of Services
• Online data and knowledge repository</td>
</tr>
<tr>
<td colspan="2">Cost structure
• Functional Units operation</td>
<td colspan="3">Funding structure
• Annual full member monetary contributions
• Host country in-kind contributions
• National and regional infrastructure funds
• Horizon 2020 and Horizon Europe
• Service provision fees
• Industry partnership contributions</td>
</tr>
</table>

Fig. 1 EMPHASIS business model canvas proposal (according to the methodology of Osterwalder & Pigneur, 2010)

4 EMPHASIS: Sustainable Funding Framework

The dynamics of an ESFRI RI follows a life cycle that includes a number of steps from a concept phase to design, preparation, implementation, operation to termination, according to the ESFRI Roadmap (ESFRI, 2018; see also Chap. 1 "The Concept of Research Infrastructure"). The single steps may vary substantially between different RIs, and community-specific demands need to be taken into account. The key elements of the business model include the development of services that address the user demand, the implementation of a legal framework that supports the operation, and a funding framework that enables coverage of all costs related to operation, especially for service provision.

Here we will focus on the development of a potential funding framework for the operational phase. The following paragraphs represent the methodology for developing such a funding framework, integrating a large number of assumptions. The presented monetary values thus do not present estimated values that have been used to develop the methodology as a basis for further discussion.

4.1 Implementation Phase

The EMPHASIS Implementation Phase should ensure a smooth transition from the preparation to operation by:

- Engaging the relevant stakeholders from the ministries/funders to establish an **Implementation General Assembly**, i.e., a main decision-making body, based on a non-binding agreement to operate an Implementation Governance.
- Enabling **decision-making** on key strategic options such as the funding and legal framework for the Operational Phase and as such enabling the transition of EMPHASIS to a sustainable long-term operation with service provision embedded into a legal model and sound financial basis.
- Illustrating the potential of EMPHASIS to generate benefits by operating **pilot services** to test the feasibility of service provision, optimise the underlying processes as well as to evaluate the demand and benefits of the services.

The EMPHASIS Implementation Phase includes ministry representatives from a number of European countries building the Interim General Assembly enabling decision-making for future operation of EMPHASIS with respect to the legal framework, host countries' Functional Units as key service providers, statutory seat country, and the required budget. EMPHASIS will support decision-making by providing a range of strategic options on these aspects to national ministries, including potential funding framework scenarios for a full operation based on the current plant phenotyping landscape (See Chap. 10 "Developing a Data-Driven Community Engagement Plan for Integrated Carbon Observation System Research Infrastructure", Sect. 2). Here it is also important to note that there will be a periodization process for services that can already be established in the implementation phase (i.e. pilot services) and continuously extended into full operation. The Implementation Phase is supposed to lead to a stable Operational Phase with a long-term sustainable funding and legal framework starting approximately 2 years after the start of the implementation Phase.

4.2 Operational Phase

The operation of EMPHASIS will be decided on by the members of the Implementation General Assembly. In order to support this decision-making process, a number of funding scenarios are developed that focus on the provision of services and the required resources (see Implementation Phase). The basic assumption is that EMPHASIS will provide a full range of services as defined in the Functional Units (see paragraph 2 above). The services may be provided and organised by the Central Services in different countries operating on a pan-European level. For the financial considerations, the focus is on the funding and costs of the Central Services and the resources such as personnel and financial contributions required to operate it and its contribution to EMPHASIS service provision.

Three different scenarios have been constructed with different financial considerations for the service provision within the framework of EMPHASIS assuming that 11 Member States will contribute financially (the number of Member States is an assumption based on preliminary survey regarding interest in participation by European countries). In all three scenarios, the full service portfolio will be offered, yet with differences in terms of service coverage. The three scenarios are regarded as a starting point for discussing a funding framework (and especially membership contributions) with countries interested in becoming members of EMPHASIS. Once these countries have signalled their expectation with respect to service coverage (quantity and quality-wise), the preferred scenario will be further elaborated.

4.3 Funding Framework Assumptions

General considerations for the scenarios take into account a few assumptions:

- Considering an annual budget for the Operational Phase of a fully operational EMPHASIS with 11 contributing Member States. The Member States are randomly selected.
- The membership fee is based on an equal share portion of 30% of the total member contributions and 70% according to the national GDP. For simplicity, other models are not taken into account for the initial scenarios, but will be developed and brought forward to ministries during future negotiations.
- Observers pay an annual fee of 25 k€, and contributions from one observer are assumed.
- The calculation of personnel costs is based on an estimate of the public service costs in Germany (as two of the authors of this article work at a German host institution), including three different payment levels: i) director (100 k€), ii) manager (85 k€), and iii) technical staff (75 k€) required to provide services in all Functional Units and management of the Research Infrastructure (Table 1).
- Each Functional Unit receives a contribution of 25 k€ as a basic budget to cover costs related to service provision.

Table 1 Functional Units with a basic description and the estimated personnel resources

Functional unit	Description	Resources for central services: Personnel	Costs (k)
I. User access	Facilitates access to plant phenotyping installations for user community from academia and industry	Access Manager	85 k€
II. Infrastructure quality	Enable quality standards for the infrastructure categories: i) controlled environment, ii) intense and iii) lean field sites	Quality Management Officer	85 k€
III. Data management	Enable a high quality of data management and access for users embedded in a sound data policy	Data Manager	85 k€
IV. EMPHASIS innovation	Support knowledge-driven innovation to the agricultural sector, seed industries, technology development	Innovation Office	85 k€
V. Communication and community integration	Foster an intense discussion with all stakeholders (e.g. annual European plant phenotyping conference)	Communication Officer	85 k€
VI. Training and education	Enable and coordinate training for users and future operators of plant phenotyping facilities	Training Officer	85 k€
VII. Support and coordination	Coordinate the interaction between Functional Units, National Nodes, Facility managers incl. legal and administrative issues	Coordinator	85 k€
Management	General strategy development, interaction with the Board, European Commission, other ESFRI Research Infrastructures, EMPHASIS stakeholders	Director	100 k€
		Project Manager (covered by grants)	–
		Administrative/ Financial Support	75 k€
		Legal support	75 k€
		Technical Support	75 k€

- In Scenario 1, 1000 k€ is included as a budget to cover the operating costs of dedicated facilities providing access in Member States.
- The overhead for the operation represents an estimated 30% of the personnel costs, including office rent, IT infrastructure, electricity, office material and equipment.
- Travel expenses are estimated on the basis that each member involved in the Central Services is doing 12 business trips per year with estimated costs of 0.5 k€/trip.
- Income in the form of fee-for-service contributions (e.g. by industry) and grants is related to the resources allocated to service provision assuming that the fee-for-service contributions and grants are in the range of 30% of the service

resources. Please note there is a substantial uncertainty with estimating the fee-for-service contributions.

- No bank loans will be acquired during the first years of operation, as the financial credibility of the then newly founded organisation is assumed to be low.

All costs are calculated in thousand € = k€.

The specific scenarios have different budgets with respect to the service provision (Table 2). The scenarios are characterised by:

- **Scenario 1—Full coverage of all services:**
- Each Functional Unit has a dedicated officer to manage the services within the Functional Unit and a Management Unit for the Research Infrastructure. Each Functional Unit has basic resources linked to the service provision. Additionally, access to facilities is managed by the Functional Unit officers based on excellence-driven access including management of respective resources to cover the operating costs of the installations providing access.
- **Scenario 2—Basic coverage of all services:**
- Each Functional Unit has a dedicated officer to manage the services within the Functional Unit and a Management Unit for the Research Infrastructure. Each Functional Unit has basic resources linked to the service provision. Access to facilities is supported by the Functional Unit officers based on excellence-driven access.
- **Scenario 3—Minimum coverage of services:**
- Each Functional Unit is operational; officers providing services may need to cover services within multiple Functional Units. In comparision to Scenarios 1 and 2, the available budget for personnel costs is significantly reduced.

The service provision within these three different scenarios requires different contributions by Member States (Table 3). Here we selected 11 different Member States as potential members of EMPHASIS, based on a preliminary analysis of potential country interests in EMPHASIS membership. The contributions are based on equal share portion of 30% of the total member contributions and 70% according to the national GDP. The calculation mode was selected for simplicity; however, there are a number of other models that can be used but are not taken into account

Table 2 Basic operational costs for three different scenarios

Basic operational costs (k€)	Scenario 1/ year	Scenario 2/ year	Scenario 3/ year
Personnel costs	920 k€	920 k€	590 k€
Services	1.200 k€	200 k€	125 k€
Travel	48 k€	48 k€	30 k€
Overheads: 30% of personnel costs(office rental, electricity, computers, etc.)	276 k€	276 k€	177 k€
Total costs	**2.444 k€**	**1.444 k€**	**922 k€**

Table 3 Financial contribution assuming 11 different Member States for the operation of the Central Services assuming 3 different scenarios of service provision

Country[a]	GDP 2017 (k€)	Scenario 1	Scenario 2	Scenario 3
Austria	369.686 k€	112 k€	66 k€	42 k€
Belgium	437.204 k€	121 k€	71 k€	46 k€
Denmark	288.981 k€	101 k€	59 k€	38 k€
Finland	223.843 k€	92 k€	54 k€	35 k€
France	2.291.705 k€	375 k€	222 k€	141 k€
Germany	3.263.350 k€	508 k€	300 k€	192 k€
Italy	1.716.935 k€	296 k€	175 k€	112 k€
Netherlands	737.048 k€	162 k€	96 k€	61 k€
Portugal	193.072 k€	88 k€	52 k€	33 k€
Serbia	36.795 k€	66 k€	39 k€	25 k€
Switzerland	601.327 k€	143 k€	85 k€	54 k€
United Kingdom	2.327.730 k€	380 k€	225 k€	143 k€
Total costs		**2.444 k€**	**1.444 k€**	**922 k€**

[a] The respective GDP numbers are from European statistics (https://ec.europa.eu/eurostat/web/national-accounts/data/main-tables)

for the initial scenarios of service provision. The reason is that further models will be presented in line with the upcoming input from ministries when negotiating potential membership contributions. It is important to note that different scenarios can also be drawn here by changing the number of contributing Member States for each scenario. For simplicity, however, we keep the number of Member States similar for all different scenarios.

4.4 Evaluation of the Funding Scenarios

The different scenarios represent a potential operation of EMPHASIS within the defined Functional Units (Table 1). The largest differences between the different scenarios are the financial support for service provision and the personnel related to the service provision (Table 2). These different financial contributions in each scenario obviously result in different contributions by the potential member States (Table 3). Within these scenarios, we assume that the Central Services have a coordinating role to enable services and particularly access to physical and virtual services. It is worth noting that physical access at the facility level in different countries may not be provided in-kind since the access costs are rather high. Thus, an important activity of the Central Services is to ensure that access facilities can be supported financially.

- **Scenario 1—Full coverage of all services:**
- In this scenario, we assume substantial financial resources (~1000 k€) available for service provision, particularly for access to phenotyping facilities. The service funding would cover the operating costs for the installations providing

access based on excellence-driven access according to the European Charter for Access (European Commission, 2016). EMPHASIS would here enable excellence-driven access based on previous experience from I3 projects such as EPPN or EPPN2020. The access would foster a competitive process for user access stimulating excellent science. Further, it would provide a strong incentive for the facility managers to provide access covering their running costs as well as implement the quality standards for best scientific practice and data policy of EMPHASIS. Additionally, it provides some return of investment for the installations by supporting the operating costs of these installations in countries contributing to the operation of EMPHASIS. We assume that this process may become an incubator for excellent science and innovation. Additionally, EMPHASIS will facilitate third-party funding to utilise the phenotyping infrastructure with dedicated research projects, which represents the key activity in scenario 2. Evaluation of the access will allow identification of upcoming trends and enable funders and policy makers to develop a national infrastructure research agenda based on the demand. The scenario will further enhance Europe's leading role in this research area.

- **Scenario 2—Basic coverage of all services:**
- In contrast to scenario 1, there is a very basic funding for service provision in scenario 2. The resources would be mostly used to facilitate access to phenotyping facilities by enabling third-party funding. EMPHASIS in this sense will facilitate the interaction between facility managers, users, and funders on the EU and national levels to enable funding research projects that utilise the phenotyping facilities and take into account the quality criteria and data policy of EMPHASIS.
- **Scenario 3—Minimum coverage of services:**
- In this scenario, we assume a very basic coverage of services with some basic resources. Some Functional Units may need to be merged and EMPHASIS officers will have to manage more than one Functional Unit. This scenario entails the least contributions by Member States but can only provide a very basic service in facilitating third party funding to utilise the phenotyping facilities in research projects.

Based on the differences in resources to provide services in each scenario, we estimate that EMPHASIS will be able to generate benefits and impacts as outlined above as well as different income due to service and data products, mostly from commercial fee-for-service activities and EU and international grants (Table 4). The general assumption is that the income generation is linked and related to the resources contributing to service provision. We assume income by fees for services and data products in the range of 30% of the service resources. This income is obviously largest in Scenario 1 with 1200 k€ service resources resulting in an income of 360 k€ + 360 k€ (fee for service and grants, respectively). This scenario will provide, as such, the largest resources, which may provide a financial margin required to continuously evaluate the phenotyping landscape and develop: i) new highly

Table 4 Estimated income of EMPHASIS

Total income (k€)	Scenario 1/ year	Scenario 2/ year	Scenario 3/ year
Yearly monetary contribution for full members	2.444 k€	1.444 k€	922 k€
Yearly monetary contribution for observers (estimated)	25 k€	25 k€	25 k€
Contribution by Functional Unit host country(estimated)	100 k€	100 k€	71 k€
Fee for services and data products(estimated 30% of the service contribution)	360 k€	60 k€	38 k€
Grants(estimated 30% of the service contribution)	360 k€	60 k€	38 k€
Total incomes	**3289 k€**	**1.689 k€**	**1.093 k€**

demanded cutting-edge services; ii) a strong basis for strategic development of the European research agenda; iii) investment in highly demanded infrastructure strengthening the plant research environment in Europe; and iv) enable scientific excellence.

It is important to note here that we are aware that the assumption of 30% revenue generation by fee-for-service activities and grants is rather arbitrary at this stage. However, plant phenotyping has been recognised as a growing market with respect to technology development for the agricultural sector at large (Market Research, 2019) and the resulting impact specifically for improvement in plant breeding may provide further increase in social welfare gain within the agricultural sector by a sustainable increase of food supply (Noleppa, 2016).

5 Outlook

EMPHASIS intends to start implementation by the establishment of the Implementation General Assembly (IGA) early 2020. The business model options, with some of them having been sketched out in this chapter, will form a basis for providing decision-making support to the IGA. A core element of the discussions will be the funding model framework, where a respective methodology for its development has been presented here. All the strategic options presented will further be modified according to the demands of the participating ministries. The interested reader will find latest information on the development of EMPHASIS on its homepage: https://emphasis.plant-phenotyping.eu.

Acknowledgements We would like to express our sincere thanks to all partners of the EMPHASIS-Prep project supported by the European Union (Grant Agreement: 39514) contributing to the business planning and strongly supporting the development of pan-European plant phenotyping community and the RItrain project (Grant Agreement: 654156) with the Executive Master in Management of Research Infrastructures (EMMRI). We are especially grateful for the support from Paola Bongini (University of Milano-Bicocca, Italy) and Michael Raess (INFRAFRONTIER) providing valuable insights and expertise as supervisors of this field project within the EMMRI programme.

References

Dodgson, M., Gann, D. M., & Phillips, N. (2014). Perspectives on innovation management. In *The Oxford handbook of innovation management*. Oxford University Press.

ESFRI Roadmap Part 1. (2018). PART1 *Roadmap & Strategy Report on Research Infrastructures*. http://roadmap2018.esfri.eu/media/1048/rm2018-part1-20.pdf.

ESFRI Roadmap. (2016). *ESFRI Roadmap Strategy Report on Research Infrastructures*. https://www.esfri.eu/sites/default/files/20160308_ROADMAP_single_page_LIGHT.pdf

European Commission. (2016). European charter for access to research infrastructures principles and guidelines for access and related services. https://doi.org/10.2777/524573.

FAO. (2017). The future of food and agriculture—trends and challenges. Rome. https://openknowledge.fao.org/server/api/core/bitstreams/2e90c833-8e84-46f2-a675-ea2d7afa4e24/content

Fiorani, F., & Schurr, U. (2013). Future scenarios for plant phenotyping. *Annual Review of Plant Biology, 64*, 267–291.

Furbank, R. T., & Tester, M. (2011). Phenomics—technologies to relieve the phenotyping bottleneck. *Trends in Plant Science, 16*, 635–644.

Houle, D., Govindaraju, D. R., & Omholt, S. (2010). Phenomics: The next challenge. *Nature Review Genetics, 11*, 855–866.

Marker Research. (2019). Plant phenotyping market size, Share and Forecast 2019–2026. https://www.datamintelligence.com/research-report/plant-phenotyping-market?gclid=EAIaIQobChMItbOar8zn5gIVFs93Ch0BCwiOEAAYASAAEgLKS_D_BwE

Noleppa, S. (2016). The economic, social and environmental value of plant breeding in the European Union An ex post evaluation and ex ante assessment. HEFFA Research GmbH (https://hffa-research.com/wp-content/uploads/2019/01/2016-03-HFFA-Research-Paper-Conclusion-The-economic-social-and-environmental-value-of-plant-breeding-in-the-EU.pdf).

Osterwalder, A., & Pigneur, Y. (2010). *Business model generation: A handbook for visionaries, game changers, and challengers*. Wile.

Pieruschka, R., & Schurr, U. (2019). Plant phenotyping: Past, Present, and Future. *Plant Phenomics*. https://doi.org/10.34133/2019/7507131

Serraj, R., Krishnan, L., & Pingali, P. (2019). Agriculture and food systems to 2050: A synthesis. In agriculture and food systems to 2050. In R. Serraj & P. Pingali (Eds.), *Agriculture & food systems to 2050 global trends, challenges and opportunities* (World scientific series in grand public policy challenges of the 21st century) (Vol. 2). World Scientific Publishing Co. Pte. Ltd.

Developing a Data-Driven Community Engagement Plan for Integrated Carbon Observation System Research Infrastructure

Evi-Carita Riikonen and Luca Brusati

Abstract

This chapter describes the development of a data-driven community engagement plan for the Integrated Carbon Observation System Research Infrastructure (ICOS RI), a distributed European Research infrastructure producing high-quality greenhouse gas data. It examines ICOS RI's complex governance model and highlights the need to strengthen internal cohesion and sense of community across its diverse members, roles, and scientific domains. Drawing on an identity study based on survey and interview data, the chapter analyses members' perceptions of the RI's purpose, motivations for participation, and expectations. These insights inform a structured engagement framework addressing emotional, cognitive, and behavioural needs across different constituencies. The chapter outlines how engagement activities can be aligned with ICOS RI's strategic objectives to enhance coordination, strengthen shared identity, and foster long-term sustainability.

1 Background

1.1 The Governance Model of ICOS RI

Integrated Carbon Observation System Research Infrastructure (ICOS RI) is a distributed Research Infrastructure established to enable high-quality climate change research and increase the usability of research data. ICOS RI describes itself as a

E.-C. Riikonen (✉)
ICOS-ERIC (Integrated Carbon Observation System, European Research Infrastructure Consortium), Helsinki, Finland
e-mail: evi-carita.riikonen@icos-ri.eu

L. Brusati
Department of Economics and Statistics, Udine University, Udine, Italy
e-mail: luca.brusati@uniud.it

E. Guarini et al. (eds.), *Research Infrastructure Management*, Management for Professionals, https://doi.org/10.1007/978-3-032-20373-1_10

"distributed pan-European research infrastructure producing high-quality data on greenhouse gas concentrations in the atmosphere, as well as on carbon fluxes between the atmosphere, the land surface and the oceans" (ICOS ERIC, 2019). ICOS RI has operational nodes in several countries and operates on several scientific domains related to atmosphere, ecosystem, and ocean greenhouse gas observations to provide timely and reliable data for research, policymaking, and the general public.

Since 2015, ICOS RI has been built in the form of an ERIC, meaning that the legal entity of the RI consists of the ERIC part, which, in the case of ICOS, means the coordinating office (ICOS Head Office, run by a Director General) and the data centre (ICOS Carbon Portal). The operational part of the RI consists of:

- Central facilities, including three domain-wise (atmosphere, ecosystem, and ocean) thematic centres and two central analytical laboratories
- National networks, i.e. the sets of measuring stations across all three domains hosted by national institutions (e.g. universities and research institutions) in 11 member and observer countries

Funding is channelled through national ministries and their agency organizations. ICOS is governed by a General Assembly that includes representatives from each national ministry and the RI itself, officially represented by representatives from the Head Office and occasionally from the central facilities in an advisory capacity. The General Assembly is supported by two advisory bodies, the Scientific Advisory Board and the Ethical Advisory Board. On top of the statutory governing bodies, two additional bodies have been established to serve in a coordinating, advisory and contributing function: first, the Research Infrastructure Committee, consisting of representatives from the central facilities and the chairs of the Monitoring Station Assemblies, which are domain-wide bodies that coordinate the national networks. Secondly, ICOS RI has appointed national focal points, who are representatives from each national network, as well as principal investigators, who are responsible for each measuring station. Figure 1 summarizes the governance model and the relationships among the components of ICOS RI.

ICOS RI has promoted the adoption of a specific terminology for the different parties associated with its activities, which is used throughout this chapter. "Stakeholder" is commonly understood as meaning the funders, e.g. national ministries and their representatives in the General Assembly. Everybody working in an ICOS-related position inside the different components of the RI is referred to as a "member", whereas the external users of ICOS data are referred to as "users". These definitions are still not entirely clarified inside ICOS, however, and competing definitions exist, causing confusion. In this respect, it is useful to remind that, as in most RIs, governance roles are entrusted to members who at the same time undertake different responsibilities; so, for example:

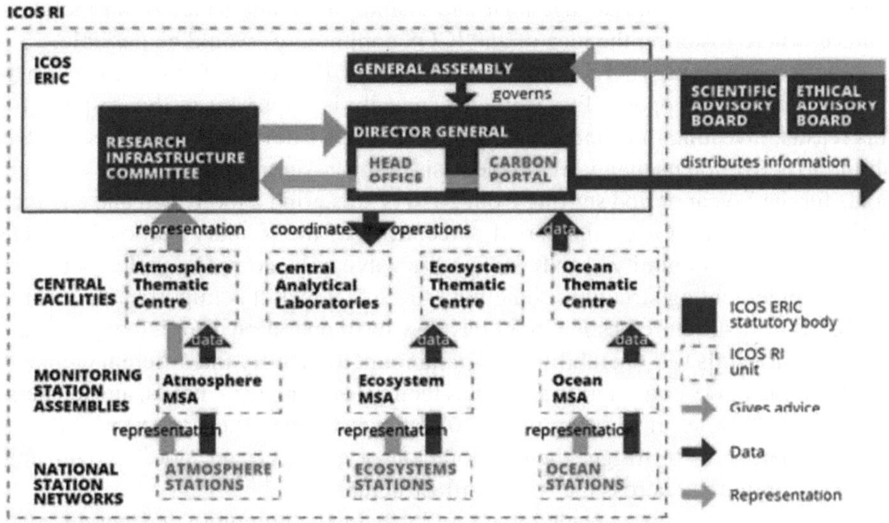

Fig. 1 Governance model of ICOS RI. Author's elaboration on ICOS-ERIC internal document

- The Director General belongs to the Head Office and the RI Committee
- Focal points belong to national networks and to monitoring station assemblies, are often station principal investigators and occasionally attend RI Committee meetings, even though they are not officially part of it
- Station principal investigators belong to national networks and monitoring station assemblies, and some of them also serve as focal points
- The chairs of monitoring station assemblies, the directors of the thematic centres, and the director of the Carbon Portal are RI Committee members

This description highlights the fact that the roles and components within ICOS are overlapping; on the other hand, the vast majority of members work in the different components of the network without being part of any specific coordination body. As a consequence, they may feel alienated from the coordination activities and information related to the work they do or the challenges they face, as this is conveyed via members with specific roles. While this specialization of labour works fine at some scale, a more interactive channel is missing between the Head Office and RI members.

1.2 Rationale and Objectives for the Intervention

Since ICOS, as most RIs, is built on several types of organizations, consisting of institutes with different agendas and histories and different cultural, political, and linguistic areas, the perceived purpose, motivation to be part of it and expected benefits associated to participation present significant variations. For this reason, it is vital to establish a shared understanding on these issues, so as to be able to facilitate community building and engagement and enable the maintenance of an inclusive culture, where fostering the idea of an "ICOS community" would be possible.

After receiving the ERIC status in 2015, one of ICOS RI's focus areas is obviously enhancing its operability. Network capacity is important in this respect; for this reason, investing time and resources in community development serves the RI's ability to deliver on its mandate. On the basis of this assumption, one of the strategic goals for the 5-year period starting from 2020 is "fostering a motivated and engaged ICOS community". Given the varied perceptions of the primary purpose of ICOS RI, the "ICOS community" can be defined as a dynamic, complex, varied but internally complementing structure: something towards which it is important to develop the ICOS infrastructure. As ICOS RI has now been operational for a few years and is moving towards full operability, it is paramount to identify the different elements that form the ICOS community, as well as their roles, functions, needs, and expectations; on these bases, it will be possible to plan how to serve them in a more customized manner, so as to trigger the development of a deeper and more recognizable sense of community across the whole infrastructure.

For this reason, it was decided that a fully-fledged community engagement plan would be designed by the ICOS Head Office as part of the EMMRI programme. The objectives of the community engagement plan were operationalized as follows:

- Describe the situation:
  - Find out what is the current "shared vision" of ICOS RI in the community, and in particular how the ICOS RI is perceived
  - Find out the community's motivation behind wanting to be part of the RI
  - Find out what expectations the community has *vis-à-vis* the RI
- Identify solutions, based on the situation:
  - Define the basic structure of the community engagement plan
  - Specify target groups and their needs, activities and their rationale, resources needed, potential barriers and bottlenecks in implementing activities, ways to monitor and evaluate community engagement, and coordination arrangements of the activities (e.g. task ownerships)
- Plan and implement practices for community engagement:
  - Identify actual tasks and deliverables for engagement activities
  - Link the community engagement plan to the broader strategic plan and theoretical framework

As it was considered important to base planning on systematic evidence generated by RI members themselves, an ICOS identity study meant to serve as a baseline for the community engagement plan was conducted in 2018. The purpose of this study was to investigate ICOS identity, i.e. the internally perceived purposes, motivations, and expectations that determine what ICOS RI is for its members. The focus was on three levels (societal, professional, and personal) and on three temporal perspectives (past, present, and future): these were considered to be the levels on which the internal members perceived the RI to operate, and on which it was

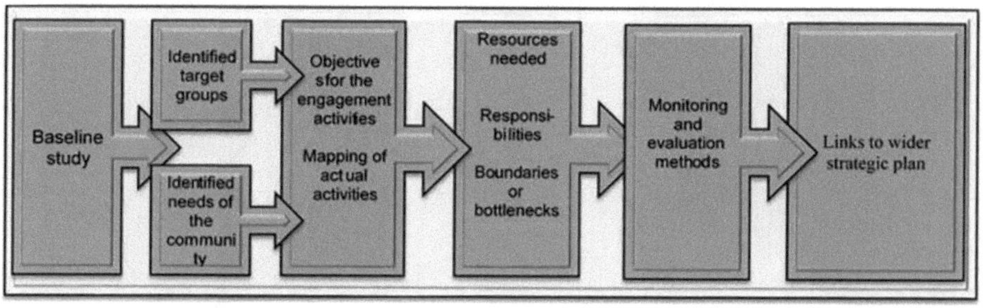

Fig. 2 The process and structure underpinning the development of the community engagement plan. Author's elaboration

considered beneficial to collect data. The study was therefore designed around these dimensions, focusing on specific areas related to the perceived purposes, abilities, functionalities, and meanings related to ICOS RI. The approach was not designed to cover all aspects of the overarching topics that were identified, but rather to give an idea of the multidimensionality of the infrastructure.

An overall view of the process and structure underpinning the development of the community engagement plan is featured in Fig. 2.

1.3 Target Groups

The presence of a unified context and common goal, i.e., to "provide harmonized and high precision scientific data on carbon cycle and greenhouse gas budget and perturbations", seems to suggest that ICOS RI could be understood as a collective shared space (Fig. 3). As it is the case in most RIs, though, ICOS RI is essentially a mosaic of nested communities (Fig. 4) taking different geographical and focus-driven forms and operating in several scientific domains.

For this reason, the ICOS identity study focused on gathering the views of RI members belonging to national networks (e.g. staff working in the host institutions, principal investigators, and focal points) and central facilities, so as to avoid focusing exclusively on governance bodies, whose views tend naturally to dominate the debate. Since the baseline study was conducted by a person working for the Head Office, it excluded on purpose the ERIC part. In turn, the community engagement plan focused on this part of the ICOS community, as it was considered important to address the expectations of this constituency (in the coming years the focus will be expanded to include the ERIC part as well as external stakeholders and users). The following target groups were identified:

- National networks:
  - Focal points
  - Station principal investigators

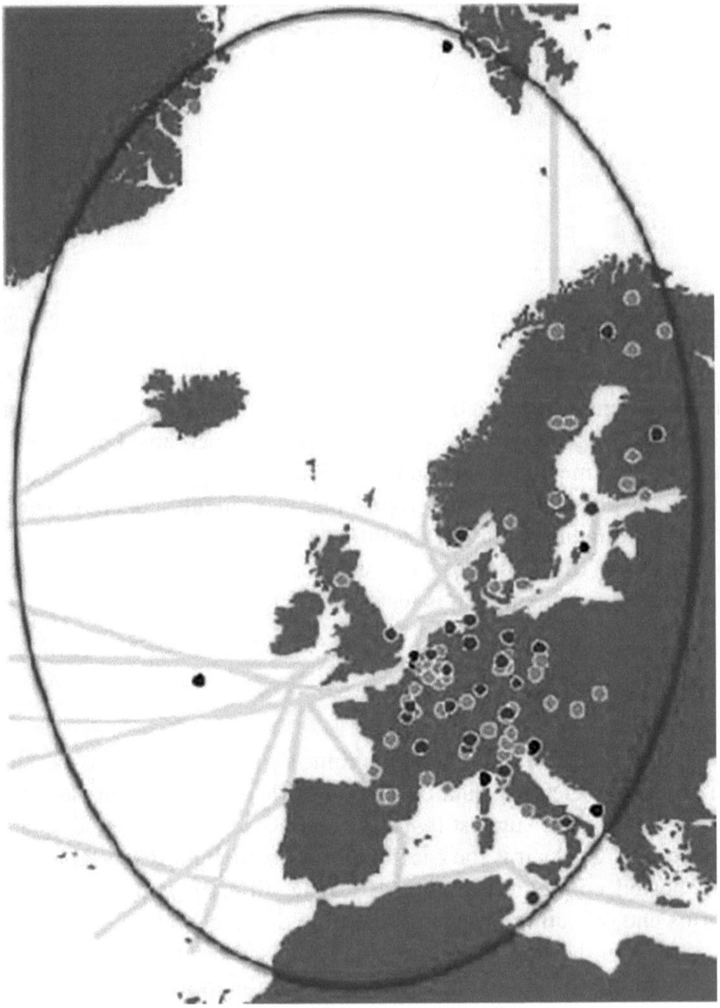

Fig. 3 The ICOS community as a single shared space. Author's elaboration

- Host institutions' staff involved in ICOS-related tasks (scientists, managerial and administrative staff, collectively referred to as atmosphere, ecosystem, and ocean communities)
- Monitoring station assemblies

- Central facilities:
  - Atmospheric, Ecosystem, and Ocean Thematic Centres
  - Central analytical laboratories
  - RI Committee

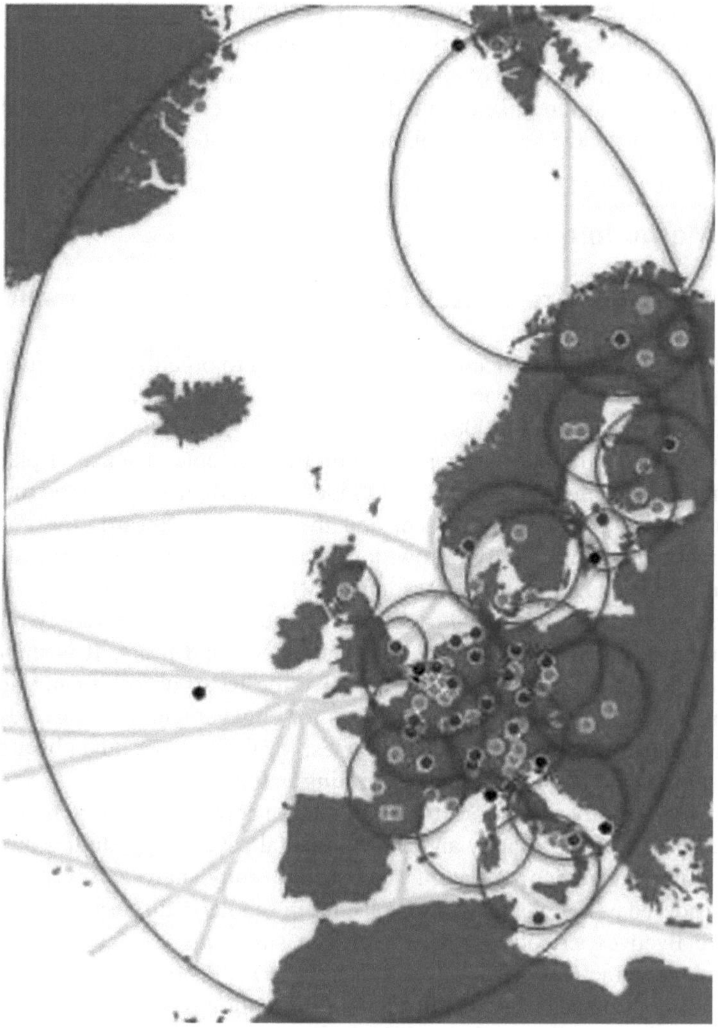

Fig. 4 The ICOS community as a collection of nested communities. Author's elaboration

To make it easier to manage the complexity of RI members, two viewpoints are adopted: roles and domains. This approach allows one to differentiate the needs related to different coordinating roles from the needs related to different scientific communities. As a consequence, the evidence generated by the baseline study reflects interpretations understood from different viewpoints by different observers. When discussing the "sense of community" in ICOS, for instance, it is easy to see from the data that it can mean closely collaborative nodes within one or more domains, communities across one domain, across two domains, or across all ICOS domains, or defined in geographic or institutional terms, or formed by people working in similar roles or in the same functional bodies (e.g. committees); it is not always possible to understand whether "ICOS community" is understood as an overarching, collective community including the whole RI or it is interpreted to mean one piece in the mosaic of communities. This is also noticeable when comparing results among different scientific domains: the level on which respondents felt there was a clear "ICOS sense of community" varied interestingly between them.

2 Methodology

2.1 Sense of Place, Sense of Community and Engagement

In the design of any data collection activity targeted to organizational change, careful conceptualization of constructs should precede their operationalization (Kraut, 2006; Macey & Schneider, 2008). In the case of ICOS RI, the interpretive framework underpinning the intervention relied on the concepts of sense of place, sense of community and engagement. The ICOS identity study first discussed the RI from the point of view of sense of place, and the approach towards the community engagement plan continued to narrow down the focus via the concepts of sense of community and engagement. The reason for such a broad approach lies in an attempt to understand holistically the nature of a distributed RI and the variety of requirements that are linked to its members, stakeholders, and users. It is important to acknowledge that not everybody will perceive the RI's purpose or mission in the same way, resulting in different preferences for engagement activities. Ideally, the RI should cater for its different constituencies; for this reason, it can be argued that a broad approach benefits community building in the long run.

The ICOS identity study is centred on the concept of "sense of place", which originated in human geography and environmental psychology studies but can also be applied in management research. The baseline study analysed several characteristics considered as being attached to "places" in scholarly discussion: in this sense, places are lived experiences, where everyday situations are faced, solutions are negotiated, and practices are developed (Relph, 1976; Proshansky et al., 1983). The understanding of places is thus built on the information received via everyday phenomena: one develops perceptions of places in relation to one's personal life history, consisting of meanings, memories, and embodied knowledge. This capital is utilized and further developed over time and in relation to different places, and every observer has a different understanding of the same place based on what is relevant about the place in relation to the individual's narrative. In this light, it is quite easy to identify similar characteristics in RIs.

Three components are recognized to contribute to the perceptions of places (Jorgensen & Stedman, 2001; Nanzer, 2004; Jorgensen & Stedman, 2011):

- Attachment, i.e. emotional bonds and sense of belonging (affective component)
- Identity, i.e. beliefs, knowledge, and identification (cognitive component)
- Dependence, i.e. behavioural commitments and intentions (conative component)

The ICOS Identity study focused on these dimensions in studying the views of members about ICOS RI: it considered perceptions and needs emerging from attachment-related factors (emotional needs), identity-related factors (cognitive needs), and dependence-related factors (conative needs). Furthermore, it differentiated needs on personal, professional, and societal levels and assumed that members experience these three types of connections in relation to the RI. While it was clear that the way ICOS RI is perceived consists of elements in all of the three components, the most interesting results emerged from the emotional bond and sense of belonging, i.e. the place attachment component.

As Peterson et al. (2008) put it, the concept of "sense of community" refers to collective experience (Pretty & McCarthy, 1991; Hughey et al., 1999). The concept is often analysed on the basis of the model presented by McMillan and Chavis (1986). In their approach, sense of community consists of four elements:

- Membership, formed by boundaries, emotional safety (security), a sense of belonging and identification, personal investment, and a common symbolic system
- Influence: Members need to feel that they have influence, and some influence by the group on its members is needed for group cohesion
- Integration and fulfilment of needs, meaning that members feel rewarded in some way for their participation in the community
- Shared emotional connection, such as shared history and shared participation, or at least identification with the history of the community

The debate around sense of place concluded that sense of community is closely linked to place attachment: the emotional connections to space and place are the result of the level of perceived satisfaction and need fulfilment that the setting provides (Low & Altman, 1992; Pretty et al., 2003; Ramkissoon & Mavondo, 2015; Adams, 2017; Alawadi, 2017; Clark et al., 2017). The results from the baseline study clearly indicated that the sense of community within ICOS is an area that needs focusing on; the resulting community engagement plan is therefore designed around this concept.

Engagement is an ambiguous construct (Macey & Schneider, 2008; Schaufeli, 2013) that can be used to describe a broad range of different behaviours (Beer et al., 2010): willingness to participate in activities, quality of effort invested, interest, motivation, and time spent on activities are all behaviours linked to engagement. According to self-determination theory (Deci & Ryan, 1985; Meyer & Gagné, 2008), two types of motivations control people's willingness to engage in activities, i.e. intrinsic and extrinsic motivation: intrinsic motivation refers to activities performed out of interest and enjoyment, whereas extrinsic motivation refers to activities performed out of instrumental reasons, for instance, in a work context or to gain benefit from the activity (Meyer & Gagné, 2008). For the purposes of this study, in keeping with Bowen et al. (2001), we define engagement as the outcome of the felt sense of community; in other words, the stronger the sense of community, the stronger the engagement, and vice versa.

While it is important to understand how engagement develops, it is also important to understand what the opposite is: if it is just lack of engagement or behaviour that rebels against engagement. From a community engagement point of view, this can also reveal vital points in planning engagement activities. Meyer and Gagné (2008: 62) highlight that this aspect is especially important when considering the types of activities that are proposed at a workplace: efforts to create engagement that threaten rather than satisfy psychological needs (for instance, by asking people to perform on a level that is too challenging) undermine rather than build engagement.

Research by Bowen et al. (2001) indicates that participation in community matters strongly influences the sense of community, but participation is not the only indicator of engagement. They identify three engagement indicators that influence the felt sense of community: community participation, community connections, and community capacity. Community participation is defined as the level at which people participate in the activities that are offered to them (e.g. number of events attended). Bowen et al. (2001), though, did not discuss the events organized by people themselves; it is possible to distinguish between active and passive participation, and both types are important, especially in the case of a distributed RI. Community connections can be seen as the ease of making contact with other community members, but also the frequency and the quality of these contacts, even though quality is more problematic to define; in the case of a RI, it can be defined by analysing meetings that reached solutions to the questions discussed or a task delivered by team effort. Community capacity, again according to Bowen et al. (2001), is defined as the extent to which members demonstrate a sense of shared responsibility and collective competence in situations that require resilience.

An interesting insight for community engagement stemming from the contribution by Bowen et al. (2001) is that capacity can be built via participation and connections. The links among engagement indicators and the sense of community are summarized in Fig. 5. This framework seems useful in pointing out that engagement consists of components that have to be understood on separate levels:

- Community participation: The actual activities that the community can be participating in
- Community connections: The ability of the community to access participatory activities and establish connections, i.e. the quality of the activities provided to the community
- Community capacity: The build-up of community competence and resilience

As a consequence, activities and their quality can be planned in the community participation and community connections areas, whereas how engaged the community is and how strongly felt the sense of community appears to be can be monitored and evaluated in the community capacity and sense of community areas.

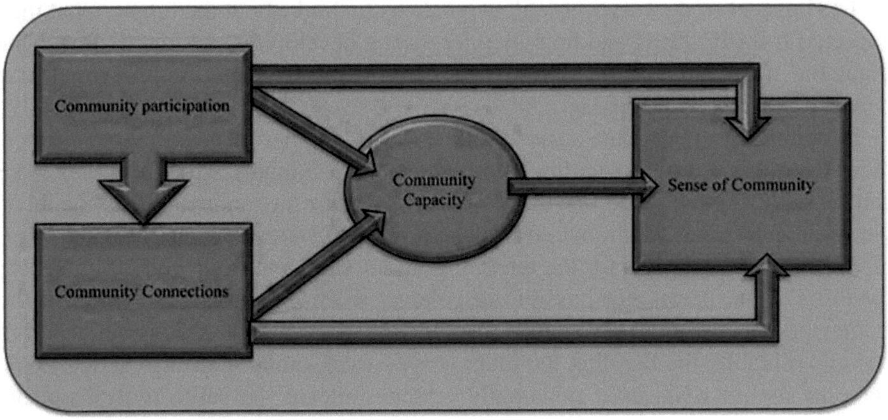

Fig. 5 Engagement indicators and their link to the sense of community. Author's elaboration on Bowen et al. (2001: 78)

2.2 Data Collection Patterns

Following careful conceptualization of constructs, evidence for the ICOS identity study was collected from the internal members of ICOS RI combining an online survey and thematic, semi-structured interviews. The survey was administered via online survey tool Wufoo and consisted of both open-ended and Likert-scale statements (1 being "strongly disagree" and 5 being "strongly agree"). It was sent to the wider ICOS community of approximately 250 people, with the understanding that active members (station principal investigators, focal points, and other active members from national networks, monitoring station assemblies, and Research Infrastructure Committee) would total around 150. The survey generated 66 responses, making the response rate 26.4% if we consider all recipients of the survey, or 44% if measured against the subsample of 150 most active members. The response rate reflects the fact that ICOS communities are fragmented around several parallel activities: it is challenging to reach the majority of the communities at the same time or within a tightly defined timeframe.

The first part of the survey invited respondents to reflect back on the time they first became involved in ICOS, either by starting to work in a specific ICOS-related position or getting gradually involved in tasks that were connected to the infrastructure. Purposefully the survey did not specify a strict timeframe; hence, for some respondents "in the beginning" can mean a decade or more ago, whereas for some it may mean as little as a year or less.

The second part of the survey focused on the currently perceived situation among the internal members of the ICOS RI. Again, there was no strictly specified setting in which the respondents were supposed to provide their answers; for instance, the instructions did not ask respondents to indicate whether they were at the end of their fixed contract or about to change roles or tasks within the infrastructure.

The last part of the survey asked respondents to think about the future: what they expected from ICOS RI and how they foresaw it developing and functioning. This time, the questions specifically invited participants to focus on the timeframe between the next 3 and 5 years.

In addition to the online survey, four in-depth, semi-structured thematic interviews were carried out, reaching members from all domains. The interviews were carried out using a method that allows interviewees to stay anonymous to the interviewer, requiring an additional effort in setting up the interview platform and organizing suitable time slots for the interviews that took between 45 and 70 min each; for this reason, it was not possible to conduct more individual interviews in the framework of this study. Despite this fact, the interview data was rich and proved to be very valuable; the fact that the interviewees were anonymous also added to the value of the answers, as it potentially erased some of the subjectivity from the analysis.

The purpose of using this interviewing method was to invite respondents to share their thoughts and ideas with the utmost feeling of anonymity. Given the fact that the interviews were carried out by a person working in the ICOS Head Office, the importance placed on the effect of subjectivity from both the respondents and interviewer is justified. A browser-based, real-time chatroom allowed respondents to answer questions by using only a nickname. To enable participation, an online registration form for available interview slots was set up, asking participants to book a suitable slot for their interview and giving instructions to enter the chatroom. Participants were provided with information about data storage and privacy related to the chatroom and given the possibility to familiarize themselves with the privacy policy before deciding to take part in the interview.

3 Results

3.1 Situation

The first objective of the ICOS identity study was to find out the current “shared vision” of ICOS RI in the community, and in particular how the ICOS RI is perceived among members belonging to national networks and central facilities. Based on resulting data, it is clear that the perceived purpose of ICOS takes several different types or forms that can be divided into two main categories, i.e. scientific and societal purposes (Fig. 6).

Interestingly, it is clearly visible from the groupings that the purpose of ICOS can be considered from a variety of perspectives. While some respondents perceive ICOS’ role as purely collecting and analysing data or harmonizing and providing high-quality data, so as to improve the standards of research, others perceive ICOS’ function as facilitating science, where ICOS’ purpose is to support and enable science either by providing facilities for conducting research or by focusing on scientific community building. What is clear from available data is the fact that the scientific purposes of ICOS RI are further fragmented into very specific areas,

Scientific purpose		Societal purpose	
Conduct science	Facilitate science	Influence policymaking	Raise awareness of climate change
Collect data, maintain high-quality data, harmonize greenhouse gas data	Support and enable science: provide facilities for research, enable scientific community building and innovative research, provide open data and resources to serve researchers Strengthen collaboration across domains OR strengthen a specific domain in ICOS OR build a sense of European research community	Influence science policy to gain resources for research OR influence decisions related to climate change mitigation	Educate, involve the general public, distribute knowledge on climate change, increase visibility in society

Fig. 6 The perceived purposes of ICOS RI

reflecting the complexity in the mosaic of constituencies involved. Those who perceive ICOS' purpose as primarily societal see ICOS' role either as an influencer to policymaking through lobbying science policy or through producing mitigation methods for policy makers for climate change prevention, or as needing to be there for raising awareness of climate change among the general public.

The second objective of the ICOS identity study was to find out respondents' motivation behind wanting to be part of the RI. It is clear from the data that some factors score very strongly among the members of ICOS RI:

- At personal level, positioning oneself according to the felt sense of community
- At professional level, factors related to one's own role in the RI
- At societal level, positioning oneself in relation to the RI in terms of its correspondence to one's world view in general

The third objective of the ICOS identity study was to find out what members belonging to national networks and central facilities expect from the RI. Respondents' expectations seem strongly related to a few themes:

- At personal level, expectations are related to individual development and support from the community
- At professional level, expectations are placed on RI's operability and its scientific and functional abilities, especially in terms of clarifying the governance structure and collaboration across domains, as well as scientific visibility and own role in ICOS, and the RI's ability to provide facilities and resources
- At societal level, expectations are placed on the RI's visibility in society in general and RI's ability to provide its services to society, for instance, in terms of data availability.

In a nutshell, ICOS is perceived as a competent, yet very complex structure, the components and interlinkages of which are considered challenging to understand. As understanding the governance structure of ICOS proved challenging, this could have resulted in the perceived unclarity of mandates to perform one's tasks and contributed to the level of perception that one's work in ICOS could contribute to decision-making at societal level.

Respondents feel proud to be involved in ICOS RI, but almost half note that the sense of community within ICOS is not felt very strongly. In other words, it was clear that members belonging to national networks and central facilities called for more engagement. There is a clear need, and also a clear demand, for more community building and professional collaboration. Overall, members believe that ICOS will have gained societal and scientific visibility, operability and geographical coverage in the next 3 to 5 years. They are keen to develop both their own skills and the collaboration across scientific domains, and most of them see themselves still involved in ICOS in the near future.

When comparing the types of perceived purposes, it appears clearly that those who perceive ICOS' main purpose to be scientific see its desired main function as consisting of services to scientists and research, either via obtaining resources and providing a platform for conducting science or influencing science policy to obtain resources; on the other hand, those who consider ICOS' main purpose to be societal see its main function as an influencer or pathfinder on multiple levels (on policy, coverage, and informative aspects).

3.2 Solutions

The situation described in the ICOS identity study allows one to identify solutions, and in particular to use a data-driven approach to define the basic structure of the community engagement plan. Such a plan should identify, define and describe the required inputs and outputs, as well as reflect on the hoped-for outcomes and select the key metrics based on which the monitoring and evaluation of engagement activities will take place. As the very first step, the headings for the content should be planned. They include:

- The target groups and the type of need to be met
- The type of objective that engagement activities are expected to achieve to meet those needs
- The existing or newly proposed engagement activities to be implemented and their type
- The type of resources needed, either already available or required
- The staff member responsible for coordinating the engagement activity and the type of tasks
- The type of potential boundaries or bottlenecks in implementing the engagement activity
- The monitoring patterns and metrics
- The type of engagement based on monitoring and evaluation results
- The link to theoretical framework

As discussed in Sect. 1.3, the focus of the community engagement plan is on the internal members of the RI and on their needs and expectations, as pointed out by the baseline study. In identifying the types of target groups, it was considered meaningful to divide members based on either their role in the components in the coordinating bodies of the RI (role-based membership) or on their scientific domain (domain-based membership). Even though the baseline study did not specifically inquire about the respondents' roles in coordinating bodies, this information was gathered from interview data, when interviewees were willing to share it.

The needs to be met were also divided based on type, i.e. emotional, cognitive, or conative. Different types of engagement activities were also identified (external, internal, or governance-related events), together with the objectives that engagement activities are expected to achieve to meet those needs (informing, enabling, supporting, developing, or interacting). Furthermore, the types of resources needed (facilities, equipment, personnel, communication, technical solutions, access, and clear work plans), the types of tasks entrusted to RI staff members organizing the activities (organizing, coordinating, or supporting), and the potential bottlenecks or boundaries were identified. These include restricted access to resources, lack of resources, imbalance of responsibilities for engagement tasks within the RI, restricted access to information or materials, lack of information or materials, inadequate or irrelevant communication channels, inadequate technical solutions or equipment, key messages not developed or communicated, inability to demonstrate RI's impact, and unclear roles and responsibilities.

Finally, methods for monitoring and evaluating the activities' occurrence and effectiveness (engagement indicators) were proposed, and the links to the theoretical framework were identified, including the four components of the sense of community identified by McMillan and Chavis (1986), i.e. membership (consisting of boundaries, emotional safety, common symbolic system, personal investment, and a sense of belonging and identification), influence, integration and fulfilment of needs and shared emotional connection, and the community engagement types suggested by Bowen et al. (2001), i.e. participation and connections contributing to capacity.

As the final step, specific practices for the actual engagement of members belonging to national networks and central facilities can be identified. This step entails identifying possible operational tasks and deliverables for each engagement activity, as well as potential indicators for monitoring the activities taking place and evaluating their effectiveness. Figure 7 highlights how the community engagement plan could be linked to the broader strategic management process of ICOS RI.

4 Lessons Learnt

As a direct consequence of their mandate, the challenge of many distributed RIs is to establish an inclusive culture where several types of communities, with varying ways of identification with the RI, can interact easily and complement each other, rather than "widen the gap". In the case of ICOS RI, the binding factor that

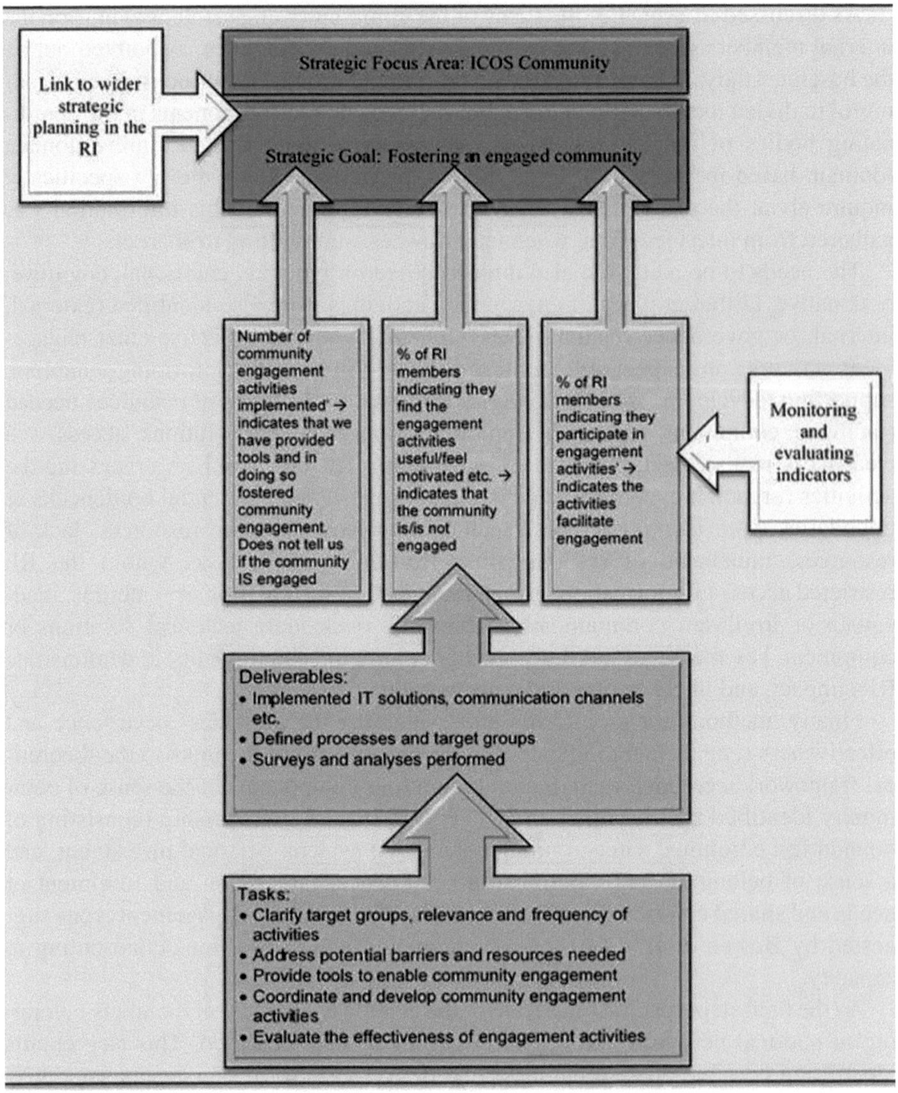

Fig. 7 The role of the community engagement plan vis-à-vis the broader strategic management process of ICOS RI. Author's elaboration

motivates people (either strongly or on a level that members would like to increase) is the sense of belonging: as one interviewee put it, being part of a "big thing". It is, therefore, extremely useful to have been able to gather the data for the community engagement plan directly from RI members, and to be able to show that this data has been taken into account in the development of the community engagement plan.

From a managerial standpoint, the direct benefit of developing a community engagement plan is the ability to link individual activities to the broader strategic planning of the RI. Because of the broad scope and extensive background research that was required to identify the areas that need focusing on, the information gathered for the community engagement plan supports not only the specific cross-cutting strategic focus area ("The ICOS community") and the strategic goal linked to it ("Fostering a motivated and engaged ICOS community"), but other focus areas as well, in particular "Sustainability" and "Services supporting science". The community engagement plan includes metrics meant to track how the goal is being acted upon and whether it has been achieved, also providing suggestions suitable to assess both the relevance of engagement activities and the level of engagement itself.

The process leading to the development of the community engagement plan showed that a clear definition of context and purpose, as well as a shared terminology must be agreed upon for any plan, before any content is envisaged. As Czarniawska-Joerges (1992: 17) pointed out, "pictures of complex organizations change depending on the standpoint". Especially in a distributed RI, the perceptions of structures, purpose, and processes can vary considerably, resulting in multiple takes on the same subject. The ICOS identity study demonstrated that RIs are socially constructed entities: people can be driven by very different ideas about why the RI exists, what it does, why they are in it, and what they expect from it, despite sharing a strongly felt identification with the RI's field. In this sense, the effort placed into the community engagement plan has served multiple purposes in the development of the RI management.

The analytical work underpinning the development of the community engagement plan proved to be a valuable exercise in understanding how complex ICOS RI actually is; it also pointed out that many engagement activities are already taking place, but they are not widely known, not communicated about, or not coordinated enough. Rather than implementing a large array of new activities, the existing ones would need to be better focused on and coordinated, with a clear assessment of required resources and potential barriers.

A comprehensive set of documents and plans has been developed by ICOS RI to support its operability and serve as the cornerstones of a sustainable RI. These include the ICOS RI Strategy, published in 2019 with a specific five-year plan (ICOS ERIC, 2019), and a management plan including a full set of key performance indicators, being finalized in 2020. As an overarching conclusion it can be argued that, by improving the common understanding of the governance structure of ICOS RI, engagement across domains becomes easier to organize, and this in turn can help strengthen the sense of community and the sense of belonging in ICOS RI.

References

Adams, P. C. (2017). Methodologies of place attachment research. In J. S. Smith (Ed.), *Explorations in place attachment* (pp. 227–240). Routledge.

Alawadi, K. (2017). Place attachment as a motivation for community preservation: The demise of an old, bustling, Dubai community. *Urban Studies, 54*(13), 2973–2997.

Beer, C., Clark, K., & Jones, D. (2010). Indicators of engagement. In C. Steel, M. J. Keppell, & P. Gerbic, (Eds.), *Curriculum, technology and transformation for an unknown future. Proceedings of ASCILITE 2010, Sydney*. (pp. 75–86). Retrieved August 3, 2020 from https://beerc.files.wordpress.com/2010/11/indicators-of-engagement.pdf.

Bowen, G., Martin, J., Mancini, J., & Nelson, J. (2001). Civic engagement and sense of community in the military. *Journal of Community Practice, 9*(2), 71–93.

Clark, W. A. V., Duque-Calvache, R., & Palomares-Linares, I. (2017). Place attachment and the decision to stay in the neighbourhood. *Population Space and Place, 23*(2).

Czarniawska-Joerges, B. (1992). *Exploring complex organizations: A cultural perspective*. Sage.

Deci, E. L., & Ryan, R. M. (1985). *Intrinsic motivation and self-determination in human behavior*. Plenum.

Hughey, J., Speer, P. W., & Peterson, N. A. (1999). Sense of community in community organizations: Structure and evidence of validity. *Journal of Community Psychology, 27*(1), 97–113.

ICOS ERIC. (2019). *ICOS strategy*. Retrieved August 13, 2020 from https://www.icos-cp.eu/sites/default/files/cmis/ICOS%20Strategy.pdf.

Jorgensen, B. S., & Stedman, R. C. (2001). Sense of place as an attitude: Lakeshore owners attitudes toward their properties. *Journal of Environmental Psychology, 21*, 233–248.

Jorgensen, B. S., & Stedman, R. C. (2011). Measuring the spatial component of sense of place: A methodology for research on the spatial dynamics of psychological experiences of places. *Environment and Planning B: Planning and Design, 38*(5), 795–813.

Kraut, A. I. (Ed.). (2006). *Getting action from organizational surveys: New concepts, technologies, and applications*. Jossey-Bass.

Low, S. M., & Altman, I. (1992). Place attachment: A conceptual inquiry. In I. Altman & S. M. Low (Eds.), *Place attachment* (pp. 1–12). Plenum.

Macey, W. H., & Schneider, B. (2008). The meaning of employee engagement. *Industrial and Organizational Psychology, 1*(1), 3–30.

McMillan, D. W., & Chavis, D. M. (1986). Sense of community: A definition and theory. *Journal of Community Psychology, 14*(1), 6–23.

Meyer, J. P., & Gagné, M. (2008). Employee engagement from a self-determination theory perspective. *Industrial and Organizational Psychology, 1*(1), 60–62.

Nanzer, B. (2004). Measuring sense of place: A scale for Michigan. *Administrative Theory & Praxis, 26*(3), 362–382.

Peterson, N. A., Speer, P. W., & McMillan, D. W. (2008). Validation of a brief sense of community scale: Confirmation of the principal theory of sense of community. *Journal of Community Psychology, 36*(1), 61–73.

Pretty, G. H., Chipuer, H. M., & Bramston, P. (2003). Sense of place amongst adolescents and adults in two rural Australian towns: The discriminating features of place attachment, sense of community and place dependence in relation to place identity. *Journal of Environmental Psychology, 23*(3), 273–287.

Pretty, G. H., & McCarthy, M. (1991). Exploring psychological sense of community among women and men of the corporation. *Journal of Community Psychology, 19*(4), 351–361.

Proshansky, H. M., Fabian, A. K., & Kaminoff, R. (1983). Place-identity: Physical world socialization of the self. *Journal of Environmental Psychology, 3*(2), 57–83.

Ramkissoon, H., & Mavondo, F. T. (2015). The satisfaction-place attachment relationship: Potential mediators and moderators. *Journal of Business Research, 68*(12), 2593–2602.

Relph, E. C. (1976). *Place and placelessness*. Pion.

Schaufeli, W. B. (2013). What is engagement? In C. Truss et al. (Eds.), *Employee engagement in theory and practice* (pp. 15–35). Routledge.

Correction to: European Research Infrastructures' Compliance with International and European Law

Carla Gulotta and Ohad Graber-Soudry

Correction to:
Chapter 7 in: E. Guarini et al. (eds.), *Research Infrastructure Management*, Management for Professionals,
https://doi.org/10.1007/978-3-032-20373-1_7

The author name was misspelled in the original version of the manuscript as Ohad-Graber Saudry. This has now been corrected to Ohad Graber-Soudry.

The updated version of this chapter can be found at
https://doi.org/10.1007/978-3-032-20373-1_7

E. Guarini et al. (eds.), *Research Infrastructure Management*, Management for Professionals, https://doi.org/10.1007/978-3-032-20373-1_11